CISTERCIAN STUDIES SERIES: NUMBER NINETY

FROM CLOISTER TO CLASSROOM

From Cloister to Classroom

Monastic and Scholastic Approaches to Truth

THE SPIRITUALITY *of* WESTERN CHRISTENDOM III

Edited by E. ROZANNE ELDER

CISTERCIAN PUBLICATIONS INC.
Kalamazoo, Michigan
1986

BV
4490
.F76
1986

Available in Britain and Europe from
A. R. Mowbray & Co Ltd
St Thomas House   Becket Street
Oxford OX1 1SJ

Available elsewhere from the publisher
Cistercian Publications
WMU Station
Kalamazoo, Michigan 49008

The work of Cistercian Publications is made possible in part
by support from Western Michigan University.

Typeset by Gale Akins, Kalamazoo
Printed in the United States of America

Library of Congress Cataloguing-in-Publication Data:
Main entry under title:

From cloister to classroom.

(Cistercian studies series ; no. 90)
1. Spirituality—History of doctrines—Addresses,
essays, lectures.   I. Elder, E. Rozanne (Ellen Rozanne),
1940-   . II. Series.
BV4490.F76 1986   248.2'094   85-30874
ISBN 0-87907-890-1

TABLE OF CONTENTS

RATIONAL RESEARCH IN THE RHETORIC
OF AUGUSTINE'S *CONFESSIO*
Raymond D. DiLorenzo

T HE LEADING IDEA of this study is that, in the activity St Augustine called *confessio,* dialectics, chief discipline of reason among the ancient philosophers, must yield its pride of place as supreme guide to wisdom. It must yield to the laws of a new guide, namely, a christian confessional rhetoric that suffuses and modifies the rational work of dialectics in the discovery of the truth.

The work of dialectics thus becomes part of an effort to rouse up human understanding, affections, and speech to God. In short, *confessio* is a rhetorical theology and, at the same time, a contemplative ascent. It imposes upon reason a new governing regime that dialectics, usually regarded as the supreme arbiter, is unaccustomed to establish for rational research in matters of God and the soul.

The argument explaining how *confessio* governs the work of reason stands upon two basic points: first, that for St Augustine philosophy had a decidedly rhetorical orientation and, second, that his *Confessions* was a particular expression of this philosophy. Before discussing these points, I wish to comment upon a few of the hypotheses that, like the stars of old, influence the argument from afar.

I

In the year 392 AD, the second year of his priesthood, Augustine began to dictate exegetical glosses on the Psalms, apparently to serve as working texts for sermons. (Many years later he would finish the huge collections of sermons we now call *Enarrationes in Psalmos.*) When he came to Psalm 7:18— 'I will confess to the Lord according to his justice'—Augustine distinguished, for the first time, it seems, two kinds of *confessio* found in Scripture: a confession of personal sins and a confession of praise for God.[1] Eight years later, in the year 400 AD, having previously become bishop of Hippo Regius, Augustine completed the thirteen books of his *Confessions.* Apparently, something in or connected with the simple notion of a twofold *confessio* in Scripture so attracted Augustine that he made it the substance of a lengthy work that many think is his greatest accomplishment as a writer and thinker.

Can we determine what it was that attracted him? Can we trace some development of the idea of *confessio* in works he composed between 392 AD and, say, 400 AD? It is possible, I think, but we cannot take that route here. There is a simpler way. During the early years of Augustine's philosophical and religious retirement, first at Cassiciacum, then at Rome and Tagaste, Augustine delimited firmly the nature and area of his philosophical interests. To him, philosophy was a search for a happy life (a *beata vita*) through wisdom; and, according to a well-known text from his *Soliloquia,* Augustine wanted to investigate only two things, God and the soul.[2] Thus, to seek a happy life meant to seek the truth by reasoned understanding and the supreme good by heart and will. But the truths that compose wisdom and the supreme good are the truths about the relationship of the soul to God. Thus,

becoming happy means knowing and loving God. This program, as Gilson has observed, is a simple map to the vast land
of Augustinism.[3] Throughout this vast land, one can observe,
without great difficulty, the co-presence of his two-fold
interest. If this is 'philosophy' for Augustine, it is also the
very form of his mind.

We may surmise, then, with some assurance, that what
attracted Augustine to the two modes of Scriptural *confessio*
was their correspondence to his master interests. Nevertheless,
to the usual ways of seeking beatitude in God by reason and '
will, the *Confessions* adds a distinctive third thing—confessional speech itself. *Confessio* is a verbal activity; although reason
and will play their parts, they are subordinated to and inte-
grated within *confessio* itself. To say this is merely to assume
that everything in the *Confessions* is an expression of *confessio*: the highly poetical flights of religious ardor, the so-called
autobiographical story of persons and events leading to Augustine's conversion, all the ratiocinative passages both in the
conversion story of the first nine books and in the inquiries
of the last four, where Augustine speaks as a bishop in the
ministry of the word and sacred mysteries. Throughout the
Confessions, Augustine makes evident that all these features
of his work are a seeking of God through speech of praise for
him and lament for personal sin, a speech both interior,
through the affections of the heart and motions of mind, and
exterior, through the tongue and pen.[4]

Insofar as confessional speech develops through praise and
blame, it is, rhetorically regarded, a kind of epideictic or
rhetorically demonstrative discourse.[5] One of the three major
kinds of rhetoric—forensic and deliberative being the other
two—epideictic discourse was essentially a process of idealization. Whatever its subject, whether trees, flowers, cities, abstract entities like justice, love, virtue, or philosophy, or persons, civil and military, like kings, emperors, conquerors,
(even the gods could be the subject of epideixis), it sought a
kind of persuasion that results from adorning and amplifying

its subject, thus making it evocative of love and praise. Especially admired by ancient rhetoricians was the paradoxical encomium. Things or persons normally blamed, held in disrepute, thought low—say, the wicked Helen of Troy, flies baldness, or foolishness (as in Erasmus' *Praise of Folly*)—all such things could be praised; and, in so doing, a speaker would at the same time be giving praise both to himself and, especially, to the wondrous power of the rhetorical word.[6]

Idealization through epideixis seeks persuasion, not conviction through dialectical reasoning, though not necessarily excluding dialectics. (I am using the word 'dialectics' imprecisely and in a generic way to denote the disciplined use of reason and word to arrive at truth. Everyone can spot its presence in a discourse, to some a keen delight, to others a disagreeable annoyance.) *Confessio* too seeks persuasion by epideictic idealization; and the sort of persuasion it seeks seems in essence to be contemplative or, if this word is not too contentious, mystical. In Augustine's own words, the aim of his *Confessions* was 'to praise the just and good God for the things good and evil of my own and to rouse up (*excitant*) human understanding (*intellectum*) and affection (*affectum*) to him'.[7]

Apart from this hypothesis, I cannot account for the remarkable expansion of Scriptural *confessio* into the elaborate work Augustine called *Confessions*—unless, of course, the word is a misleading title. But perhaps we ought to give Augustine the benefit of the doubt and trust that he knew what he was doing. If we do, there must have been in his mind some impetus to expand scriptural *confessio* into a supple, powerful, and profound form of theological discourse. It seems the *confessio* of the *Confessions* derives from some integration of the simple modes of scriptural confession with, first, the procedures and aim of epideictic rhetoric and, second, with the ideas of Augustine developed in the philosophical pursuit of his master interests, God and the soul, especially *after* his sudden conversion to the rhetorical offices of a priest in 391 AD.

The plausibility of this hypothesis can be strengthened by an analysis of the *Confessions* itself from the standpoint of literary criticism, though, again, space cannot be taken here to do what is necessary.[8] Nevertheless, some idea of what I have in mind may be helpful. The most famous part of the *Confessions* is the conversion story in Books I–IX. These books amount to a demonstration (in the rhetorical sense) of God. He, not Augustine, is the protagonist of the *Confessions,* and he is rhetorically idealized as a persuasive speaker. It is God's persuasive speech that converts a worldly rhetorician into a minister of the Word. And God speaks in the *Confessions* through several media—through the events of Augustine's life, through the perturbations of his soul, through the created world, and through Sacred Scripture. Augustine's *confessio* is itself stimulated by God's speech persuading him to reintegrate his tongue and pen to his heart and mind, they being also persuaded to break from the glue of deceiving opinions and loves.[9]

The conversion of Augustine's tongue is, in point of the plot, the completion of all that has been narrated in the first nine books. Structurally considered, the story comprises episodes selected from periods of Augustine's life from infancy to manhood. What Augustine confesses—demonstrates through praise and blame—is the potency and mercy of God's own persuasion. The famous conversions of Books VII and VIII do not complete the process. Book IX is the climax, and Book IX is about the conversion of the tongue.[10] Augustine's baptism is only a minor part of this book. (I do not imply, of course, that it is a minor part of Augustine's life.) The major part of Book IX is an example of the transformed rhetorical powers of Augustine. The eulogy of Monica—eulogy being a species of epideictic rhetoric—is primarily about God, not Monica.[11] It is a vivid illustration of the way God's persuasive speech converts the tongue to his praise. Even the so-called vision at Ostia, which is part of the eulogy, is not so much a

vision as a verbal dialogue, the Word speaking in the souls of
Monica and her son.[12] So much else in Book IX—Augustine's
toothache, his pulmonary problems, the moving words of
psalm four, Augustine's early literary activity (still somewhat
breathing the pride of the schools, he says)—all these things
have unmistakable reference to the aural and oral, chief sen-
sory components of the phenomenon of speech. Historians of
philosophy and theology have understandably emphasized the
conversions of intellect and will in Books VII and VIII respectively. But even the crucial episodes in these books are attended
by examples of divinely inspired speech—the chaste eloquence
of St Paul's letters in Book VII and the famous voice saying
'tolle, lege' in the garden at Milan in Book VIII. The intellectual and moral conversions of these books are necessary but
still preliminary stages in the conversion of the tongue, the
fulfillment of this process. In this way Augustine prepares us
for the last four books, where, again, the primary object of
confessio is God speaking in the soul and in the Sacred Scriptures, but now to one who seeks him as a christian bishop,
minister of the Word and of sacred mystery. What ultimately
the *Confessions* do is, first, to project epideictically an ideal
of God—a God who speaks persuasively—and, second, to provide at the same time an interpretation of God's speech.

Let us now turn to the main argument and the two points
on which it stands: that Augustine's understanding of philosophy has a rhetorical orientation and that the *Confessions*
are an expression of this philosophy.

II

Inseparable from the confessional projection of God as an
ideal to be loved and praised are excursions of dialectical reason in searching out the truth. As every reader knows, they
occur everywhere in the *Confessions,* some of them more elaborate and systematic than others. Spontaneously, it seems,
Augustine's epideictic *confessio* becomes inquiry into abstract
general questions—for example, the kinds of divine law and

their relation to historical circumstances, the nature of evil, of spiritual substance, the psychology of sin and free choice, the interrelations of being to truth, goodness, and beauty, what memory, time, and eternity are, indeed, what God is, this last being the major question, as I have suggested, of the whole work. There is, clearly, a research of reason in *confessio*. To be sure, we must never forget that *confessio* rhetorically demonstrates how God's search for the soul precedes and englobes man's search for Him. Nor must we forget that the dialectical issues Augustine raises, some of which I have just listed, comprise all that obstructs praise for God by men. In rhetorical terms, these issues are the dialectical *topoi* of confessional epideixis. However, insofar as *confessio* is rational research for the true, it appears to be what we call philosophical inquiry. How, then, does Augustine philosophize within *confessio*? Put in another way, the question is, under what conditions does rational research proceed in the *Confessions*?

I have already described the general understanding of philosophy that informs *confessio*. In this century the preoccupation of scholars has been to assess Augustine's debt to and use of the platonic philosophical tradition. We need not raise here the very complex questions of specific sources and teachings. What attracted Augustine to this tradition was its general inclination, as it were, toward the good to be contemplated and lived. It does not, of course, neglect knowledge of the true, but it seeks the true for the sake of the good. Hence, the platonic tradition regards psychological, moral, political, and religious considerations as the consummation of philosophy more emphatically than, say, Aristotelianism, for which Platonism looks like a subordination of theoretical science, the truth of things known for their own sake, to practical sciences of the good; and it is not uncommon for commentators to categorize Augustine's view of philosophy from an aristotelian standpoint and call it practical, though the category has no historical applicability whatever to

Augustine's own thinking.[13]

However much Augustine owed to the tradition of Plato, he was not uncritical in his use of it, and I would like to recall one general assessment he made of it, in order to stress a sometimes neglected point: what drew Augustine away from Platonism but toward Christianity was the *rhetorical* impotency of ancient philosophers to span the chasm between *vita* and *doctrina* in their own religious lives and in the lives of men they sought to persuade. This criticism is all the more telling since, in the platonic tradition, Ciceronianism was a conscious attempt to enhance platonic teaching with the power to persuade by adjoining eloquence to the wise teachings of the original Academics.

Augustine's treatise *De vera religione,* written shortly before he became a priest in 391 AD, begins with a critique of Plato's religious contribution to the human desire for beatitude, which, we remember, initiates in men the love of wisdom. The first sentence appears to summarize all that Augustine had learned from the time Cicero's encomium of philosophy first inspired him to seek wisdom, whatever it might be. He was then nineteen years old (373 AD). Some two decades later, a baptized Catholic living a quasi-monastic life in the company of a few friends, Augustine wrote the opening words of the treatise *De vera religione:*

> ... the entire way of the good and blessed life is
> constituted in true religion, in which one God is
> worshipped and, with the most purified piety,
> is known to be of all natural things the source,
> by which the universe is begun, perfected, and
> contained.[14]

No doubt about it in Augustine's mind: this is the way. But what of those who worshipped many gods and, among them, those platonic philosophers who seem to have come so close to knowing the way to the blessed life? Augustine says:

> . . . hence more evidently grasped is the error
> of those peoples who preferred to worship many
> gods rather than the one true God and Lord of
> all—that their wise men, whom they call philo-
> sophers, kept to conflicting schools and com-
> mon temples. For to neither people nor priests
> was it unknown how diverse were the things about
> the nature of the gods the philosophers thought,
> since each of them did not fear to profess his
> opinion publicly and each tried, if he could, to
> persuade everybody; nevertheless, all of them,
> along with their sectaries thinking things both
> adverse and diverse, came to the common rites,
> no one of them putting up opposition. The matter
> now is not who among them thought more truly,
> but surely this one thing appears certain enough—
> that they upheld one thing in religion and de-
> fended in private another thing, with the very
> same people listening.[15]

Augustine is pointing to an inconsistency in the lives of philosophers. However much they differed about the gods, they all
participated in the public rites, even though they did not
share the religious views of the people and priests. Why?
Augustine's answer includes a review of the religious heritage
of Platonism to prepare for his main thesis: religion is not to
be sought from the philosophers, not even the Platonists, but
from the Christian Catholic Church.

  Why did the philosophers participate in the public rites,
though they did not believe in the public religion? Augustine
observes that they did not have the power to persuade the
people to accept their eccentric and unorthodox religious
views. Socrates, for example, was bolder than other philosophers in his attempts at persuasion. Yet his coy irony and
even his death had little effect. For example, he often swore
oaths upon dogs, stones, or some nearby object. Augustine

supposes that Socrates knew very well how much better these objects were than the images made by craftsmen and worshipped in the temple. By so swearing, Socrates might expose to intelligent men the superstition of most other men and of customary religious practices. Even more was possible. Those who worshipped the natural world as the supreme god might see that to consider a stone or a dog as a particle of god was objectionable and, therefore, might conclude that god is superior to the world, to every soul, and to our minds. 'Plato afterwards', says Augustine, 'wrote [all this], rather more sweet in reading than potent in persuading. These men [the philosophers] were not so constituted in nature that they might turn the opinion of their own peoples from the superstitions of images and the vanity of this world to the true worship of the true God.'[16] Socrates himself, in spite of everything he did, venerated temple images. 'After his condemnation and death', Augustine writes, 'no one dared to swear by a dog or to call any stone Jupiter.'[17] For Socrates, everything backfired, reinforcing, it seems, the public worship he sought to change. 'These things were merely transmitted by memory and in writings. Whether this was due to fear or to some awareness of the times', Augustine concludes, 'it is not for me to judge.'[18]

Imagine now, Augustine says, that one of Plato's own disciples were to question him about the people's reluctance to worship according to his teachings. Let this disciple admit that Plato has persuaded him to accept many doctrines. At this point, Augustine makes a summary of the philosophical heritage of Plato as it bears upon religion: the truth is seen not by a bodily eye but by the mind; the soul that adheres to truth is made happy and perfect; nothing hinders knowledge of truth more than a life of lust and the deceptive images of sensible things in the world, for these images derive from the body and cause diverse opinions and errors; the mind must be healed, then, in order to behold the immutable form of things whose beauty remains unchanged and unchangeable

by space or time, abiding one and the same; it alone exists
supremely, though men do not believe in it; all other things
are born and die, dissolve or break apart, but these things owe
what existence they have to the eternal God who created
them in his truth; the rational and intellectual soul is given
to man so that it might enjoy and contemplate God's eternity
and thereby obtain eternal life, but the love of things that
come to be and pass away causes the soul to become vain
among vain images and to scorn those who say that something
exists not capable of being seen by the eyes or of being contained in any phantasm: the mind alone can see it. Such
platonic teachings seemed to Augustine quite concordant
with the christian religion.

What, then, if Plato's imaginary disciple, having been persuaded to accept these teachings, were to ask his master about
the possible existence of a certain great and divine man?

> . . . who might persuade the people that such
> teachings were to be at least believed, if they
> could not perceive them, or, if any could per-
> ceive them, that they, involved in the base
> opinions of the multitude, might not fall into
> vulgar errors . . . . [19]

Would not such a man be worthy of divine honors? Augustine
imagines Plato's reply: no man could do it, unless especially
favored and strengthened by God. The man would himself
have to despise all that wicked men covet, suffer all that they
fear, accomplish all they admire, and, with the greatest love
and authority, convert the human race to a sound faith. Such
a man, being the bearer and instrument of God's own wisdom,
would deserve a place beyond all humanity.

Plato might have imagined the need for a great and divine
man who could persuade the human race. But, says Augustine, that man has in fact appeared. He was God's Word and
came into the world, persuading peoples all over the world.

The marvel, however, is not merely that he persuaded multitudes but that he persuaded them to believe what the Platonists maintained but could not establish as a public piety for all. And if Plato were to come to life now and see that Christians everywhere were believing and living out teachings that called them away from transient temporal goods to abiding spiritual and intelligible goods, what would Plato say? What would his disciples say? They would say, Augustine imagines, 'these are the things about which we dared not persuade the people, and we yielded to their custom rather than draw them to our belief and preference'.[20] Augustine then concludes that, however much the philosophers may boast, anyone can see that religion should not be sought from them. Any philosophy that does not lead to a public piety in accord with it should be repudiated.

Augustine's argument demands that philosophy must, to be complete, terminate in a public piety. Herein lies what I have called the rhetorical orientation of his view of philosophy. The failure of the Platonists in this respect testifies to the rhetorical superiority of Christianity. The philosophers were unable to persuade the many to accept philosophical teachings attractive only to the few. What the Platonists were unable to do, lacking the power to persuade and, perhaps, fearful of a public backlash, Christianity did, in spite of persecution. It effected a transition between words and deeds, life and doctrine, which is the whole meaning of persuasion. Augustine thinks it should be obvious, even to Plato, were he to come to life, that the one who could persuade people to live according to teachings so terribly abrasive of their customary superstition and materialism would have to be a *magnus vir et divinus.*

Augustine has, no doubt, put words into Plato's mouth, though that may not be as unfair to Plato as it seems. Augustine, I believe, was very alert to an epideictic ideal within Platonism itself: the perfect wise man. In the platonic dialogues, he was projected by means of the portrait of Socrates, who, however, likely is not that ideal wise man but the image by which his form is apprehended. Socrates was not beyond criticism. Aristophanes and Isocrates did not think he was. Nor did Cicero, whose criticism we will momentarily recall. It is perhaps too cynical of us to think that Plato refers indirectly to himself as the ideal man. One reason he concealed his own views by writing dialogues in which he does not speak may have been a desire to direct attention to and develop admiration for the ideal. Later platonic sects, especially the Stoics, were keen to discuss the wise man. But it was Cicero who undertook a major revision of the ideal. He insisted that eloquence, for which rhetoric was an aid, be united with wisdom. Plato drew the image of Socrates as a contrast to sophists like Gorgias and Protagoras. They were presented as relativists, morally, politically, and metaphysically. Thus, to them the power to persuade had no restraint other than their own desires. The dialectical talk of Socrates was the antidote to the dangerous illness of soul and city they caused. Dialectics lead to an intuition of abiding forms or ideas that were the norms of thinking and acting. Dialectics, in short, must rule rhetoric. However, Cicero projected an ideal orator as a contrast to Socrates, who was charged with the crime of divorcing words and things, thinking and speaking, wisdom and eloquence. The philosophers since Socrates had, in Cicero's view, done nothing to reunite things that belonged together.[21]

To restore what were truly interdependent was Cicero's program. In his youthful work *De inventione,* he attributed the discovery of eloquence to a mythical man in some far off time—a certain *magnus vir et sapiens* who first realized the power of eloquence in men's souls and used it to transform savages roaming in the field into civilized men. No mute wisdom could have transformed their lives. No mute wisdom could have persuaded the naturally stronger to submit in law to equalization with the weaker. Alone, without wisdom, eloquence could be dangerous. Without eloquence, wisdom

inadequacy of their ability to overcome through persuasion the materialism and superstition of almost all men.

could do no harm, but then it could not do what eloquence could—fashion a great city.[22] Rome was no fabulous city dreamt by greek philosophers.

Cicero's most mature rhetorical works, *De oratore, Orator,* and *Brutus,* amplify his youthful thoughts. It is not commonly realized that these dialogues are basically epideictic, much like Plato's socratic ones, for they seek to envision the intelligible form of the perfect orator (*perfectus orator*) who, Cicero insists, has perhaps never existed and never will. Yet he is the model, and to Cicero he might as well be called a philosopher, though the philosophers try always to separate *orator* from *philosophus.* Nevertheless, he is both of them in one. In this way Cicero attempted to correct the great ideal of the Old Academy and to enable its teachings to persuade multitudes.

But even this ciceronian vision was vain. This is not the place to review the argument of Augustine's *De civitate Dei,* which, though written long after the *Confessions,* is yet like it in being an epideictic form of christian theologizing.[23] Augustine's attitude toward the ciceronian ideal may be gathered from his early dialogue *Contra Academicos,* as it is usually called. Augustine here refutes the skepticism of the third Academy, to which Cicero adhered. But the refutation is complicated by the famous conjecture that the Academics were not skeptics at all. They may have maintained an esoteric teaching, which Augustine thinks, was none other than the Old Academy's—Plato's—teaching. Skepticism may have been a defense against the dogmatism and materialism of the Stoics and Epicureans.[24] It was, moreover, a sort of rhetorical tactic to deal more effectively with the crude opinions of the multitude who might otherwise not give Academics a hearing. Augustine's attitude seems to be that, if the Academics did maintain skepticism, he has refuted them. If they did not, then their skepticism is one more testimony to the inadequacy of their ability to overcome through persuasion the materialism and superstition of almost all men.

It is not surprising, then, that, when Augustine wrote *De vera religione,* he had come to a point where Christ, the Word of God—indeed, the whole plan of redemption—could appear as the fulfillment, not only of the jewish hope for a Messiah, but also of the classical ideal of a perfect orator and philosopher. Christianity included whatever wisdom the Platonists discovered and added to it a persuasive power that was only possible for God's own Word. In Augustine's mind the rhetorical superiority of Christianity is historically indisputable.

It remains for us to see in what the rhetoric of Christianity consists and how it affects the work of rational research by one ardently seeking truths about God and the soul. As I have suggested, the *Confessions* are an epideictic search to understand and praise God in the manner and media of his divine speech to the soul; and in so far as Augustine has recounted for us the impediments he faced as a seeker of the truth, he has allowed us to observe how reason must operate while God is speaking to the soul, teaching, delighting, and moving it in the fashion of some supremely loving and compassionate speaker.

III

That to the soul God speaks, persuading it and, in fact, enabling it to overcome whatever obstructs it from turning to him as the source of its beatitude, is not an easy idea to appreciate, still less to see as the consummation of philosophy; but it is the chief idea communicated by the *Confessions.* The *Confessions,* thus, are an elaborate affirmation and interpretation of the mysterious ways of divine grace; and, though not itself a systematic theology of grace, the work everywhere testifies to the operations of grace, so much so that, to the observant reader, God, not Augustine, is the protagonist or leading actor. Consequently, we are liable to misread the *Confessions* if we expect to read his autobiography in it or if we do not understand that, for Augustine, philo-

sophy completes itself in a persuasive power capable of ful-
filling the desires that evoked it in the first place, these
desires being seen finally as the first effects of divine speech
spoken to and within the soul.

In the *Confessions* philosophy is a three-fold search for
beatitude: by the mind and reason for the truth; by the heart
and will for the tranquility of the supreme good; and by the
tongue for the beautiful and praiseworthy. The experience
which initiates it is disquiet of soul; and, from within this experience two beliefs arise spontaneously: that, surely, there is
a God, the supreme good for the soul; and that he has a care
for humankind.[25] Indeed, as if from his mother's milk, the
infant Augustine drank the name of Christ, and that name
would remain for him, amidst all his difficulties, one of the
primary religious claimants upon his soul.[26] Augustine's
philosophical search, then, does not begin in any systematic
or heroic effort to doubt and thereby abstract himself from
the given situation of his life. He will have his doubts and feel
the allure of skepticism, but such doubt does not start his
search for beatitude. His experienced privation of it does.

In the remaining few pages, I will outline only Augustine's
intellectual search within the general model of philosophy he
expressed in the story of his conversion. The pattern emerging from his search will be an authoritative model of christian
intellectuality for the Middle Ages. This search for the true
began in earnest, as everyone knows, when, after reading
Cicero's exhortation to philosophy in the dialogue *Hortensius,*
he ardently desired wisdom and only wisdom itself, whatever
it might be, not the teachings of some sect of philosophers.
The climax of his intellectual search comes in Book VII. The
story of the impediments he faced up to that point, may I say
again, shows us what obstructs *confessio* as the laudatory
revelation of God's potent and merciful persuasions of the soul.

In general, what obstructs the discovery of the truth is
intellectual pride (*superbia*). Pride also affects the heart and

tongue, though we cannot now take these into account. In this respect, then, the story of the discovery of truth amounts to uncovering the reasons for intellectual humility. So important is humility for Augustine that, if we fail to see its role, we will completely misunderstand philosophy. Without rational humility, the soul cannot see the reasons to advance or rise up to a knowledge of God through comparison and contrast between it and the external world of sensible things, and then, between it and God. Moreover, without humility, the soul will not see the need or the suitability of what Christianity is basically all about—the humility of God's mode of redemptive love—the sending of his Word to man by the Incarnation of his Son, the supreme instance of the divine speech by which men are turned to God as the source of their beatitude. Intellectual humility is the prerequisite for the praise of God because without it the reasonableness of believing in God before one knows much at all about him does not occur to the soul. For St Augustine *any increase in knowledge about God and the soul that does not, at the same time, encourage increasing awareness of the limitations of the human intellect comes to naught.* For the soul deafens and blinds itself to the illuminating Word being spoken to it. Thereby, the soul wanders into error, both in the logical sense and in the moral and psychiatric sense of the word.[27] Even the tongue is afflicted, since, without humility it serves the disordered loves of a heart by attracting glory and aiming for worldly success, which are things the confessing bishop laments in his educational experience and in his career as a professor of rhetoric. The *Confessions* show us the redemption of rhetoric, not its damnation.

The impediments to the truth intellectual pride constructs are scientific rationalism and imaginative literalism, and both of them emerge in Augustine's struggle to liberate himself from Manicheanism. The Manichees promised him truth about God and the soul. They did not require of Augustine what the Catholic Christians did, namely, faith *before* one

knew the truth. But, then, what the Manichees delivered as
the truth was an elaborate comic and religious mythology
whose meaning puzzled Augustine. Though he could at first
find no expositor of the myths to answer his questions, he
was told that the erudite Faustus, a manichean bishop, could
resolve his difficulties.

The failure of Faustus is the first occasion in the *Confessions* for Augustine the narrator to confess the meaning of
what I have called scientific rationalism and imaginative
literalism, the two major forms of intellectual *superbia* with
which Augustine deals. In fact, the model of augustinian
intellectuality comes into full view here. Subsequent episodes,
including those in Book VII, only give it definition in fuller
detail.

While awaiting a meeting with Faustus, Augustine was
reading the pagan philosophers. When he compared the
teachings of their books with the splendid phantasms of
manichean myth, he discovered that for natural phenomena,
solstices, equinoxes, and the eclipses of the great celestial
lights, the myths he was given contained no rational account
confirmable by number or eyesight. Pagan physics, relying on
reason, sense perception, and the laws of number seemed to
him more probable. However, Augustine did not yet know
whether, with Faustus' help, he could transform into true
food the splendid phantasms of the Manichees as he had often
transformed the verses and songs of the poets.[28] Augustine
was in search of what we would call a method of allegoresis
that would make images respond to a questioning intelligence concerned with truth. But Faustus proved unable to do
so, having little knowledge of the liberal disciplines, though
he did possess a certain smoothness in speech.

As Augustine recollects the failure of Faustus, he does not
hesitate to give credit where it was due—to the pagan philosophers who helped him expose the irrationality and allegorical impermeability of manichean religious myth. Yet these
same philosophers who spoke truly of the world failed either

to find the Lord of the world in what truths they did discover or, when they did find him, failed to honor him as Lord. Augustine does admit that, in the language of St Paul, reason can know the power and glory of God as it inspects the visible things of the world. It can, but as a matter of historical fact, it did not, since the ancient philosophers failed. They failed, says Augustine, because in their pride 'they did not seek piously'.[29] Thus, for Augustine the method of philosophical physics—dialectical reason founded upon the laws of number and the evidence of sensible experience—is not the method by which one religiously attaches himself to God in proper worship. Something more than reason is required.

A sort of law, very different from any rule of dialectics, comes into effect when the soul is seeking God. This law is announced in the very first sentence of the *Confessions,* and Augustine echoes it as he meditates upon the way of philosophical science:

> You are great, O Lord, and regard things
> humble, but the exalted you keep far from
> knowing: nor do you draw near except to
> the contrite in heart, nor are you discovered
> by the proud, not even if they by curious skill
> number the stars and sand and measure the
> sidereal regions and trace out the ways of the
> stars.[30]

A pride (*superbia*), born of success, impeded the piety necessary to any relationship of the soul with God. The success of the pagans was their downfall in this respect, for, as Augustine says, 'they did not religiously seek whence they had the talent by which they sought [the truths of the world]'.[31] Thus, piety implies the humility which recognizes that reason's power to discover the truth is not explainable by reason itself. Later, in Book VII, we find out why: truth possesses an unchangeability and permanence not possessed either by the things of the world that fall into corruption or by the mind itself, so often changed as it learns, so often affected by forgetfulness and illusion.[32]

The plain fact is that for Augustine wisdom is piety, not a rational science. Vergil once said that happy is the man who knows the causes of things. Indirectly alluding to Vergil's text, Augustine allows that human beatitude is independent of increase in rational science. In fact, to find wisdom one does not need at all the rational science of the so-called philosophers:

> O Lord God of Truth, is he who knows these
> things [of rational science] thereby pleasing
> to you? Surely unhappy is the man who knows
> all these things but does not know you. Blessed
> is he, rather, who knows you, even if he does not
> know these things. Indeed he who knows both you
> and them is not happier because of them but because
> of you alone is he blessed, if as he is thinking of you,
> so he glorifies you and gives you thanks and does
> not become vain in his thinking.[33]

This text is not anti-intellectualism, but it does clearly indicate that God, the source of beatitude, is not a conquest of reason operating apart from a contrast between God and the seeker, a contrast that evokes humility and the giving of glory to God, all of which is piety. In a paradoxical fashion, it is necessary to praise God as one gets to know much of him, in order to get to know him and love him more. In other words, looking at this matter from the standpoint of rhetorical praise, the grounds or reasons for praise of God are discovered only if the soul is disposed to praise and does praise while it seeks to know *what* he is who is being praised. Plato and Aristotle had taught antiquity that the question of essence must precede speech which bestows praise or blame.[34] That makes good sense generally, but in the matters of God and the soul, where human happiness is at stake, that sensible law does not hold. God must be praised as one seeks to know him, and he gives already both in the visible universe and in the evident wretchedness all men experience enough suggestion that he exists to get the whole process started in faith. Piety demands faith.

The reasonableness of faith as a starting-point for reason Augustine will discover later on, after hearing Ambrose lift the mystic veil from the Scriptures and reveal that Catholic Christians did not hold the crude and materialistic teachings that the Manichees ridiculed in the Old Testament.[35] Augustine would then realize how deeply reason is implicated in a network of belief that it cannot prove but that makes human life and society possible. Following authority for what is difficult to understand is not unreasonable, given the condition of reason in human life. Here, then, is another awareness productive of intellectual humility, not pride.

Moreover, suddenly to find in christian mythology, so to speak, a spiritual interpretation that was not, like the myths of the Manichees, impermeable to a rationally inquiring mind was a liberation. As Augustine knew from his own experience in the schools, the fictions of the poets could be transformed into true food for the soul. That the Sacred Scriptures permitted reasonable interpretation, that they produced rational insights into truths of reason independently seen, that they in fact provoked the mind beyond its own limits in a way not confounded by imaginative and figurative language—all these things are a permanent legacy of the augustinian model of intellectuality.

Even the books of the Platonists, famed in augustinian scholarship, did not provide Augustine with a list of doctrines as much as they showed him a sort of philosophical myth corresponding in many ways with the beginning of St John's gospel and other parts of the New Testament. Though compatible in so many ways with the gospels, platonic rational myth fell short in the one most important thing: the humility of the Word's descent to men that they may ascend to God.

There was no conception of the divine rhetoric of redemption in the Platonists.

But these experiences were to come in the future. While the narrator bishop recollects his experience with Faustus, he observes that the pagan philosophers did not come to know the humble way shown to men in the divine speech of the Incarnation. Thus, in foolish pride, their hearts deluded by deceiving phantasms, the philosophers reversed the way of humility, and by exalting themselves descended into psychic vanity and corrupted God's incorruptible glory:

> . . . they [the philosophers] think themselves
> exalted with the stars and brilliant, but, see, they
> have plunged to the earth. And they say many true
> things about the creature, but the truth, artificer of
> the creature, they do not seek piously and so they do
> not find; or if they do find him, recognizing God,
> they do not honor him as God or give thanks and
> grow vain in their thinking and say they are wise
> by attributing to themselves what is yours and in
> this way by a very perverse blindness attribute to
> you what is theirs . . . and convert your truth into
> lies and so worship and serve the creature rather
> than the creator.[36]

The whole model of augustinian intellectuality emerges clearly in the episodes dealing with Faustus the Manichean. There is no need here to recount the way Augustine resolves the issues of evil and spiritual substance, for both issues are occasions of intellectual humility in their solution and open the way for the brilliant analysis of Scripture as the speech of God in the latter books of the *Confessions.*

The University of Dallas

NOTES

1.   'Confitebor Domino secundum iustitiam eius'; *Enarrationes in Psalmos* 7. 19 (v. 18), edd. D. Dekkers and J. Fraipont, in *Corpus Christianorum Series Latina [CCSL]* 38 (Turnhout: Brepols, 1956) 48. The editors (p. xv), following S. Zarb's study of the chronology of the *Enarrationes,* ascribe the dictation of comments upon the first thirty-two psalms to the year 392.

Whenever I could, I have cited Augustine's words in the critical editions of the *CCSL.* Otherwise I have relied upon J. P. Migne, *Patrologiae Cursus Completus, Series Latina [PL]* (Paris, 1844–64). Augustine's works are in tomes 32–47. All translations into English are mine.

2.   *Soliloquia* I. 2. 7 *(PL* 32: 872).

3.   Etienne Gilson, *The Christian Philosophy of Saint Augustine,* trans. L. E. M. Lynch (New York: Random House, 1960) p. x.

4.   Consider, for example, the text of *Confessiones* X. 2. 2: 'Et quo fructu tibi confitear, dixi. Neque id ago uerbis carnis et uocibus, sed uerbis animae et clamore cogitationis, quem nouit auris tua . . . Confessio itaque mea, deus meus, in conspectu tuo tibi tacite fit et non tacite. Tacet enim strepitu, clamat affectu.' Ed. Lucas Verheijen, in *CCSL* 38 (Turnhout: Brepols, 1981) 133.

5.   The ancient theory of epideictic or demonstrative rhetoric is summarized in Quintilian, *Institutio Oratoria* III. 4. 12-16 and III. 7. 1-28. See also the useful synthesis of epideictic theory in Josef Martin, *Antike Rhetorik: Technik und Methode* (Munich: C.H. Beck, 1974) 177-210.

6.   The paradoxical encomium is best treated in Theodore Burgess, *Epideictic Literature,* University of Chicago Studies in Classical Philology, vol. 3 (Chicago: University of Chicago Press, 1902) 157-166.

7.   *Retractationes* II. 6 *(PL* 32: 632): 'Confessionum mearum libri tredecim, et de malis et de bonis meis Deum laudant justum et bonum, atque in eum excitant humanum intellectum et affectum'.

8.   By 'literary criticism' I mean, not a particular school of thought, but a general outlook attentive to the author's design implicit in the pattern of action (plot), characters, dialogue, and setting of a narrative.

9.   That God moves man to confess is made immediately evident by Augustine in *Confessiones* I. 1: 'Tu [Domine] excitas, ut laudare te delectat [homo]'. The point is affirmed by Pierre Courcelle, *Recherches sur les Confessions de Saint Augustin,* nouvelle édition, (Paris: E. de Boc-

card, 1968), 14, in light of *Conf.* XI. 1. 1: 'Tu prior uoluisti, ut confiterer tibi'.

10.   *Confessiones* X. 1. 1: 'Laudet te cor meum et lingua mea; X, 4, 7: Et venit dies, quo etiam actu soluerer a professione rhetorica, unde iam cogitatu solutus eram. Et factum est, eruisti linguam mean, unde iam euras cor meum . . . ' . The metaphor of the 'pen of the tongue' (*lingua calami,* XI. 2. 2) emphasizes that Augustine is conscious of *confessio* as an act of writing a text which will be read by others.

11.   Because the eulogy of Monica forms a part of Augustine's *confessio,* he emphasizes that he will speak not of her gifts, but of God's in her (*Conf.* IX. 8. 17: 'Non eius, sed tua dicam dona in eam').

12.   Augustine stresses the interplay between thought, desire, and the conversation (*sermo*) and words (*verbum*) of him and Monica, all leading to their conjectures about the speech of the *Verbum* directly to their souls; see *Confessiones* IX. 10. 24-25.

13.   See Gilson, *Christian Philosophy of Saint Augustine,* pp. 115-126. St Augustine speaks of differences between *scientia* and *sapientia,* to which the Aristotelian's distinction between theoretical and practical knowledge has little pertinence. *Sapientia,* wisdom, may involve *scientia,* knowledge—whether theoretical or practical, in the Aristotelian senses— but wisdom confers happiness by leading one to the loving possession of God and does not necessarily need science. See below, n. 30.

14.   *De vera religione* I. 1: '[cum] omnis uitae bonae ac beatae uia in uera religione sit constituta, quo unus deus colitur et purgatissima pietate cognoscitur principium naturarum omnium, a quo universitas et incohatur et perficitur et continetur . . . ' . Ed. K. D. Daur, in *CCSL* 32 (1962) 187.

15.   *De vera religione* I, I (*CCSL* 32: 187): ' . . . hinc euidentius error deprehenditur eorum populorum, qui multos deos colere quam unum uerum deum et dominum omnium maluerunt, quod eorum sapientes, quos philosophos uocant, scholas habebant dissentientes et templa communia. Non enim uel populos uel sacerdotes latebat, de ipsorum deorum natura quam diuersa sentirent, cum suam quisque opinionem publice profiteri non formidaret atque omnibus si posset persuadere moliretur; omnes tamen cum sectatoribus suis diuersa sentientibus ad sacra communia nullo prohibente ueniebant. Non nunc agitur, quis eorum senserit uerius, sed certe illud satis, quantum mihi uidetur, apparet aliud eos in religione suscepisse cum populo et aliud eodem ipso populo audiente defendisse priuatim.'

16.   *De vera religione* II. 2 (*CCSL* 32: 188): ' . . . suauius ad legendum quam potentius a persuadendum scripsit Plato. Non enim sic isti nati erant, ut populorum suorum opinionem ad uerum cultum ueri dei a

simulacrorum superstitione atque ab huius mundi uanitate conuerterent'.
17.   *De vera religione* II. 2 (*CCSL* 32: 188): ' . . . et post eius damna-
tionem mortemque nemo ausus est iurare per canem nec appellare
quemcumque lapidem Iouem . . . '.
18.   *De vera religione* II. 2 (*CCSL* 32: 188): ' . . . sed haec tantum-
modo memoriae litterisque mandare. Quod utrum timore an aliqua
cognitione temporum fecerint, iudicare non est meum'.
19.   *De vera religione* III. 3 (*CCSL* 32: 189): ' . . . qui talia populis
persuaderet credenda saltem, si percipere non ualerent, aut, si qui pos-
sent percipere, non prauis opinionibus multitudinis implicati uulgaribus
obruerentur . . . '.
20.   *De vera religione* IV, 6 (*CCSL* 32: 192): 'Haec sunt, quae nos
persuadere populis non ausi sumus, et eorum potius consuetudini cessi-
mus quam illos in nostram fidem uoluntatemque traduximus.'
21.   See Raymond DiLorenzo, "The Critique of Socrates in Cicero's
De Oratore: Ornatus and the Nature of Wisdom', *Philosophy and
Rhetoric* 11 (1978) 247-261.
22.   Cicero, *De inventione* I. 1. 1-2. 3.
23.   We ought to note that Augustine's purpose is to praise the glorious
city of God. Once again the aim and techniques of epideictic rhetoric
fuse with Augustine's apologetic and theological intentions.
24.   See *Contra Academicos* III. 17. 37-19. 42 (*CCSL* 32: 57-60).
25.   Augustine notes in *Conf.* VI. 5. 7 (*CCSL* 27, p. 78) that never did
he forsake the beliefs that God exists and that He governs human affairs.
26.   See *Confessiones* III. 4. 8 (*CCSL* 27: 30).
27.   The moral and psychiatric senses of *error* come to Augustine from
the philosophical psychiatry of Cicero's *Tusculan Disputations*. See, for
example, *Tusc. Disp.* III. 1. 2: 'nunc autem simul atque editi in lucem et
suscepti sumus, in omni continuo pravitate et in summa opinionum per-
versitate versamur, ut paene cum lacte nutricis *errorem* suxisse videamur'.
Ed. J. E. King, Loeb Classical Library (London and Cambridge, Mass.:
W. Heinemann and Harvard University Press, 1927, rpt. 1966).
28.   See *Confessiones* III. 6. 11 (*CCSL* 27: 32).
29.   *Confessiones* V. 3. 5 (*CCSL* 27: 59): 'non pie quaerunt et ideo
non inveniunt . . . '. See Raymond D. DiLorenzo, '*Non Pie Quaerunt:*
Rhetoric, Dialectic, and the Discovery of the True in Augustine's
Confessions', *Augustinian Studies* 14 (1983) 119-129. A similar analysis
of the importance of the Faustus-episode is made here.
30.   *Confessiones* V. 3. 3 (*CCSL* 27: 58): 'Quoniam magnus es, domine,
et humilia respicis, excelsa autem a longe cognoscis nec propinquas nisi
obtritis corde nec inueniris a superbis, nec si illi curiosa peritia numerent
stellas et harenam et dimentiantur sidereas plagas et uestigent uias astrorum'.

31. *Confessiones* V. 3. 4 (*CCSL* 27: 59): '. . . non enim religiose
quaerunt, unde habeant ingenium, quo ista quaerunt . . . ' .
32. See *Confessiones* VII. 17. 23 (*CCSL* 27: 107).
33. *Confessiones* V. 4. 7 (*CCSL* 27: 60): 'Numquid, domine deus
ueritatis, quisquis nouit ista, iam placet tibi? Infelix enim homo, qui
scit illa omnia, te autem nescit; beatus, autem, qui te scit etiamsi illa nesciat,
qui uero et te et illa nouit, non propter illa beatior, sed propter te solum
beatus est, si cognoscens te sicut te glorificet et gratias agat et non
euanescat in cogitationibus suis.'
34. This priority of the question of nature (or essence) to that of
quality or kind is the major theme of Vinzenz Buchheit, *Untersuchungen
zur Theorie des Genos epideiktikon von Gorgias bis Aristoteles* (Munich:
Max Heuber, 1960).
35. See *Confessiones* VI. 4 (*CCSL* 27: 76-77).
36. *Confessiones* V. 3. 5 (*CCSL* 27: 59): '. . . putant se excelsos esse
cum sideribus et lucidos, et ecce ruerunt in terram, et obscuratum est
insipiens cor eorum. Et multa uera de creatura dicunt et ueritatem,
creaturae artificem, non pie quaerunt et ideo non inueniunt, aut si
inueniunt, cognoscentes deum non sicut deum honorant aut gratias
agunt et euanescunt in cogitationibus suis et dicunt se esse sapientes sibi
tribuendo quae tua sunt . . . et conuertunt ueritatem tuam in mendacium
et colunt et seruiunt creaturae potius quam creatori.'

BEDE'S STRUCTURAL USE OF WORDPLAY
AS A WAY TO TEACH
Lawrence T. Martin

'REMARKABLE' is the word Dom Jean Leclercq uses to describe the achievement of the Venerable Bede, an eighth-century Anglo-Saxon monk of Jarrow in the far north of England, a location of practically maximum distance at that time from Rome, the center of Christianity and christian learning as well as of the remnants of the classical tradition of latin learning and literary excellence. 'It is remarkable', says Leclercq, 'that, less than one hundred years after the arrival of St Augustine of Canterbury, this grandchild of pagans should become a Doctor of the Church, and one of the classics of our Christian literature. This child of barbarians knew and quoted Pliny and other authors of classical antiquity . . . . He was very well acquainted with the Fathers of the Church . . . and he unites all these treasures in an harmonious synthesis.'[1] Dom David Knowles found it remarkable that Bede, who 'probably never went further south than York, nor further north than Lindisfarne', was so learned. 'Living on the edge of the world, in a land

with no tradition of learning [which had been] converted to
Christianity only half a century before, he had no books save
for the collection that had been assembled by his first abbot
. . . . yet with this collection Bede made himself the most
learned man in Western Europe.'[2]

Bede's genius was contagious. It produced a climate of
intellectual productivity in northern England that is sometimes referred to as the 'Northumbrian Renaissance', and
Bede himself was indeed a sort of 'Renaissance man', for his
interest and knowledge extended to many fields—natural
science, mathematics, astronomy, grammar, history, theology,
and above all exegesis or interpretation of Scripture. Today
Bede is recognized chiefly as an historian, the author of *The
Ecclesiastical History of the English People,* but in his own
time and throughout the Middle Ages he was valued primarily for his exegetical works, which were studied and copied
in monastic centers of learning all over Europe. At the end of
the Middle Ages or at the dawn of another renaissance, Dante,
in canto 10 of the *Paradiso,* included Bede among the circle
of twelve lights, the learned 'men through whom the Word of
God was mediated in wisdom to the world'.[3]

My concern here is not directly with the theological
content of Bede's exegesis, but rather with the style and
artistry which he exhibits in his exegetical writing, specifically in his commentary on the Acts of the Apostles. The
extremely high quality and sophistication of Bede's latin
writing is just as remarkable in a way as his great learning, for
he was a native speaker of Old English and very far removed
from the sphere of the latin language. How, we may ask, did
Bede acquire his remarkable command of Latin?[4] He clearly
did not, like his continental contemporaries, learn Latin as a
spoken tongue. There is some evidence that the high quality
of latin (and greek) teaching brought to the school of Canterbury by Archbishop Theodore and Abbot Hadrian had pene-
trated as far north as Jarrow, where Bede probably entered
the monastic grammar school at the age of seven. Nevertheless,

the primary explanation of Bede's excellent Latin is probably what is still the best means of language learning, viz., a combination of a gifted mind interested in language, and an atmosphere of immersion in the target language. From his seventh year Bede lived in an atmosphere of Latin, especially the Latin of the Scriptures. The Divine Office with its chanted latin psalms and scriptural readings, took up several hours of the day. In addition, an important feature of the monastic life was the *lectio divina,* or private, meditative reading of Scripture and the Fathers. Not only the quantity of latin reading, but also the reading technique used in the *lectio divina* is important in accounting for Bede's latin competence, and also for the particular feature of his style that I am concerned with in this paper, his use of wordplay of various sorts. Private reading at this time was done aloud, either murmured or at least with physical mouthing of the words. Benedict's *Rule* cautions monks who want to read not to disturb others,[5] and Augustine recalls his astonishment at Ambrose's peculiar habit of reading in complete silence.[6] Silent reading as we know it is a recent development. The mouthing of the words in the *lectio divina* is probably the basis of a frequent metaphor—the monk must 'feed on the Word of God' as he feeds on the Eucharist. A variation on this metaphor is the notion of *ruminatio,* a comparison of reading, especially reading of the Scriptures, to the way a cow chews its cud, munching continuously and relishing the delight of sweet grass and also regurgitating the previously chewed cud to re-relish its sweetness. Likewise the reader chews on the words of Scripture (literally moving his lips and jaw), and relishes their spiritual sweetness. The analogue to the cow's regurgitation process is the reader's summoning back to his memory earlier reading, associating that with the text before him. The *ruminatio* metaphor was related to the definition of clean animals, those which may be eaten, in the Law of Leviticus (11:3) and Deuteronomy (14:6) as those which have a cloven hoof and chew the cud (*ruminant*). Bede's most familiar use of this

metaphor is in the story of Caedmon, the first English poet,
in the *Ecclesiastical History*,[7] but Bede also uses the *ruminatio* metaphor frequently in his exegetical works, practically
every time a cow or ox or deer is mentioned in his text. There
is a good example in one of Bede's homilies, where he urges
us to imitate 'the clean animals, now ruminating by vocalizing
with the mouth, now drawing back up from the innermost
reaches of the heart'.[8] The technique of semi-aloud reading
in the *lectio divina*, along with his fondness for the *ruminatio*
metaphor, was probably responsible for certain features of
Bede's latin style which will be explored in this paper. The
vocalizing and chewing upon the words of Scripture produced in Bede a delight in the physical sound and shape and
sweetness of the individual word, and the *ruminatio* or cow-
chewing-its-cud notion is reflected in Bede's reluctance to let
a good word go; instead he repeats it and plays with its various
forms or alternative meanings. The regurgitation aspect of the
ruminatio notion is also reflected in Bede's constant allusions
to other passages in Scripture where a key word in the text
under consideration also occurs. For Bede, as for monastic
exegetes in general, the technique of reading *lectio divina*,
reading not only with the eyes and mind, but with the muscles
of the vocal system and the ears as well, led to a knowing of
the Bible 'by heart', so that Bede was able to supply a text or
word from elsewhere in the Scriptures to correspond to the
text he was commenting upon. He was, in Leclercq's words,
'a sort of living concordance'.[9]

Bede typifies monastic exegesis, which Leclercq has
characterized as 'inseparably literal and mystical', literal
because of the importance given to individual words, and
mystical because each word was regarded as addressed by God
to each reader for his salvation.[10] Bede had a consuming
interest in and love for words. He regarded the individual
words of his scriptural texts on the one hand as 'mysteries',
or sacraments of divine meaning if properly read, and on the
other hand as intriguing linguistic problems demanding solu-

tion. Elsewhere I have discussed Bede's competence as a scientific linguist,[11] dealing there with his comments of an etymological sort, chiefly concerning proper names and mostly borrowed from Jerome or Isidore, and also with Bede's more original comments in which he rigorously compares the greek and latin words in his interlinear text of Acts in order to clarify syntactic or referential ambiguity in the Latin, or to explore differences in the semantic fields of greek and latin synonyms. In the present paper I am concerned, not with Bede as a linguist and not with his scientific interest in language, but rather with Bede as a lover of words who in his own latin style manifests a genuine delight in words and wordplay of various sorts, in etymological puns and in creative exploitation of the polysemous nature of many latin words in order to delight his readers and at the same time to make his message the more effective.

Monastic exegesis is a kind of literary criticism which aims both to explain the sacred text and to move the reader, to produce appreciation and delight as well as understanding. One of Bede's earliest works is a little treatise, *De schematibus et tropis,* a 'textbook' on figures of speech written for his students.[12] In the introduction Bede announces his basic thesis, that the Bible surpasses classical literature not only in its content, but also in its artistic composition, even when judged against the very standards of classical rhetoric. The body of the work is a classified list of figures of speech known to classical rhetoricians, but illustrated by scriptural examples. 'Schemata' are manipulations of the position of words, various types of repetition, and similar devices used for the sake of embellishment. 'Tropes' refer to metaphorical uses of words, where a word's specific, narrow, concrete meaning is replaced by an extended or figurative meaning. In *De schematibus et tropis,* Bede's purpose is clearly not only to teach appreciation of the artistic use of language in the Bible, but also to teach his students how to write elegantly by imitating the verbal artistry and figurative language of the Bible. My purpose here is to

examine certain stylistic features of Bede's own writing in his
Commentary on Acts. In order to move and delight his
readers, as well as to teach them, Bede employs the sorts of
stylistic devices which he had described in *De schematibus et
tropis.* His own practice, however, is far more sophisticated
than his theory. I will focus on two features of Bede's style,
both of which we might label 'wordplay'. The first of these
features is a *schema*—Bede's use of patterns of *repetition* of
certain words to build a sort of framework around which to
structure his comment on a particular Acts verse. Sometimes
this repetition involves *variation* between two (or more)
derived forms of the same root, and at other times Bede plays
off words of similar sounds (puns) or words of only apparent
etymological connection (etymological puns).

The second feature of Bede's style which I wish to discuss
is a *trope* which Bede frequently employs in conjunction with
the repetition and variation schemata just described. Here he
juxtaposes two or more occurrences of the same word, or its
etymologically related forms, but in addition he plays upon
the layers of meaning which one and the same word often
carries, from concrete and specific to abstract and figurative.
Here again the wordplay functions in a structural way relative
to the design of the comment as a whole. The Commentary on
Acts is full of such wordplay, often used as a structural device,
but I have time here to give only a few examples which illustrate four general types of structural wordplay.

Let us begin by looking at some examples of Bede's use of
repetition schemata as a kind of structural framework for a
comment on a particular Acts verse. These examples are taken
from Bede's commentary on the story of Paul's visit to Athens
in Acts 17. The first is a simple example, showing Bede taking
off from an unusual word in the Acts verse, a compound–
derivative of the root *semen* ('seed'), then moving to the root
form used in a metaphorical way, and then by way of the
regurgitative or memory aspect of *ruminatio,* or concordance
exegesis, ending his brief comment with an allusion to 1 Corin-

thians, where Paul used a verbal derivative of *semen,* also
with a figurative meaning:

> Acts 17:18 QUID VULT SEMINIVERBIUS HIC DICERE?
> 1) Recte *seminiverbius,* id est, stermologos, vocatur,
> 2) quia *semen* est verbum dei,
> 3) et ipse dicit, 'Si nos vobis spiritalia *seminavimus.'*
> [CC 121:71,26/8]

In the Acts verse Paul is called a 'sower of words' (*seminiverbius*) contemptuously, in the sense of a chatterbox. Bede
picks up on the etymology of this unusual word and reverses
its use, referring to the greek equivalent term in the process,
and working in the root *semen* used metaphorically: 'Paul is
rightly called a *seminiverbius,* i.e., *stermologus,* because the
seed (*semen*) is the word of God'. Then, in line 3, Bede refers
to Paul's own use of an etymologically related verb, used with
similar metaphorical sense in 1 Cor 9:11: 'We have sown
(*seminavimus*) for you spiritual things'.

The next example, from Bede's commentary on Acts 17:23
(Paul's sermon to the Athenians) is a good example of Bede's
use of repetition and variation schemata as a structural framework for his comment:

> Acts 17:23 INVENI ARAM IN QUA SCRIPTUM
> ERAT: 'IGNOTO DEO.'
> 1) *Notus* in Judaea deus sed non receptus,
> 2) *ignotus* in Achaia deus quamvis per multa
>   quaesitus.
> 3) Et ideo qui *ignorat ignorabitur,*
> 4) qui praevaricatur damnabitur.
> 5) Neutri inmunes a culpa, sed excusabiliores
> 6) qui fidem non *obtulere* Christo quem *nesciebant*
> 7) quam qui manus *intulere* Christo quem *sciebant.*
>   [CC 121:71,29/34]

Several words for 'to know' and their negative forms are here
arranged in neatly balanced syntactic structures to develop a
basic contrast between two kinds of non-response to the revelation of God in Christ. The comment itself does not greatly
clarify the literal sense, nor does it make a profound moral
or allegorical point. It seems to exist primarily for the sake of
the aesthetic delight provided by the wordplay structure.
Some of the wordplay can be captured in translation, e.g.,
notus/ignotus ('known'/'unknown') in lines 1–2; and *nescie-*
bant/sciebant ('not know'/'know') in lines 6–7. We can also
keep the wordplay of *ignorat/ignorabitur* in line 3 by translating both words with 'not recognize' or 'ignore', but in
either case we lose Bede's further play on the etymological
connection between these words and the other forms of the
root *noscere* ('to know') which Bede used in lines one and
two. It is also impossible to capture in translation the clever
playing with the contrast between the two derivatives of the
basic verbal root *ferre* ('to bear') in the perfect verbs *obtulere*
and *intulere* in lines 6 and 7. I would translate *fidem non*
obtulere as 'not put faith in,' and *manus intulere* as 'lay hands
on,' but this unfortunately loses Bede's effect, for in using
two etymologically related words in parallel constructions,
he highlights the contrast between the two radically different
responses taken toward the new 'knowledge' of God made
available in Christ—that of the Athenians, who 'did not put
their faith' (*fidem non obtulere*) in Christ because they did
now know him, for he was their 'unknown God' (*ignoto deo*),
and that of the Jews, who 'laid hands on' (*manus intulere*)
Christ although they had knowledge concerning who he truly
was.

Next, I would like to look at some examples of a second,
more elaborate, type of schema, in which Bede uses etymologically related words, not only to provide aesthetic delight,
but to reinforce the theological content of his interpretation.
These examples come from the story of Philip's baptism of
the ethiopian eunuch who was a minister of the court of

Queen Candace, on the desert road from Jerusalem to Gaza.
Bede's commentary on this story is many-faceted, but basically he highlights the contrasts inherent in the situation: salvation (i.e., fruitfulness) found in a desert, the blackness of
the Ethiopian's skin versus the whiteness of his soul, and so
forth.

First, a simple illustration of the technique under discussion:

> Acts 8:27 ET ECCE VIR AETHIOPS EUNUCHUS
> POTENS
> Pro *virtute* et integritate mentis *vir* appellatur . . .
> [CC 121:41,62/3]

The Acts verse reads: 'And behold, an Ethiopian man (*vir*), an
influential eunuch.' Bede comments: 'He is called a man (*vir*)
because of his *virtue* (*virtute*) and wholeness of mind (*inte-
gritate mentis*),' in spite of his lack of physical vir-ness and
wholeness.

Presently I want to look at a more complex example of
this same technique of etymological wordplay used to reinforce a metaphorical interpretation. This will be taken from
the same Acts story, but first a little background is necessary.
Bede was evidently intrigued by an etymologically related
family of words which included the verb *colere* and the nouns
colonus, colonia, cultus, and *cultura.* These words all had a
triple-leveled meaning which is still available to us in English
loanwords:

1) *an agricultural meaning:* 'to till the soil' ('cultiva-
tor,' 'under cultivation')

2) *an urbanization meaning:* 'to inhabit,' often with
overtones of city dwellers being civilized, educated,
well-mannered (as in 'a cultivated person,' or 'a cultured person')

3)   *a religious meaning:* 'to worship the gods' ('cult')

All of these levels of meaning are attested in classical texts. In his commentary on Acts 16:12, Bede gives a straightforward etymological explanation, that is, purely the linguistic facts, with no allegorical application, and here he establishes the etymological connection between *colonia* and *cultus/cultor,* a relation which is not immediately evident from the surface forms:

> Acts 16:12 QUAE EST PRIMA PARTE MACEDONIAE CIVITAS COLONIA
> 'Colonia est quae defectu indigenarum novis *cultoribus* adimpletur, unde et a *cultu* agri *colonia* dicta est.' [CC 121: 69,23/5]

Meanings #1 and #2 are involved here. The Acts verses refers to Philippi, 'which is the principal city of part of Macedonia, a colony *(colonia).*' Bede's comment, borrowed from Isidore, is: 'A *colonia* is a place which, because of a lack of original dwellers, is filled with new inhabitants *(cultoribus),* and thus it is called a *colonia* from the cultivation *(cultus)* of a field.'

Now, returning to the story of the Ethiopian eunuch baptized on the desert road from Jerusalem to Gaza, we see Bede fully exploiting the range of meanings of this *colere* word-family, and he uses this etymological wordplay to reinforce a fundamental metaphoric comparison he wishes to make between pagans and the desert as an image of spirituality aridity. This comment also incorporates similar wordplay between another pair of etymologically related words, the noun *deserta* ('desert') and the participle *deserta* (from *deserere,* 'to remove from'):

> Acts 8:26 AD VIAM QUAE DESCENDIT AB HIERUSALEM IN GAZAM, HAEC EST DESERTA.
>   1)   Non via sed Gaza *deserta* dicitur . . .

2)   quae allegorice gentium plebem designat,
3)   olim a dei *cultura desertam,*
4)   neque ullius prophetarum praedicationibus
      excultam. [CC 121:41,52/7]

The Acts verse reads: 'An angel of the Lord spoke to Phillip, saying, "Arise and go south to the road that goes down from Jerusalem to Gaza." This is a desert.' On the literal level, of course, a desert suggests both a lack of inhabitants or civilization, and a lack of agricultural fruitfulness. Bede points us to the spiritual analogy: 'Allegorically this designates the people of the gentiles, who were once a desert (*deserta,* line 1), removed from (*desertam,* line 3) the worship of God (*dei cultura,* line 3), and not brought to fertility (*excultam,* line 4) by the preaching of any of the prophets.' Bede's choice of *excultam,* a derivative of the *colere* family, suggests all three *colere* meanings at once: The gentiles were, of course, removed from the worship of the true God (meaning #3), and the juxtaposition with another *colere* word, clearly modified (*dei cultura,* line 3) makes this religious meaning primary. However, the metaphoric comparison of the gentiles to a desert calls on the other two *colere* meanings as well—the gentile desert, even in the worldly, civilized (meaning #2) world of manners at a court like that of Candace, is, through the eyes of faith, uncivilized, or 'uncultured.' (*Excolere* can also mean to improve a person's mind or manners.) Finally, such a gentile desert is also unfruitful, not put under cultivation (meaning #1), and therefore unproductive of virtuous behavior.

We move now to a third type of stylistic technique involving wordplay used as a structural device. Here, Bede combines repetition schemata with metaphorical tropes involving playing with two levels of meaning of the same word, concrete and abstract. Bede's interpretations frequently move from some clarification of the literal, historical facts of an Acts event to a moral or mystical truth signified by these

literal facts, and he sometimes echoes or reiterates his metaphorical connection between the tangible facts of the physical
world and their spiritual meaning by repeating certain words,
using them in their physical, concrete sense in the literal part
of the comment, but repeating them with an extended, abstract, psychological, moral, or mystical sense in the allegorical part of the comment. It is as though the words themselves, with their dual layers of meaning, mirror the dual
nature of Bede's medieval view of reality, in which this physical, concrete world is a sign of another, spiritual world beyond
this one. An example will clarify this:

> Acts 12:8 PRAECINGERE ET CALCIA TE GALLI-
> CULAS TUAS
>
> 1) Et prophetas et apostolos cingulis usos fuisse
>   legimus,
> 2) cujus sibi Petrus ligamenta propter *rigorem* car-
>   ceris ad horam *laxaverat,*
> 3) ut tunica circa pedes dimissa frigus noctis utcum-
>   que *temperaret,*
> 4) exemplum praebens infirmis:
> 5) cum vel molestia corporali vel injuria *temptemur*
>   humana
> 6) licere nobis aliquid de nostri propositi *rigore*
>   *laxare.* [CC 121:58,33/8]

When Peter was imprisoned (in Acts 12), an angel appeared
to him by night and said: 'Gird yourself and put on your san-
dals.' In his commentary Bede first explains the literal sense:
'Peter had undone (*laxaverat,* line 2) the ties of his waistband
on account of the chilliness (*rigorem,* line 2) of the prison at
that hour, so that his tunic, lowered about his feet, might
lessen somewhat the cold of the night.' Bede then offers a
moral interpretation which repeats the noun *rigor* and the
verb *laxare,* but both with abstract senses appropriate to his
moral interpretation. 'This provides an example to the weak:

When we are tried by bodily afflictions or unjust treatment
by men, we are permitted to relax (*laxare,* line 6) somewhat
from our intended asceticism (*rigor,* line 6).' It seems likely
that Bede is here also punning upon the similarity of the verb
temperaret ('to lessen,' line 3) in the literal interpretation to
the verb *temptemur* ('to try' or 'test,' line 5) in the moralization. Because of the linear, one-thing-at-a-time nature of discourse, a commentator generally is forced to discuss first the
literal sense of a scriptural text, and then its spiritual significance, resulting in a kind of fragmentation of the scriptural
message. Bede, however, breaks through this linear constraint
by his pattern of repetition of the same words, first with literal
meaning, then with abstract, psychological meaning. In this
way he can point to both levels of meaning, but at the same
time remind his readers that both meanings are present in the
scriptural text simultaneously and integrally.

The examples that we have examined up until now have all
illustrated Bede's use of wordplay as a structural device within
a single comment on an individual Acts verse. My final example will show the same types of structural wordplay (repetition,
variation of etymologically related forms of the same word,
and exploitation of a word's several layers of meaning, from
concrete to figurative). In this final example, however, the
wordplay functions structurally to achieve a kind of thematic
coherence throughout a whole series of comments on successive verses, all part of a single story, viz., Peter's cure of the
lame beggar at the gate of the Temple. In this example the
wordplay also serves to enrich a basic metaphorical structure
which governs Bede's interpretation of this miracle story.

I am forced to present only a few sentences from Bede's
commentary on this story. This might give a misleading impression that the commentary on the story is quite brief.
Actually the commentary stretches over several pages, and
the lines which we will be looking at are separated from each
other by other material. When one is reading the entire commentary, the lines which we will see function like a musical

theme, reappearing now and again to draw us back to Bede's governing theological metaphor and enriching that metaphor by wordplay.

> Acts 3:1 PETRUS AUTEM ET JOHANNES ASCEN-
> DEBANT IN TEMPLUM, etc.
>> Apostoli nona hora templum ingressuri primo *claudum* diu *debilem salvant* . . . [CC 121:23,1/3]

This is Bede's opening sentence in his treatment of the story of the cure of the lame beggar. The sentence gives us an overview of the entire story, and at the same time Bede uses his introductory sentence to place before us three words which will reappear as leitmotifs throughout his entire interpretation of the story: *claudus* ('lame'), *debilis* ('enfeebled'), and *salvare* ('to heal'). In this introductory sentence all of these words are used with their primary, physical meanings, since they refer to the literal story.

We now skip over some further commentary on verse one, and pass to verse two:

> Acts 3:2 ET QUIDAM VIR QUI ERAT CLAUDUS EX
> UTERO MATRIS SUAE BAIULABATUR.
>> 1)   Quia populus Israhel non solum domino incarnato,
>> 2)   sed a primis etiam legis datae temporibus, rebellis extitit,
>> 3)   quasi ex utero matris *claudus* fuit. [CC 121:23, 8/11]

The Acts verse tells us that the beggar had been lame 'from his mother's womb'. Bede's commentary on this verse begins by immediately asking us to make a metaphorical leap—the lame beggar is the people of Israel. This people, says Bede, were 'as if lame (*claudus*) from the mother's womb because they were rebellious not only after the Lord's incarnation, but even from the earliest times, when the Law was given'.

Here obviously *claudus* is used in an extended sense, but it is not yet clear just what this sense is. Why 'lame' Israel, when we are talking about rebellious Israel? In a sort of riddling fashion, Bede invites us to ponder what semantic features of lameness are appropriate to Israel's spiritual rebelliousness in rejecting Christ. Only gradually do we learn the answer to this riddle. (In *De schematibus et tropis,* Bede labels such gradual revelation of the full significance of a metaphorical use of a word 'metalepsis'.)

The next sentence from Bede's comment on verse two gives us a first answer to our question, Why is the adjective *claudus* ('lame') applied to Israel?

4) Quod bene Jacob cum angelo luctante
5) benedicto quidem sed *claudicante* figuratur.
    [CC 121:23,11/12]

This answer to our question is an allusion, the product of Bede's 'concordance exegesis', or the regurgitation-via-memory aspect of *ruminatio.* Typically Bede expects his readers not only to recognize the passage to which he refers, but to be familiar with the entire passage, even though he gives only a brief and cryptic allusion. The allusion is to a rather odd story in Genesis 32, in which Jacob wrestled with an angel (or with Yahweh himself according to modern critics), and Jacob's hip was dislocated in the course of the wrestling match. Jacob finally prevailed and forced his opponent to bless him. The blessing was the change of Jacob's name to 'Israel'. This is the key to Bede's application of the adjective *claudus* ('lame') to the people called Israel, as the continuation of Bede's commentary on verse two makes clear:

6) Quia populus isdem domino in passione
    praevalens,
7) in quibusdam per *fidem* benedictus,
8) in quibusdam vero est per *infidelitatem*

claudus. [CC 121:23,12/14]

Since Jacob, who was 'blessed indeed though lamed' (*benedicto quidem sed claudicante,* line five), was named 'Israel,' so also the beggar in Acts, who was lame but blessed, i.e., healed, by Peter, appropriately represents Israel as a people who 'prevailed over the Lord in his passion' (*praevalens,* used in line six, is the word used in the Genesis story to describe Jacob's wrestling victory), and as a result this people was 'blessed in some of their members through faith' (line seven), but 'in other members lamed (*claudus*) through lack of faith' (line eight). Notice the etymological wordplay on *fidem/infidelitatem* in lines seven–eight, as well as the skillful pattern of repetition of *benedicto . . . claudicante* (line five and *benedictus . . . claudus* in lines seven–eight.

We should perhaps pause here to note how Bede's comment on Acts 3:2 is built around three uses of the word *claudus,* one in each sentence. In the first sentence (lines one–three) and the third sentence (lines six–eight), *claudus* is used metaphorically in reference to rebellious Israel. In the second sentence (lines four–five), a derivative of *claudus, claudicante* is used as a clue to the allusion to the story of Jacob's wrestling, which explains, at least on one level, the legitimacy of applying the adjective *claudus* ('lame') to the noun Israel, which has a double reference, to the re-named Jacob and to the people of Israel. It is noteworthy that *claudus* is not used anywhere in this comment on verse two to refer directly to the lame beggar of the Acts story, who must, however, be present to our minds throughout this commentary as the literal point of the theological comparison which is the essence of the overriding theological metaphor upon which Bede's interpretation of the Acts story is built. The beggar's presence before our mind is maintained by the resonances of the word *claudus* which were set up in the introductory summary of the literal Acts story given in Bede's opening sentence on verse one.

Moving now past some intervening material, we come to verse six, which describes Peter's cure of the lame beggar, who then leaped up and walked with Peter and John into the temple through the gate where he had been lying every day begging, unable to enter. Bede's comment on verse six reads, in part:

1) Populus ille, qui ante auratos postes mente *debilis jacuerat,*

2) in nomine crucifixi *salvatus* templum regni caelestis ingreditur. [CC 121:24,26/8]

Bede's commentary on this verse continues his fundamental metaphor of the lame beggar as the people of Israel, and this commentary now gives us a second, deeper justification for the application of the adjective 'lame' to Israel. Israel was lame because, like the lame beggar, Israel in her unredeemed state was unable to enter the temple, which here becomes the temple of the heavenly kingdom (*templum regni caelestis,* line two). But now Israel, saved (*salvatus*) in the name of the crucified one (line two), is able to enter that heavenly kingdom, just as the lame beggar was healed (*salvatus*) by Peter and thus enabled to enter the earthly temple with Peter. In this comment Bede does not use *claudus,* but instead the synonym *debilis* ('enfeebled'), which he had paired with *claudus* in his introductory theme sentence (see above comment on 3:1). In that same introductory sentence Bede used the verb *salvare* in its physical sense ('to heal'), which was appropriate to the physical lameness of the beggar. In the comment on verse six Bede repeats a derived form of *salvare, salvatus,* but here it has the spiritual meaning 'saved,' which is appropriate to lamed, i.e., unredeemed Israel.

Pressures of time compel me to skip over some fascinating and theologically rich structural wordplay in the rest of Bede's treatment of this story. I will conclude by drawing attention to Bede's final word on the story of the cure of the lame

beggar. This comes several pages later, after a good deal of
commentary on Peter's sermon:

> Acts 4:22 ANNORUM ENIM ERAT AMPLIUS
> QUADRAGINTA HOMO IN QUO FACTUM ERAT
> SIGNUM ISTUD SANITATIS.
>   1) . . . Allegorice autem populus Israhel . . .
>   2) semper idolorumque ritus *claudicabat.*
>   3) Vel, si numerus quadragenarius geminae legis
>   plenitudinem significat
>   4) (quater enim deni quadraginta faciunt),
>   5) utriusque transgressor velut quadragenariam per-
>   fectionem *debilis jacendo* transcendit.
>   [CC 121:26,43–27,52]

This Acts verse refers back to the lame beggar, adding the
information that he was more than forty years old. Bede's
comment on this verse is based on number symbolism which
need not concern us here, but what is interesting is the way
in which Bede links this final comment with the metaphorical
theme that he had developed earlier. He does this by repeating
once again a verbal derivative of *claudus*—during the forty
years in the desert the people of Israel 'had always limped
along (*claudicabat,* line two) with the worship of idols.'[13]
Bede also repeats once more the phrase *debilis jacendo*—a
transgressor of the two-fold law as it were 'lies enfeebled'
(*debilis jacendo,* line five), transcending a forty-fold perfection. Notice that in this comment on 4:22 both *claudicabat*
and *debilis jacendo* are rather odd word choices if read only
in relation to the immediate context of the sentence in which
they occur. Clearly Bede chose these words in order to close
his interpretation of the story of the lame beggar by calling
our minds back to the rich theological metaphor which he had
built around these words in his comments on Acts 3:1, 3:2,
and 3:6.

   In conclusion, for a scholastic philosopher the ideal vehicle for seeking the truth would be, it seems, a language of precision, a one-to-one correspondence between word and concept, so that a particular word would always mean a specific thing and nothing more—an ideal perhaps realized later in the algebraic notation of symbolic logic or in other sorts of artificial language. For a monastic writer like Bede, on the other hand, such artificially precise language would not be unambivalently regarded as a tool of thought, but it would probably be taken as something of a limitation, for not only would it lack a necessary affective dimension, but as a way to truth it would also fall short of the richness provided by the rich ambiguity of natural human language and metaphor.

The University of Akron

NOTES

1.   Jean Leclercq, *The Love of Learning and the Desire for God* (New York, 1961) p. 45.

2.   David Knowles, *Saints and Scholars* (Cambridge, 1962) 13-14.

3.   Dorothy L. Sayers and Barbara Reynolds, trans., *The Comedy of Dante Alighieri, Paradise* (Middlesex, 1962) 139.

4.   Andre Crepin offers some interesting suggestions regarding this question in his article, 'Bede and the Vernacular,' in Gerald Bonner, ed., *Famulus Christi, Essays in Commemoration of the Thirteenth Centenary of the Birth of the Venerable Bede* (London, 1976) 170-192.

5.   *St. Benedict's Rule for Monasteries,* ch. 48.

6.   Augustine, *Confessions* 10. 3.

7.   Bede, *Historia Ecclesiastica* 4. 24.

8.   Bede, *Homelia* 2. 7 (CC 122: 231, 246-248).

9.   Leclercq, 83.

10.   Leclercq, 85-86.

11.   'Bede as a Linguistic Scholar', *American Benedictine Review* 35 (1984) 204-217.

12.   CC 123: 142-171.

13.   Bede here makes an additional allusion to 1 Kings 18:21, where Elijah confronts the Israelites with a choice: 'How long', he asked, 'do you mean to hobble first on one leg then on the other? If Yahweh is God, follow him; if Baal, follow him.' The word which triggers the allusion is *claudicatis,* here rendered by the *Jerusalem Bible* with 'hobble'.

TRUTH IN SPIRIT AND LETTER:
GREGORY THE GREAT, THOMAS AQUINAS, AND
MAIMONIDES ON THE BOOK OF JOB
Mary L. O'Hara, CSJ

W HEN IN THE LATTER HALF of the thirteenth
century, St Thomas Aquinas composed his *Literal
Exposition on Job,* he had in mind two earlier
works, one the recent work of the jewish sage Moses ben
Maimon or Maimonides (1135–1204), and the other the
commentary composed six centuries earlier by Pope St Gregory the Great (540?–604), the *Morals on the Book of Job.*[1]
Each of the works presented its specific challenge: Gregory
had set out to make a literal, as well as an allegorical and
moral, commentary on the work, but he soon lost interest
in the letter and pursued the spirit. Maimonides offered his
own personal solution to what he took to be the central issue
of the book: the possibility of divine providence caring for
human individuals.

Comparing the works of these great thinkers is as stimu-
lating and rewarding as it is difficult. Although all three men
speak of Job, their treatments differ in many respects,

Maimonides' being not a commentary at all, but a few pages
in a very large work devoted to a discussion of the whole of
scientific knowledge in his time as it related to the hebrew
bible. For this reason it is principally Gregory's *Morals* and
Thomas' *Exposition* that will be considered here, but with some
advertence to the way in which 'Rabbi Moses', as Thomas
referred to him in the *Summa of Theology,* influenced
Thomas' way of considering the question of providence in
his work on Job.

The dialectic between Thomas and Gregory grows out of
their respective emphasis upon, in Gregory's case, the two
'spiritual' senses, i.e., the allegorical and moral, and, in
Thomas', the literal. The notion that a given passage of
Scripture could have many senses was an old one already in
Gregory's time, going back through Origen to the New Testament itself. But many different formulations and lists of
senses had appeared by the time Thomas established among
them the order that would become classical in the first
question of the *Summa of Theology.*[2] There he made it plain
that for him the spiritual senses rest upon the foundation of
the literal, and that the literal sense, thanks to the dispositions of divine providence, makes possible the spiritual senses.
In the case of Scripture alone, Thomas taught, providence can
so dispose events that things, and not merely words, can be
the signs of things, and thus the basis, for spiritual interpretation.

> literal: words signs of things
>
> ↗
>
> Senses:
>
> ↘
>
> spiritual: things signs of things
> (allegorical, moral, and anagogical)

It is not to be expected, then, that even christian theologians like Gregory and Thomas would understand the cate-

gories of the senses of Scripture in exactly the same way.
Gregory set up three categories, Thomas, four; and although
both regarded the literal sense as in some way fundamental,
they did not entirely agree with respect to the precise extension of the literal sense. Of two quite different intellectual
outlooks and living in different historical eras and philosophical ambiences, they nevertheless shared a common doctrine;
but their expression of it and the context in which they
placed it was often very different. Gregory is warm, personal,
edifying. Thomas is scientific, detached, only occasionally
and indirectly affording a glimpse of his personal spiritual
outlook. Yet both men, Doctors of the Church, were regarded
as mystics and spiritual masters in their own times.

It is the thesis of this paper that Thomas' *Exposition* was
based on two insights:

1) the spiritual senses of Scripture are possible only if,
first, there is in every case a literal sense underlying them,
and, second, there is a providential ordering of events extending to every creature. The doctrine of providence, being
derived, like other doctrines, from Scripture, is supported by
a literal interpretation of Scripture, since this alone is adequate
to the needs of scientific argument;

2) the knowledge of God's providential care is particularly important for one who suffers innocently, lest, overcome
by sorrow, such a person fail to grow in intimacy with God.

Thomas' doctrine makes it clear, in reference to Gregory,
that not all the senses of Scripture are of equal value, and that
there is an inner causality operating among them such that the
very possibility of the spiritual senses depends upon the literal.
Thus Gregory's own 'moral' commentary can be securely
established only if it is founded upon a literal commentary and
upon an adequate doctrine of providence.

Maimonides' understanding of providence was that of a
jewish Aristotelian of his time, though a more neoplatonic
Aristotelian than was Thomas. Thomas, acting as a christian
theologian using aristotelian principles, took up in his *Exposi-*

tion, not the doctrine of providence in general, but the
objections that can be made against it on the basis of the
suffering of the good, showing Job as a type of the suffering Christ. Thomas' work thus at once illustrates his doctrine
of the literal sense and furnishes a critique of Gregory's
method and of some of his conclusions, and at the same
time gives a christian answer to Maimonides' view of providence.

Gregory had tried, to the extent possible for each portion
of the Book of Job, to expound the words of his text according to all three senses, the literal (or historical), the allegorical (or typical), and the moral. He attempted

> . . . as far as the Truth should inspire me . . . to
> lay open . . . those mysteries of such depth; and . . .
> not only unravel the words of the history in alle-
> gorical senses, but . . . to give to the allegorical
> senses the turn of a moral exercise, . . . [3]

Some parts, he found, were more susceptible of spiritual (i.e.,
of allegorical or moral) than of literal interpretation; others
admitted of no historical treatment whatever:

> Yet it sometimes happens that we neglect to
> interpret the plain words of the historical account,
> that we may not be too long in coming to the
> hidden senses, and sometimes they cannot be
> understood according to the letter, because
> when taken superficially they convey no sort
> of instruction to the reader, but only engender
> error . . . . [4]

Whereas Gregory had thus attempted to give as complete
an interpretation of the Book of Job as possible, explaining
it in one or more senses as occasion warranted, Thomas gave
only a literal interpretation of the same work, since 'Pope

Gregory has so subtly and eloquently opened up its mysteries
that it seems nothing could be added to them'.[5] After this
reference to Gregory in the prologue of his *Exposition,*
Thomas scarcely adverts to him again in this work. Why?
Perhaps because the discussion, six and a half centuries after
Gregory, necessarily included other wise men than Gregory
(notably Maimonides), and widening the circle required that
he set the entire discussion on a different basis, but perhaps
also because Thomas differed in some respects from his monk
predecessor, and he showed his difference of opinion by his
silence rather than by directly engaging him in discussion.

Gregory's interest in the moral sense of Scripture is reflected
by his treatment of truth as referring to moral integrity, and
his preoccupation with the allegorical sense by his taking the
words 'truth' and 'wisdom' to refer to Christ. In preferring
these spiritual senses to the literal or historical senses Gregory
reflected the influence of stoic and neoplatonic currents of
thought prevalent in his time. Thomas' literal commentary
departed from these earlier philosophical tendencies, generally
favoring an aristotelian stance. The reason for Thomas' silence
in reference to Gregory's literal commentary will be sought in
an investigation of his use of Gregory in one part of the *Summa of Theology.*

Contrasts among the three works being considered here are
more striking than their likenesses: Gregory's *Morals* is much
longer than Thomas' *Exposition,* which in turn is some ten
times the length of the twenty or so pages Maimonides devoted
to Job.

In what follows, Gregory's *Morals* will first be discussed,
principally from the point of view of his use of the word
'truth'; next, some parts of Maimonides' *Guide of the Perplexed* will be discussed; and finally Thomas' *Exposition* will
be shown to be a reply in some respects to Gregory's and
Maimonides' works. Soundings in each work will illustrate
both likenesses and differences between Gregory's typically

monastic–patristic and Thomas' scholastic commentaries, and suggest some of the reasons for the differences. It will be seen that, whereas Gregory treated his subject principally as a moralist and psychologist, Thomas acted as a speculative theologian.

PART I. GREGORY: *MORALS ON THE BOOK OF JOB*
Begun in Constantinople while he was papal legate there, Gregory's work was finished at Rome during his papacy. Asked by his fellow monks to 'set forth the book of blessed Job', an 'obscure work . . . hitherto . . . thoroughly treated by none before us',[6] he undertook to expound the work according to as many of the various senses of Scripture as he could, but excusing himself from giving all three (historical, allegorical, and moral) in more than a few instances. Although he at times makes interesting remarks about matters pertaining to the letter of Scripture, about Arabic and Latin translations, it is clear that his interest did not lie here, any more than it did with the 'Academicians' and 'Mathematicians'. It was the practical—moral and psychological—aspect of his subject that interested him.

As an example of his pointing a moral, one may cite a remark he made on the reason Job offered sacrifice for his children in case they might have sinned in their daily banquets (Jb 1:5):

> . . . whatever stains the sons had contracted in
> their own persons at their feasts, the father wiped
> ·out by the offering of a sacrifice; for there are
> certain evils which it is either scarcely possible or . . .
> wholly impossible, to banish from feasting. Thus
> almost always voluptuousness is the accompaniment
> of entertainments . . . . [7]

Gregory was an astonishingly gifted practical psychologist. Examples of his expositions according to each of the three senses will illustrate this. In his allegorical commentary on Jb 18:3 he described the mental mechanism today known as 'projection':

> It is natural to the human mind to suppose that
> the thing that it does is done to itself. Thus they
> believe themselves to be despised, who are used
> to despise the ways of the good . . . . [8]

Again, he described the stratagems of the liar in his moral commentary on Jb 15:24:

> Another man, forsaking truth, makes up his
> mind to tell a lie . . . but what great labour it is
> to guard with sufficient heed, that his deceit itself
> may not be found out! For he sets before his eyes
> what answer may be made to him by those that
> know the truth, and with great effort he makes
> out how . . . he may surpass the evidence of truth.
> . . . he looks about for an answer resembling truth,
> whereas if he had been minded to tell the truth,
> assuredly he might have done it without pains. For
> the path of truth is smooth, and the road of false-
> hood grievous.[9]

The effect of falsehood on the man who loves truth was described in the historical explanation of Jb 21:33:

> The friends of blessed Job could not console
> him, in whom they gainsaid the truth by their
> discourse, and when they called him a hypocrite
> or ungodly, by the very fact that they themselves were
> thus guilty of sin, assuredly they augmented the chastise-
> ment of the righteous man . . . . For the minds of the
> Saints, because they love the truth, even the sin of
> another's deceit wrings. For in proportion as they
> see the guilt of falsehood to be grievous, they hate it

not only in themselves, but in others also.[10]

The liar, unable to make his point against the truth, falls to uttering truisms, as Gregory points out in his literal commentary on Jb 22:2:

> Those persons, who being opposed to the words
> of truth, get the worst in making out a case, often
> repeat even what is well known, lest by holding
> their tongue they should seem defeated.[11]

For the most part Gregory emphasized the moral or typical senses. The most usual sense of 'truth' found in many chapters in the *Morals* is 'God' or 'Christ' who speaks in Scripture. Occasionally 'truth' is contrasted to the many untruths or forms of ignorance possible for human beings, and so principally in the moral sense. As the 'doctor of contemplation', who 'never separates the practice of virtue from contemplation',[12] Gregory intended to lead his readers to God. Thus he showed the relation of humility and patience to truth:

> For he, who states of himself good qualities,
> which are true, when necessity compels, the
> more closely is united to humility, the more he
> adheres also to truth . . . . everything which he said,
> he uttered not from the sin of impatience, but from
> the virtue of truth . . . . [13]

Patience and humility have nothing to do with self-denigration.
    This emphasis upon truth as related to moral character is in keeping with Gregory's affinity for stoic values. Although no theoretician himself, Gregory was no doubt influenced, through Augustine, by Neoplatonism, and by Stoicism through Ambrose.[14] His own humane outlook, however, influenced no doubt by the *Rule of St Benedict*, tempered the stoic attitude of indifference toward suffering. This is indicated in the

following passage:

> Thus because blessed Job observed the rule of
> the true philosophy, he kept himself from either
> extreme with the evenness of a marvelous skill,
> that he might not by being insensible to the pain
> contemn the strokes, nor again, by feeling the
> pain immoderately, be hurried madly against the
> visitation of the Striker.[15]

'Almighty God gives the word of truth to those that do it
and takes it away from those that do it not.'[16] The righteous
are anxious 'that day by day they should try their actions by
the ways of truth . . . ' .[17] Job's friends, on the other hand,
Gregory represented as heretics, who 'hold not the solid substance of truth . . . ' .[18] To the word 'wisdom', which can be
considered to belong to the same epistemological 'family' as
'truth', he usually gave a moral or allegorical meaning as well.
It is used, for example, to designate prudence: 'By anger
wisdom is parted with, so that we are left wholly in ignorance
what to do, and in what order to do it . . . ' .[19]

Gregory's tendency to hurry over the literal sense to one of
the spiritual senses is illustrated by the comments he made on
Jb 28:12-17. Here, speaking of the verses, *Where shall wisdom
be found?* and *Gold and glass cannot equal it,* he wrote:

> For it is plain to all that neither can this wisdom
> of man be held in a place, nor be bought with riches.
> But the holy man being full of mystical ideas sends
> us on for the making out other things, so that we
> should look for not wisdom created but Wisdom
> creating; for except in those words we search the
> secret depths of allegory, surely those things that
> follow are utterly deserving of disregard, if they be
> estimated according to the historical narration alone.
> For . . . while . . . glass is far and incomparably of

> lower price than gold, wherefore . . . did he say that
> 'glass' too is not equal to wisdom? So by the mere
> difficulty of the letter, we are forced that we be
> quicksighted to the mystical sentiments in these
> words. So then what wisdom is it . . . but . . .
> *Christ . . . the Wisdom of God?*[20]

Besides being a name for God, 'wisdom' might mean for
Gregory 'our faith', or the gift of the Spirit.

Gregory's Job is principally a model of moral goodness,
especially patience. In portraying Job in this way, Gregory
reflected some of the popular non-canonical versions of the
story current at the time.[21]

As the elder contemporary of Mohammed the Prophet,
Gregory could not guess what a different world the coming
of Islam was to create. He gave little attention in the *Morals*
to the Jews who were present in his world, seeing them
mainly in their role in past history: ' . . . the Jews, . . . before
the Lord's Incarnation were "truthful" in that they believed
that he was to come, . . . but when he appeared in the flesh,
they denied that it was He.'[22]

Gregory's commentary with its emphasis on the spiritual
was meant to help Christians of his troubled century attain
the highest perfection of union with God. It came to serve for
centuries as a basic text in moral theology and as the classic
source of much of later christian mystical theology. It is noteworthy that in the *Morals,* which became a standard text in
moral theologies for later centuries, and a classic source of
mystical theology, Gregory almost never used the word
'providence'. He did in a neat sentence sum up the christian
answer to the question that can be raised about God's providential care for one who suffers: 'Let no one, then, who is not
speedily heard, believe that he is not cared for by God's providence.'[23] Again, he said that 'there are some who consider that
God is not concerned about human affairs, and think that they
are carried on by accidental movements'.[24] Still these remarks

do not constitute a major theme of the *Morals;* Maimonides, on the other hand, who lived six hundred years after Gregory, saw providence as the major concern of the Book of Job.

PART II.
MAIMONIDES: *THE GUIDE OF THE PERPLEXED*

By writing his great work in Arabic with hebrew letters, the Jew Maimonides underscored his intention of making it inaccessible to any but the most learned: he did not wish to violate the prohibition against divulging sacred secrets. In his baffling *Guide* he summed up much of aristotelian (and neo-platonic) philosophy, moslem thought, and jewish biblical lore. Even the few pages devoted to the Book of Job have their puzzling passages.

The Book of Job, and its setting outside the land of the Chosen People, appears atypical of Old Testament books. It contains no cultic references that would relate it to the books of the Law and the Prophets. It can even appear contradictory to the teaching of Deuteronomy:

> If Yahweh set his heart on you and chose you, . . .
> It was for love of you . . . that Yahweh brought you
> out . . . . Know then that Yahweh your God is . . .
> the faithful God who is true to his . . . graciousness
> for a thousand generations towards those who
> love him and keep his commandments, but who
> punishes in their own persons those that hate him.
> (Dt 7:7-10) . . . if you love Yahweh your God and
> follow his ways, if you keep his commandments,
> his laws, his customs, you will live and increase
> . . . . (Dt 30:16)[25]

But it was not principally questions having to do with the place of the Book of Job among other biblical books that concerned Maimonides in his *Guide.* He preferred to answer challenges to the teachings of the Law raised by moslem philosophy invoking the doctrine of Aristotle. As moslem thinkers either decried the teachings of the philosophers or tried to reconcile them with the Qur'an, so Maimonides strove to find the proper relation between Aristotle and other ancient thinkers on the one hand and the hebrew bible on the other.

To understand how Maimonides went about doing this we must recall the aristotelian order of learning the sciences: after beginning with logic, the student should go on to study physics before coming to the study of metaphysics. These disciplines, along with mathematics, astronomy, and medicine, constituted the scientific knowledge of the time. As a person interested in instructing his disciple in the very highest spiritual doctrine, Maimonides wrote his book in the order in which he did to emphasize that everything which might have a bearing upon the understanding of the word of God was important to the person who wished to grasp the truth of Scripture.[26]

These sciences had not been important to Gregory. He exemplified the learning of the rhetors, having received what was for his time an excellent education. But apart from Aristotle little systematic study of physics was possible, and it was stoic and neoplatonic philosophy rather than aristotelian that was known in Gregory's roman world.

In the arab conquest the conquerors took possession of spiritual riches as well as of lands, and learned men of the former byzantine empire were employed in translating works of the ancient greek philosophers, some never translated into Latin, from the Greek and Syriac into Arabic. The question of the bearing of Aristotle's works upon the Qur'an thus became the subject of fierce controversy. And the theoretical controversy had its practical consequences: Maimonides himself suffered exile from his native Spain at the hand of a fanatical moslem ruler and ended his life as physician to a more hospitable egyptian court.

The philosophical foundations of exegetical work on religious scriptures is by no means a merely abstract issue, then; and not only do such foundations influence the mode of scriptural exegesis, but they also enter into the very fabric of the theological system the exegete brings to his work.

No attempt will be made here to follow the *Guide* in all its intricate detail, or even to speak of Maimonides' use of the word 'truth'. Only that portion of the work devoted to consideration of divine providence and centered on the Book of Job will be studied here.

The Problem of Providence

For medieval thinkers who studied Aristotle's philosophy the problem of providence concerned the perfect Being engaged in ceaseless contemplation of its own perfection.[27] How, without losing perfection, can such a divine Being take thought for lesser beings, those human beings who, along with other, incorporeal, intelligences, and non-intelligent beings, share existence in the present uncreated eternal universe? One solution envisioned a God who provided for species but not for individuals.[28]

Maimonides' solution was distinctive: besides providing for species, God also exercises providential care over intelligent individuals, he held, but only to the extent to which they exercise their own intelligence. In the last chapter of the *Guide,* dealing with the meaning of 'wisdom', he mentioned (in addition to learning arts, acquiring moral principles, and having an aptitude for stratagems) knowing things that lead to knowledge of God, and cited the Book of Job for two of these meanings.[29] A few chapters earlier, after musing on God's care for Moses and the patriarchs, he stated his solution not only to the problem of providence but to the difficult problem of articulating the solution in the conceptual framework of the time. He said:

> A most extraordinary speculation has occurred
> to me just now through which doubts may be

dispelled and divine secrets revealed. We have
already explained . . . that providence watches
over everyone endowed with intellect proportion-
ately to the measure of his intellect. Thus providence always watches over an individual endowed
with perfect apprehension, whose intellect never
ceases from being occupied with God. On the other
hand, an individual endowed with perfect apprehension, whose thought sometimes for a certain
time is emptied of God, is watched over by providence only during that time when he thinks of
God; providence withdraws from him during the
time when he is occupied with something else.
However its withdrawal then is not like its withdrawal from those who have never had intellectual
cognition. But in his case that providence merely
decreases because that man of perfect apprehension
has, while being occupied, no intellect in actu; but
that perfect man is at such times only apprehending
potentially, though close to actuality. . . . If this is
so, the great doubt that induced philosophers to
deny that divine providence watches over all human
individuals and to assert equality between them and
the individuals of other kinds of animals is dispelled.[30]

Thus, on the basis of aristotelian principles, Maimonides
shows how a person who—possessing divine science—can
actually contemplate God at any time, is protected provi-
dentially during the time in which he is engaged in contemplation. He safeguards a providential care for human individuals while denying it to lower creatures. He found a point of
contact between Aristotle's wise man, the metaphysician,
and the wise man of jewish faith, the prophet, asserting
that in a certain act, that of contemplation, they can be one
and the same.

Using the neoplatonic notion of divine emanation, Maimonides had earlier distinguished three sorts of men: those who receive an influx from God into the rational but not into the imaginative faculty, and these are scientists; those who receive an influx into the imaginative but not into the rational faculty, and these are those who govern cities or are soothsayers or dream veridical dreams. Finally there is the class of those in whom 'this overflow reaches both faculties . . . and if the imaginative faculty is in a state of ultimate perfection owing to its natural disposition, this is characteristic of the class of prophets'.[31]

Aristotle had distinguished in his *Ethics* between two kinds of virtue: those perfecting the intellect (understanding, science, wisdom, art, and prudence); and those perfecting the moral nature of a human being (justice, courage, and temperance).[32] The moral virtues, in this theory, exist for the sake of the intellectual, and the various intellectual virtues for the sake of wisdom, which has to do with the divine science, that is, with theology or metaphysics. If the metaphysician, Maimonides seems to have been saying, is also endowed with the gifts of the prophet, 'this individual is protected because he hath known Me and then passionately loved Me'.[33] There are 'those who set their thought to work after having attained perfection in the divine science, turn wholly to God, . . . This is the rank of the prophets'.[34] These, it turns out, are persons who have studied logic and physics before coming to the study of metaphysics.

Aristotle's theory of deductive scientific knowledge relinquishes individual history in favor of universal theory. Beginning with corporeal things, Aristotle went on to explain how from them could be derived universal truth, set forth in an organized way in the sciences and culminating in a universal wisdom. The function of wisdom is thus to judge and order all the various sciences, and, through them, all things. It can do this because it stands above other sciences in the sense that, whereas these begin by assuming certain principles (as mathematics assumes axioms), wisdom undertakes the defense

of these principles themselves in addition to the properly
scientific function of drawing conclusions. In this theory,
clearly, wisdom is eminent science, drawing conclusions like
every science but in addition defending the principles themselves. Wisdom, science, and understanding, the virtue of first
principles, begin with the individual; but apart from the first
insight into the principles governing an individual situation,
these intellectual habits tend to deal with the abstract and
general rather than with concrete realities. For this reason it
may happen that scientists neglect the individual in favor
of the general.

Adopting Aristotle's distinction between potential and
actual thought, Maimonides found in it a key to understanding why the good suffer evil. If Job had known the cause of his
suffering he would have been wise. If he had acted upon this
knowledge, providence would have cared for him. For it is
when those who know God, and whose thoughts should be
fully engaged with him, willingly withdraw from this loving
contemplation (and thus only potentially contemplate him)
that providence abandons them.

It is clear from the above remarks that while Maimonides,
like Gregory, wrote of Job, he did so very differently, taking
up questions and using methods of interpretation quite different from any found in the *Moralia*.

Why do the good suffer? If there is no relation between
good and bad actions and rewards and punishments in this
life, the universe may be thought to have had no providential
creator at all; everything may result from chance. This, according to Maimonides, was the opinion of Epicurus.

Among those who acknowledge providence, on the other
hand, Maimonides found four possible theories, that of
Aristotle, that of the Moslem Ash'ariyya, that of another
moslem theological school, the Mu'tazila, and finally that of
'our Law'.[35] To each of these opinions he assigned one of the
principal characters of the Book of Job: to Job, what he took
to be Aristotle's theory; to Eliphaz, the opinion based upon

Dt 30:14-20; to Zophar, that of the Ash'ariyya; to Bildad, that of the Mu'tazila. For Maimonides' Aristotle providence could extend only to that which is *constant* in the universe, not to events in the lives of individual human beings. 'All the various circumstances of the individuals among the Adamites are considered by Aristotle as due to pure chance, by the Ash'arite as consequent upon will alone, by the Mu'tazila as consequent on wisdom, and by us as consequent upon the individual's deserts . . . . '[36]

According to the Ash'ariyya there is no possibility of finding a reason for the dispositions of the divine will. For the Mu'tazilites, however, every being, even an ant, 'receives a compensation for good or evil'.[37]

Maimonides himself seems finally to have adopted as his own view that of Elihu—that it is impossible for a human being to know the mind of God.[38] Maimonides found it remarkable that Job is never called 'wise' in Scripture.[39] Rather, he is regarded as just. David Bakan has remarked that the 'question of the Book of Job really is, as indeed the Rabbis of the Talmud took it to be, whether Job was as righteous as Abraham'.[40] Maimonides died in Cairo in 1204, half a century before Thomas wrote his *Literal Exposition on Job*. Maimonides did not find Job to be a wise man. St Thomas does.

PART III. THOMAS: *EXPOSITION ON JOB*

In undertaking to write an *exposition,* Thomas intended to explain the text before him in terms of grammar and of the meaning of words, and upon this to base his interpretation and doctrine.

Gregory's *Moralia* remained popular and influential throughout the Middle Ages. Thomas would have heard it read publicly in the refectory or as part of the Divine Office when he was an oblate at Monte Cassino. In the *Summa of Theology* I. 1. 10, Thomas cited Gregory on the subject of the senses of sacred Scripture, in the authoritative *Sed contra,* usually reserved for

Scripture itself.[41] Yet Thomas set himself the task of supplementing Gregory's work with the literal commentary Gregory had considered impossible. What did Thomas hope to accomplish in a literal commentary that Gregory had not done?

Thomas at once distanced himself from Gregory by holding that all other senses of Scripture are founded upon the literal; no portion of Scripture is not susceptible of literal interpretation.[42] The various senses of Scripture have different uses, he wrote in his very early commentary upon the *Sentences* of the Lombard: the literal, for destroying error; the moral, for instruction in morals; the allegorical, for contemplating the truth of things belonging to this life (i.e., the life of Christ and of the 'primitive Church');[43] and finally, for contemplating the things of heaven, the anagogical sense.[44] The last three, 'spiritual' or 'mystical' senses of scripture, can occur only because a provident God is able to make not only *words* but *things* meaningful.[45]

When one speaks of 'refuting error', one is in the realm of logical disputation, of trying to prove one's point. The writings of purely human sciences, established by the effort of human thinking, can have only a literal sense; God alone, and no human being, can give a meaning to *things* as well as *words,* and God, the Holy Spirit, is the author of sacred Scripture. But when Scripture speaks of a 'lion', this could be taken in one context to refer to Christ, and in another, to the devil.[46] Because of this ambiguity, no argument can be made scientifically on the basis of this word.[47]

Thomas evidently saw a need to 'destroy error' about divine providence, which he, like Maimonides, saw as the central question of the Book of Job. The 'defense of truth is everyone's business, and each one should do his part according to his ability', he said later.[48]

Thomas spoke, in the very first sentence of his *Exposition on Job,* about growing in knowledge of truth: as animals are born imperfect and little by little come to perfection, so human beings come to know the truth—at first, only a little is known, and so much error is possible. One of the subjects about which error is possible, he goes on to say, is divine providence, and the Book of Job has as 'its total intention' to show through probable reasons that human affairs are ruled by divine providence. The question is of utmost importance: without an awareness of providence, human beings would lack their strongest motives for doing good and avoiding evil: love and fear.

The greatest objection that can be raised to the reality of providence is the suffering of the good—the subject of this book.[49]

Taking the Book of Job as a theological drama or dialogue, Thomas interpreted it as a scholastic disputation, and noted Job's freedom of spirit:

> Now a disputation is between two persons,
> opponent and respondent; so Job entering
> upon his disputation with God, gives him the
> option of choosing the person of the opponent
> or respondent . . .
> . . . from now on, he speaks as though having
> God present and disputing with him. Now it
> might seem unfitting for a human being to dis-
> pute with God because of the excellence with
> which God surpasses man, but it should be
> considered that truth does not vary with the
> variation of persons, wherefore when anyone
> speaks the truth he cannot be overcome no
> matter whom he disputes with . . . [50]

Elsewhere Thomas observed that 'the greatest solidity comes through truth'.[51] But it is unfortunately not easy for human beings, who 'do not perceive the wisdom of truth through simple apprehension [as do angels] . . . but come to it by the investigation of reason . . . '[52] and so it is that 'philosophers excel in consideration of truth'[53]—a claim familiar to Maimonides.

Wisdom belongs not only to philosophers, however; theologians can acquire a wisdom through study, in their case a study based on faith. And there is another, infused wisdom, a gift of the Holy Spirit, available to all children of God.[54] Thomas continued, ' . . . but Job was certain that he spoke the truth inspired in him by God through the gift of faith and inspired by wisdom, wherefore without diffidence he asked that he not be oppressed by divine strength . . . ' .[55]

It is precisely this inspiration that is the source of Job's wisdom, Thomas seems to say. How does inspiration come to one? *The breath of the Almighty has vivified me,* Job can say, because God 'moves and perfects him to works of life among which the understanding of truth is foremost'.[56]

One of the properties of a wise person is the ability to judge of the truth and discern what is false.[57] Thomas pictured Job, in contrast to Sophar, longing to open his heart to God who is the teacher of all truth. But for the human heart, remaining firm in truth is difficult.[58] One might think it good to praise God on account of something not true; but this would in fact be to act against God.[59] What might keep a person from defending the truth? St Thomas found two sources: bodily molestation and, in the soul, fear, or some similar passion.[60]

If Thomas was defending the truth against error in offering this first literal interpretation of the great spiritual classic, just what error was he here confuting?

It is, as we mentioned above, the error that would deny a providential care for individual human beings and so cause them, by the weight of sorrow at seeing the just suffer, to lose love and fear. God in his providence does permit the just to suffer. In this way, their good lives become manifest to others. Whereas those who merely pretend to be just without really being so can be seen, when trials come, to be without virtue, the just stand firm. ' . . . and as gold is not *made* true gold by the fire, but its truth is made *manifest* to human beings, so Job was proved by adversity that his virtue should be manifested to men . . . '[61]

Job was a good man; was he wise? The answer to this question will depend upon how one regards the various goods of which Job was deprived. Goods proper to human beings are three: those of soul, of body, and of exterior things; and they are ordered in such a way that the exterior goods are for both body and soul, while those of the body are for the soul.[62] The Stoics, Thomas pointed out, regarded exterior goods as not true goods for human beings, and so they determined that loss of these goods could not make a wise person sad; the Peripatetics, on the other hand, regarded these exterior goods as less than the goods of the mind, but ordered to them, and so they conceded that a wise person could be sad, but moderately so, at the loss of such goods.[63] 'And this opinion is truer and agrees with church doctrine, as is clear from Augustine', Thomas concluded.[64] There is, in fact, need to avoid the vice of insensibility: not to weep at the death of a friend would be hardness of heart.

The virtuous person, then, will be, not the one who does *not* suffer, either because of stoic endurance or because he is totally innocent, but rather the one who, in the face of even overwhelming calamities, is not so absorbed by sorrow as to cease to be ruled by reason. Thomas acknowledged that contemplation of divine things can be a powerful help in turning one away from the thought of one's loss; yet even contemplation itself can be interfered with by great sorrow.[65]

To say that it is possible for the wise to suffer is also to agree with Scripture, which puts 'sorrow in Christ, in whom is the fullness of all virtue and wisdom'. It is even usual for the wise to express their sorrow in words, as Christ did, saying 'My soul is sorrowful even unto death'.[66] Such an expression of sorrow is moderate. When a person speaks from the impetus of passion, however, it is not he who opens his mouth; he is acted upon by the passion, for 'it is not by passion that we are rulers of our acts, but by reason alone'.[67]

One whose possession of the goods of the future life is

assured can bear with greater equanimity the loss of the goods
of this life. It is precisely because they lack hope in a future
life that Job's friends fail to realize that he is a friend of God.
It is clear from what has been said that while both Maimonides
and Thomas held that providence presides over human life,
for the jewish doctor this was so in great measure because
the human being actually occupies his mind with God; and
Maimonides seems finally to have accepted the view he attributed to Elihu—that it is impossible for man to come to know
the mind of God. Thomas, on the other hand, saw that if there
were no providence there could be no human knowledge of
God, no fruitful prayer—and no spiritual sense of sacred
Scripture![68] This last paradoxical point contrasts with Gregory's view. Thomas evidently saw an implicit contradiction
in Gregory's refusal to acknowledge a 'literal' sense to every
portion of Scripture. Why did Thomas not say explicitly that
he differed from Gregory on this point, if it is true that he did?

Gregory was a frequent contributor—particularly through
his *Morals on the Book of Job,* where he appears clearly as a
spiritual master—to those portions of the *Summa of Theology*
in which Thomas treated of the gifts of the Holy Spirit, especially the questions concerning the 'family' of gifts and virtues
that includes wisdom, understanding, charity, and their opposites. Thomas' use of Gregory is highly nuanced, however: at
times, as in the question on 'Blindness of mind and dullness
of sense' (2-2, 15: vices contrary to the gift of understanding),
Thomas cited Gregory in the weighty *Sed contra* position in
each of the three articles and embraced Gregory's teaching
unreservedly, while giving a logical defense of it. In other
cases Thomas interpreted Gregory benignly in one or more
of the *Replies* to objections (1-2, 68, 8, *ad* 2 & 3: on gifts
and virtues). Again, when the authority of Gregory was
claimed in *Objections,* Thomas sometimes replied with his
own differing opinion, without citing Gregory by name in
his *Reply* (2-2, 24, 11 *ad* 3; ibid., 6 *ad* 3: on charity).

It would seem that Thomas' silence on the Job commentary,

analogously with that in the *Summa,* indicates that his differences with Gregory were sufficiently serious to be irreconcilable with Gregory's. Thomas chose to pass over these differences in silence, rather than to gloss over them by some benign interpretation.

For Thomas the story of Job is that of the friend of God, called upon to suffer for a mysterious reason he does not understand, afflicted in body, having lost all his children and his wealth, but not overcome in mind, since his hope is in God.[69]

What sort of person is Thomas' Job? He is a thoroughly aristotelian man in his natural endowments, but one who lives in a universe populated by good and evil spirits who at times try to influence his actions. Thomas distributed the dramatic roles differently than did Maimonides: for Thomas, Job is the Peripatetic, to be sure, but all the more admirable for this; Eliphaz, on the other hand, is the Stoic, not the one who speaks for the jewish Law.[70] Job is not insensible of pain, and so his fortitude and patience are those of a human being, not of a stone. One cannot entirely deny nature; even animals naturally express their affliction.[71] A person who remains silent above sorrow he is experiencing can be somehow 'consumed by silence';[72] it can also happen that one experiences the movement of some passion and decides reasonably to refrain from expressing it.[73] To say the wise never feel sadness is to adopt the stoic posture; but it is true that the wise endeavor to moderate their sadness in order not to be led by it into sin.[74] The experience of friendship, shown most by compassion in adversity, is most delightful. One might hope, therefore, for comfort from friends; but Job is disappointed even in this expectation.[75] Thomas, unlike Gregory, did not merely speak of the sins associated with feasts; he also pointed out that Job was confident of the chastity of his daughters or he would not have permitted them to attend their brothers' banquets.[76]

To say that Job is 'peripatetic', or aristotelian, then, is to

deny that he is stoic in his emotional life. It is also to say that
his emotional life is rooted in a body animated by a rational
soul, the soul being source at once of life and of understanding.[77] To attribute to the human being what belongs to the
soul is not to identify the person with the soul, as if the
human being were a soul using a body, but simply to say that
the soul is the principal part of the human being. The soul is
united to the body as form to matter.[78] The soul is not the
human being: ' . . . not only my soul will see God, but *I myself* who subsist from body and soul.'[79]

    Thomas' anthropology, fundamentally that of Aristotle, is
grounded in an aristotelian physical universe. If Thomas'
anthropology was fundamentally that of Aristotle, he endowed Job however with the gifts of a man of faith; Job
was also distinguished from his friends by the virtue of hope,
for he put his trust not in earthly goods or rewards visible to
human eyes, but rather in eternal life.[80] Finally, Job is shown
as the loving servant of God.[81]

    Eliphaz objected that Job both wished to dispute with God
and also to pray to him: two things that seem incompatible.[82]
Thomas defended Job, however, on the ground that he disputed with God not through pride but through confidence in
the truth. It can thus happen that individual persons judge
God's actions in reference to human beings and their responses very differently: God may allow a person to be afflicted for his own good, and the person may not realize this,
since the bitter medicine is what the senses grasp, rather than
the ultimate benefit.[83]

    In sacred Scripture God is said to 'come' to human beings,
Thomas wrote, when he generously bestows his benefits: when
he enlightens the mind, or inflames the will, or in whatever
other way he benefits them. But God may permit tribulations
or spiritual defects for their salvation. In this case it can happen that a person may not perceive that God is 'coming'.[84]

    Such a person may pray to be relieved and, not being

relieved (because God knows this to be for the person's good), may think his prayer unheard, whereas it *is* heard. But if a person in this situation can see a reason for being afflicted, that it is for his salvation, for example, he can believe he is heard.[85] In all of this, it is clear that unless we could be sure that God is provident for us, all basis for prayer and for knowledge of God would be taken away,[86] and the profound paradox of the Book of Job in relation to the Law of Love in Deuteronomy would remain unresolved.

Every saint, Thomas said, excels in some one individual virtue, in regard to which no one can compare to him, except 'Christ, in whom there was excellent perfection'.[87] The virtue in which Job is seen to excel is wisdom.

Like Aristotle, Thomas connected wisdom with eminent knowledge, with understanding of principles, with judgment, and with experience. But, for Thomas, wisdom belonged especially to the person who demonstrates a profound knowledge of God, with a loving devotion that makes it evident that for the wise, nothing in all of creation approaches God in goodness. Humility and hope are thus virtues that distinguish the wise from the stupid or ignorant.[88]

Wisdom in a sense includes all spiritual goods;[89] it is the honor and ornament of a human being.[90] Stupidity or folly makes a person like an animal; it is the characteristic of the foolish and the proud to take credit themselves for what they have received.[91] They hate wisdom and flee the light,[92] They despise the poor, placing their own happiness in the things of this earth.[93] In Thomas' chilling presentation, folly or stupidity is seen as a kind of compendium of all vices.

More than age is required for wisdom: the inspiration of the Holy Spirit is its real source.[94] The thought of God is accompanied by a kind of inexplicable joy, imperfect in this life but perfect in the life to come.[95]

What is striking about Thomas' presentation of the virtues and vices is the way in which each is somehow brought into relation with wisdom, intellect, reason, while these functions

and habits themselves are seen to belong to the human
individual.

CONCLUSION

Enough has now been said to make it clear that Thomas'
teachings on matters of doctrine are not generally different
from those of Gregory, but the ambience in which they exist,
the philosophical language in which they are expressed, reflects
a different world. In response to the challenge of moslem and
jewish writers influenced by Aristotle, Thomas moved to the
level of scientific disputation, but disputation in support of a
spiritual goal. Maimonides and some of his moslem predecessors were not simply aristotelians, not mere 'philosophers',
they were on the contrary genuinely concerned spiritual men,
but men not satisfied simply to ignore human learning.[96] In
dealing with spiritual matters as a learned man of his time,
Thomas was able to elaborate his own solution to the problems
they posed.

What he undertook in this *Exposition* Thomas made clear
in the very first lines: a development of truth. Gregory was
not uninterested in the literal or historical sense of Scripture:
he called attention to the meanings of greek words in the text,
and he contrasted the 'old' and 'new' translations from 'Syriac
and Arabic'. But the very title of his work makes it plain that
his heart was elsewhere.

Thomas, unlike Gregory, seems to have been vividly aware
of the jewish and moslem worlds as he wrote this commentary;
he emphasized certain elements I have characterized as 'aristotelian' in contrast to the prevailing stoic and neoplatonic
view typical of western spiritual literature before his time.
These elements—the realization of the possibility and goodness of scientific knowledge of the world, an emphasis upon
cosmology, upon the bodily and human things, especially
human emotions as good in themselves—can be seen best as a
response to new questions that had emerged after the time of
Gregory.

Conrad Pepler, in *The Basis of the Mysticism of St. Thomas,*
says ' . . . there is nothing in St. Thomas to suggest that he regarded Aristotle as having established the need for holy indif-
ference, that apathy . . . popularized by the Stoics and
canonised by the platonically-minded Christians'.[97] In his
commentary on the Book of Job, Thomas explicitly rejected
this stoic attitude as unbefitting a Christian. This is one of his
principal differences from Maimonides. Few spiritual writers
today, however, would emphasize the virtue or the gift of
wisdom as a summary of the highest spiritual good for human
beings. Thomas' emphasis upon wisdom reflects, no doubt,
his own professional interest in the life of the mind as well
as his need to defend the life of learning against those who
attacked it. Wisdom was also the particular virtue in which
he himself excelled.[98]

In his *Exposition,* Thomas showed, against someone who
would urge that 'philosophers' are inimical to the spiritual life,
that there are many wisdoms, each with its proper claims to value.
To respond properly to suffering requires a mature spirituality,
wise, energized by charity and informed by the greatest possible
freedom and awareness. Thomas' own functioning as a contemplative theologian is more evident in this work than in the
strictly structured *Summa of Theology.* Here, Thomas was
close to Gregory in his exemplification of monastic spirituality.
With it, he combined a scientific theology able to speak to the
learned world of his time. Against Maimonides, he showed
that it is not beneath God to provide for even the least of his
creatures.

Most of all, Thomas set the edifice of spiritual commentary
established by Gregory upon the firm foundation of the literal
sense of the text, thus removing it from the danger of being
swept away by the floodtide of aristotelian learning coming
from the East.

In dealing with the story of a man neither Jew nor Moslem
nor Christian, Thomas considered the question of spirituality

in the context of the entire world, recognizing God's providence for each of his creatures, for the man from Uz 'in the oriental lands', as much as for his 'chosen' people.

St. Paul, Minnesota

NOTES

1. S. Gregorii Magni *Moralia in Job,* cura et studio Marci Adriaen, CC 143, 143A (Turnhout, Belgium: Typographi Brepols Editores Pontifici, 1979; ET: Library of the Church Fathers (Oxford: John Henry Parker, 1844-50). St. Thomae de Aquino, *Exposito super Iob ad Litteram,* cura et studio Fratrum Praedicatorum, *Opera Omnia,* 26 (Rome: ad Sanctae Sabinae, 1965). Both doctors used the Vulgate of St Jerome as their basic text. See Pierre Salmon, 'Le Teste de Job utilisé par S. Grégoire dans les "Moralia" ' in *Miscellanea Biblica et Orientalia R. P. Athanasius Miller,* OSB, cura Adalbarti Metzinger (Studia Anselmiana, Fasc. XXVII-XXVIII; Rome: Pontificium Institutum S. Anselmi, 1951) 193.
2. *Summa Theologiae,* I. 1. 10. Cf. Gal 4:24, Hb 9:9, 12:22. See C. Spicq, *Esquisse d'une Histoire de l'Exégèse Latine au Moyen Age* (Paris: Librairie Philosophique J. Vrin, 1944) 273-88. Origen, see Henri de Lubac, *Exégèse Médiévale* (Paris: Aubier, 1959-64) 1:202-204.
3. *Moralia, Epistola ad Leandrum,* 1. 45-50; ET 18:4-5.
4. *Ibid.,* 3,120-123; ET 18:7.
5. *Expositio super Iob* (hereafter: *Iob*), Prologus, 99-102 (my translation). de Lubac, *Exégèse* 4:298 sees no irony in Thomas' statement here.
6. *Mor., ad Leandrum,* 1-2,45-55; ET 18:4-5.
7. *Mor.,* I. viii. 10,8-15; ET 18:36.
8. *Ibid.,* XIV. iii. 3,2-4; ET 21:119.
9. *Ibid.,* XII, xlii, 47,2-15; ET 21:74.
10. *Ibid.,* XV, lxiii. 73,1-10; ET 21:224.
11. *Ibid.,* XVI, lines 1-2; ET 21:225.
12. Dom Jean Leclercq, 'The Teaching of St. Gregory' in *The Spirituality of the Middle Ages,* edd. J. Leclercq, F. Vandenbroucke, and L. Bouyer (New York: The Seabury Press, 1968) 6-7.
13. *Mor.,* XXVI. v. 5; xlvii. 85; ET 23:136, 197.
14. See Dom Robert Gillet, *Morales sur Job,* deuxième édition, revue et corrigée, Introduction, (Paris: Cerf, 1975) pp. 86, 104, *et passim.* On Gregory's education, see also H. de Lubac, 'Saint Grégoire et la Grammaire', *Recherches de Science Religieuse,* 48 (1960) 185-226, and Claude Dagens, 'Grégoire le Grand et le Monde Oriental', *Rivista di Storia e Letteratura Religiosa,* 17 2 (1981) 243-52.
15. *Mor.,* II. xvi. 29,23-27; ET 18:87.

16.   *Ibid.,* XI. xv. 23,8-9; ET 21:16.

17.   *Ibid.,* XVI. xxxiv. 42,4-7; ET 21:252.

18.   *Ibid.,* XVI. v. 8,59-60; ET 21:228.

19.   *Ibid.,* V. xlv. 78,14-16; ET 18:303.

20.   *Ibid.,* XVIII. xl. 61,22-37; ET 21:362. Thomas, in a characteristic departure from Gregory's spiritual interpretation, remarks that gold is valued for its splendor, glass for its transparency: *Iob* 153:217-219.

21.   See Lawrence L. Besserman, *The Legend of Job in the Middle Ages* (Cambridge: Harvard University Press, 1979) 55.

22.   *Mor.,* XI. xv. 24,30-33; ET 21:16.

23.   *Ibid.,* XXVI. xix. 34; ET 23:158.

24.   *Ibid.,* XXVII, xvii. 34; ET 23:225.

25.   Jerusalem Bible translation.

26.   Moses Maimonides, *The Guide of the Perplexed,* trans. with an Introduction and Notes by Shlomo Pines (Chicago: University of Chicago Press, 1963), pp. 374-78. Maimonides treats first the account of creation which he relates to Aristotle's *Physics,* and then Ezekiel, to which he relates the *Metaphysics.* See Zwi Diesendruck, 'Samuel and Moses Ibn Tibbon on Providence', *Hebrew Union College Annual,* 11 (Cincinnati: 1936) 346-51.

27.   Aristotle, *Metaphysics,* xii. 9. See Harry Wolfson, 'Maimonides and Halevi: A Study in Typical Jewish Attitudes towards Greek Philosophy in the Middle Ages', *Jewish Quarterly Review* 2 (1911-12) 297-337.

28.   Maimonides, *Guide,* III. 17, p. 473, attributes this opinion to Aristotle through Alexander of Aphrodisias.

29.   *Guide,* III. 54, p. 632; see Aristotle, *Metaphysics,* i. 1.

30.   *Ibid.,* 51, pp. 624-25.

31.   *Ibid.,* II. 37, p. 374; on the importance of the imagination in Maimonides' account of human functions, see S. Daniel Breslauer, 'Philosophy and Imagination: The Politics of Philosophy in the View of Moses Maimonides', *Jewish Quarterly Review* 69 (1978-79) 153-171.

32.   Aristotle, *Nicomachean Ethics,* vi. 2, 1138b35-1139a2, *et passim.* See M. L. O'Hara, 'The Connotations of Wisdom', Diss., Catholic University of America, 1956.

33.   *Guide,* III. 51, p. 627.

34.   *Ibid.,* p. 620.

35.   *Ibid.,* 23, p. 494.

36.   *Ibid.,* 17, p. 469; 'by us' evidently refers to a scripturally based opinion (Dt 30), but not necessarily Maimonides' own.

37.   *Ibid.,* pp. 468-70.

38.   *Ibid.,* pp. 471-74; 23, pp. 494-97. Maimonides refused to acknowl-

edge any analogy between the perfection of God and that of human
beings, and thus his conclusion on this point is different from that of
Thomas, although Thomas would have agreed that no human mind can
comprehend the divine or even know precisely *what* God is.

39.   *Ibid.,* 22, p. 487.
40.   David Bakan, 'Sacrifice and the Book of Job', in *Disease, Pain,
& Sacrifice: Toward a Psychology of Suffering* (Chicago: University of
Chicago Press, 1968) 95-128.
41.   The *Sed contra* of what is thought to have been a question disputed at Thomas' inception as Master at Paris, *Quodlibet* VII, Qu. 6,
art. 16, cites the same passage of Gregory's *Morals,* XXII, as the *Summa
Theologiae.* See J. A. Weisheipl, *Friar Thomas d'Aquino: His Life,
Thought, and Work,* (Garden City, N.Y.: Doubleday & Company, Inc.,
1974) 104-06 and 368. Weisheipl points out the relation between the
Expositio Super Iob and the *Summa Contra Gentiles,* III, 64-113.
42.   *Summa Theologiae,* I. 1. 10, *c.*: *Quodl.* VII, Qu. 6, art. 14, *ad* 1.
43.   *Quodl.* VII, Qu. 6, art. 14, *ad* 5.
44.   Thomas gives examples of four ways of understanding the sentence, 'Let there be light', according to the four senses of sacred Scripture he has distinguished, in his commentary on the Letter to the
Galatians, 4:7.
45.   *Sum. Theol.,* I, 1, 10, *c.; Quodl. VII,* Qu. 6, art. 16, *c.*
46.   *Quodl. VII,* Qu. 6, art. 14, *ad* 4.
47.   *Commentum In Primum Librum Magistri Petri Lombardi,* Prol.
S. Thomae. Qu. 1, art. 5, *c.* It should be noted that for Thomas the
'literal' sense included the use of metaphor, but argument cannot
be based upon metaphoric use.
48.   *Iob* 32: 17,157-59.
49.   *Iob* Prol. 40-57.
50.   *Ibid.,* 13:20,307-10; 283-90. see also 6:28,307-09; 7:21,524-27;
9:3,25; 22:2,10-15; 23:5,50-51; 34:34,387-99.
51.   *Ibid.,* 31:5,73.
52.   *Ibid.,* 28:27,340-42.
53.   *Ibid.,* 12:20,313.
54.   *Sum. Theol.,* I, 1, 6; II–II, 45; see Anthony J. Kelly, CSSR, 'The
Gifts of the Spirit: Aquinas and the Modern Context', *The Thomist,*
38:2 (April, 1974) 193-231.
55.   *Iob* 13:19:290-94; 28:27:345-46.
56.   *Ibid.,* 33:4:32; 28:27:345-46.
57.   *Ibid.,* 12:16:243-47.
58.   *Ibid.,* 11:11:177-79.
59.   *Ibid.,* 13:10:128-42.

60.   *Ibid.,* 13:20:292-306.

61.   *Ibid.,* 23:10:165-70; 1:8:458-524; see Tobit 12:11 for a possible source of Thomas' interpretation here, see John Damascene, *Orthodox Faith,* II. 29 (ed. P. Boniktius Kotter, OSB, *Schriften* 2 (Berlin: de Grayter, 1969, 1973) 101, 29-30.

62.   *Iob,* 2:1,1-5.

63.   *Ibid.,* 1:20,742-49; 6:8,78-116.

64.   *City of God,* XIV.9.

65.   *Iob* 17:11,159-70.

66.   *Ibid.,* 3:1,1-40; see Mt 26:38. Thomas seems to approach here the opinion described by Maimonides as that of the 'sufferings of love' (see *Guide,* III. 17, p. 471).

67.   *Iob,* 3:1,30-35.

68.   *Iob,* 5:8,136-47; 27:9,107-26; *Sum. Theol.,* I, 1, 10, *c; Quodl. VII,* Qu. 6, art. 14, *ad* 1; on the history of the four 'senses' of Scripture, see de Lubac, *Exégèse Médiévale,* and *The Sources of Revelation* (New York: Herder and Herder, 1968) 50-56 *et passim.* See also Charles and Dorothea Singer, 'Jewish Elements in Thirteenth-Century Scholasticism', in Jacob I. Dienstag, ed., *Studies in Maimonides and St. Thomas Aquinas* (Ktav Publishing House, Inc., 1975) 169-183.

69.   *Iob* 5:19,324-44.

70.   *Ibid.,* 6:11,150-68.

71.   *Ibid.,* 6:5,66-77.

72.   *Ibid.,* 13:1, 276-79.

73.   *Ibid.,* 10:1,26-37.

74.   *Ibid.,* 6:7,95-104.

75.   *Ibid.,* 6:13,187-241; 10:16,350-51; 2:12,220-71.

76.   *Ibid.,* I:4,114-25.

77.   *Ibid.,* 26:4,48-50.

78.   *Ibid.,* 4:19,461-90.

79.   *Ibid.,* 19:29,323-24.

80.   *Ibid.,* 2:10,175-215.

81.   *Ibid.,* 1:8,430-33.

82.   *Ibid.,* 15:3,31-39.

83.   *Ibid.,* 9:11,317-19; 1:21,847-55; 3:2,89.

84.   *Ibid.,* 9:11,303-17; cf. Rm 8:28.

85.   *Ibid.,* 9:17,430.

86.   *Ibid.,* 5:8,136.

87.   *Ibid.,* 1:8,444-53.

88.   *Ibid.,* 12:1,28-34; 12:16,243-45; 15:19,167-70; 15:27,260-61; 28:12, 156; 27,339-65; 38:36,622.

89.   *Ibid.,* 28:1,3-8

90. *Ibid.,* 18:3,29-31.
91. *Ibid.,* 15:18,161-63; 12:21,344-46.
92. *Ibid.,* 24:13,125-51.
93. *Ibid.,* 19:18,172-75.
94. *Ibid.,* 32:8,78-95.
95. *Ibid.,* 33:23,265-306.
96. The moslem mystic al Ghazālī is particularly important here. See *Freedom and Fulfillment: An Annotated Translation of al Ghazālī's al Munqidh min al-Dalāl,* trans. Richard J. McCarthy, SJ (Boston: Twayne Publishers, 1980).
97. [Oxford]: Blackfriars, 1953, p. 18. See *Summa Theologiae,* II-II, 142. 1.
98. Wisdom might profitably be considered today as an organizing principle by those who seek a suitable method for the study of spirituality. See Edward Kinerk, SJ, "Toward a Method for the Study of Spirituality', *Review for Religious,* 40 (1981) 3-19, Jordan Aumann, OP, "Spiritual Theology in the Thomistic Tradition', *Angelicum* 51 (1974) 571-98, and M. L. O'Hara, 'The Monastic Matrix of Apostolic Spirituality', *Sisters Today* 52 (1981) 596-99.

THE ROLE OF THE EREMITIC MONKS IN THE DEVELOPMENT OF THE MEDIEVAL INTELLECTUAL TRADITION
Patricia Ranft

B RUNO OF COLOGNE was born around 1030 of an unknown noble family. He was educated at St Cunibert in Cologne and completed his studies at Rheims, where he was asked to remain as master. Soon thereafter his proficiency in the arts and theology brought him to the position of chancellor. By 1080 he had decided to abandon the academic life and embarked on a search for a religious life that culminated in the foundation of the Grande Chartreuse.[1]

Robert of Arbrissel was born in 1055 in Brittany. He studied under Anselm of Laon in Paris and taught at Angers from 1090 to 1092. He then withdrew to the forest of Craon to live the life of a hermit. Four years later he established his first monastic house at La Roe and sometime around 1100 made a foundation at Fontevrault.[2]

Peter Damian was born probably in 1007 and spent most of his young adulthood in the schools of northern Italy. His studies included grammar, rhetoric, and law, most likely under the tutelage of Peter the Scholastic at Ravenna. In 1035, however, he chose to leave the academic world for life at Fonte Avellana. Under his able priorship Fonte Avellana was transformed into one of the most respected and influential eremitic groups in Italy.[3]

Examples of similar behavior are numerous. Stephen of Muret was educated in Italy, but rejected the intellectual life in favor of a monastic life with eremitic tendencies, for which he founded Grandmont around 1100.[4] Stephen Harding, educated at Dorset and then Paris, was involved in the foundation of Cîteaux.[5] Bernard of Tiron studied grammar and dialectics, but later decided to embrace the eremitic life in the Craon forest and subsequently established Tiron.[6] Indeed, so numerous are the examples of students-turned-founders of eremitic communities that the point may more dramatically be made by mentioning the exception to the rule: of all the major founders of eremitic groups of the late eleventh and early twelfth centuries, only John Gualbert of Vallombrosa apparently had no schooling.[7] Otherwise, the founders share this common history: exposure to and/or deep involvement in the new learning, followed by withdrawal and the establishment of a religious community with strong eremitic tendencies.

This relationship between education and the foundation of eremitic communities should be seriously considered. Little discusses one aspect of this relationship in his article, 'Intellectual Training and Attitudes toward Reform, 1005–1150'.[8] His focus is much broader and deals with all eleventh and twelfth-century reformers and the influence the schools exerted on these men, but some of his thought-provoking conclusions are relevant to our concerns here. If 'attendance at an urban school was the deciding factor in the creation of a radical religious reformer',[9] is it not likely that the reformer, particularly the eremitic reformer, in turn influenced the intellectual community? Is it not conceivable that these educated men and the communities they established contributed, albeit subtly, to the development of the medieval intellectual tradition even after their withdrawal from the academic world? We will explore these possibilities here and will argue that many sensitive members of the urban schools withdrew from society in part because they perceived there a tension within the relationship between knowledge and the sacred. In solitude they contemplated some of the fundamental aspects of the contemporary educational situation. Not the least of these reflections pertained to the linguistic symbols of the academic world. Specifically, the eremitic reformer grew in the realization that as an intellectual, his goal was linguistically and symbolically expressed by the word truth.[10] The traditional expression of his goal as a monk was stated differently: union with Christ. If, however, Christ and truth are one and the same, as indeed many of the Fathers claimed, then the attainment of truth is one and the same as union with Christ.[11] This was, in essence, the conclusion of the scholar hermits.

These reflections were not trivial, yet they were not particularly evident to their contemporaries and, in fact, were not in all instances readily accepted.[12] Nevertheless, they were conclusions which had far reaching repercussions because they dealt with symbols, and symbols are vehicles for change. Symbols provide the individual with access to new dimensions of awareness, and only after the individual experiences transformation through symbols can society as a whole 'absorb, incubate and give birth to new ideas' and institutions.[13] Thus, when the scholar hermits were able to revive traditional symbols and infuse them with new meaning, the symbols became vehicles for cultural evolution. The christian intellectual then felt free to pursue academic knowledge without fear of distraction from his search for Christ, thus allowing the educational transition from cloister to classroom to proceed unhindered.

This process can be documented by looking anew at two of the most influential scholar-hermits of the period: Bruno of Cologne and Peter Damian. Bruno's career will be examined

and indications of his awareness of the tension between
learned truth and lived truth will be noted. Scrutiny of Peter
Damian's works will reveal one of the ways in which scholar
hermits resolved this tension. Lastly, the ways in which these
opinions were communicated to society will be reviewed to
show how these monks actually did contribute to the medieval
intellectual tradition.

Bruno of Cologne, as we noted above, was a respected
scholar at the cathedral school of Rheims from 1056 to
1077.[14] During this period Rheims was one of the most
respected and advanced schools north of the Alps; this means
that Bruno was exposed to the educational innovations of the
day. In 1075 Bruno was made chancellor, and yet by 1077 he
had made a vow to abandon the world. Since Bruno left us
no autobiographical writings, we cannot know all his reasons
for this dramatic move, but we can at least reconstruct his
environment to learn his major concerns prior to this decision.
When Bruno assumed the chancellorship, the diocese of
Rheims was in upheaval over the controversies surrounding
its bishop, Manasses I. Accusations of simony followed
Manasses' installation, as did complaints about bad admini-
stration, clerical incontinence, and lay investiture. Only
Manasses' contact with the school remained above reproach;
there he continuously encouraged the pursuit of knowledge.
Sometime around 1075 the situation grew acute, and Bruno
and Manasses were soon bitter opponents. Within two years
Bruno resigned his post as chancellor and went to Rome to
plead his case against Manasses.[15] Once the matter was
resolved and Manasses was in exile, Bruno executed the vows
made at the time of his resignation and embraced the eremitic
life.
To a sensitive scholar such as Bruno, the dichotomy between what was preached and what was practised in the diocese was, no doubt, disturbing. While Manasses gave his full
support to the school and its pursuit of truth, he admitted

no contradiction between that and his behavior in other
areas. To Manasses, the activities of the school and the activities of life were separate and unrelated. Surely this attitude
must have frustrated Bruno and encouraged his inclination to
withdraw and reflect upon the nature of truth and knowledge,
and their relationship to life.

We know something else about Bruno's intellectual environment. The Berengarius controversy coincided chronologically
with Bruno's tenure at Rheims, a school almost next door to
Berengarius' Tours. There may even have been contact between the two, for something prompted their contemporaries
to claim that Bruno was a student of Berengarius.[16] Perhaps
there was contact around 1080, when Bruno was in Rome
pleading his case against Manasses and Berengarius was there,
summoned by Gregory VII.[17] In any case, it is not necessary
to prove actual contact between the two to appreciate the
import the Berengarius controversy must have had for Bruno—
is there a european theologian today who has remained un-
affected by the Hans Küng dilemma? Such controversies
always call forth personal re-evaluation of goals and methods,
and Bruno was not likely an exception.

So we find Bruno in the 1080s seeking radical separation
from this world, and argue that his perception of problems
within the academic milieu likely contributed to that decision. Bruno was soon joined by friends 'all of which', their
contemporaries claimed, 'were the most learned men of their
time',[18] and a community was established. But if perception
of problems within the academic world contributed to Bruno's
decision to withdraw, it certainly did not prompt him to for-
swear intellectual endeavor. To the contrary, the community
Bruno established esteemed intellectual activities highly.
Reading was fostered, books were treasured and collected,
and a library established and frequented.[19] More significant,
though, was the creation of a mentality which respected and
acknowledged man's intellectual capacities and sought ways to
use them profitably. Bruno himself never scorned his educa-

tion, but sincerely believed that his education brought him
closer to Christ because 'the treasures of knowledge and wisdom are in Christ'.[20] Pursuit of knowledge he viewed as a
means of attaining union with the sacred, not as a dubious
activity, for truth and the sacred are one. Guigo I, prior eight
years after Bruno's death, wrote: 'Truth is life and eternal
salvation, therefore you ought to pity anyone whom it dis-
pleases, for to that extent he is dead and lost.'[21]

Bruno and the Carthusians were not alone in realizing
this; indeed, this process of reflection and subsequent awareness was common among eremitic founders and their communities. Many of the brightest men in the adolescent schools
of the West were struck by a certain reluctance, a certain confusion, concerning the pursuit of knowledge within the classroom. What is the relationship between knowledge acquired
through reason and knowledge attained through faith? What
place does the search for knowledge have in the Christian's
life? These pressing questions do not belong to the thirteenth
century, when there was an urgency to define the precise
nature of truth within a critical philosophy;[22] no, the questions at this earlier age were less formal and more practical.
They were simply queries of hesitant Christians unsure of
themselves and worried that their search for truth would
jeopardize their search for salvation. The eremitic founders
who had spent the first part of their lives searching for academic truth and the latter part of their lives questing
after Christ offered reassuring conclusions to society: knowledge and the sacred are ultimately one. This conclusion they
reached primarily through discussions on the word truth.

Intuitively aware of language as symbol, the monks infused
that symbol with new life by defining truth in such a way
that division between knowledge and the sacred would be less
likely. Peter Damian did this well. In various works he talks
about truth, particularly in his treatise, 'Concerning True
Happiness and Wisdom'. According to Damian truth is Christ
Himself,[23] and wisdom is 'found in her essence only in God'.[24]

Anyone who seeks truth outside Christ renders his search fruitless and 'deserves to perish'.[25] Pursuit of truth without acknowledging the oneness of knowledge and the sacred is worldly prudence, not spiritual wisdom, and, Damian maintains, 'heavenly wisdom makes spiritually minded and abiding sons of the church; earthly prudence makes them bastards and preoccupied with matters of the flesh'.[26] Damian further contends that if truth is identified with Christ, secular learning may be pursued with the blessings of the church 'which has united the wise men of this world'.[27] Christ as truth would be given its rightful position, and secular learning a secondary but respected position as a reflection of that same truth. 'Any knowledge of human art . . . must serve with a sort of submission like a servant to her mistress, lest it should walk ahead, wander about, or lose the light of internal strength and the right road to Truth . . . ' .[28]

Thus, through such reasoning the relationship between spiritual faith and natural reason became clearer. Both must be appreciated and both may be used, but only within a hierarchy of values which places faith above reason, heavenly wisdom above earthly prudence, and at all times identifies Christ and truth as one. Secular learning is a 'captive woman' who, if properly purified and properly placed within the hierarchy, could be of tremendous service in the search for salvation.[29] This means that rhetoric and logic must not intrude obstinately on sacred laws, nor dialectics be used to interpret dogma.[30] But it also means that dialectics may be employed to help one perceive truth in a clearer light, as Damian himself did in his treatise 'Concerning Divine Omnipotence'.[31] He made extensive use of his secular education, in fact. 'When I write a thing that I wish especially to preserve, surrounded by an extensive library of various volumes, I call to mind the opinions of the masters and always resort, when necessary, to their work'.[32] He tells us in 'The Lord Be with You' that the method he used to reach his conclusions was one advocated at the schools.[33]

Damian was not conscious of being himself an exception; he coaxed others to proceed likewise. He advised Hildebrand to consult the poets and the philosophers to gain a proper understanding of the Scriptures,[34] and he offered this same advice to the general public in one of his sermons.[35] He sent his favorite nephew to Cluny for an education in the *trivium* and *quadrivium*,[36] believed that those secular clergy and bishops who guide their flock towards Christ should themselves be educated in secular knowledge,[37] and even chided one priest for letting his zeal for secular knowledge cool.[38] Again, though, all this is acceptable only if fundamental to it is the principle that Christ and truth are one. 'Our philosophy is Christ crucified',[39] Damian stoutly reminded the schoolmen of his day, and again, 'My grammar is Christ Himself'.[40] Grammar and philosophy outside this context is the work of the devil and will produce only false wisdom that blinds.[41] That is why Damian tells us in an oft-quoted passage that he spurned Plato and Pythagoras, renounced the books of Euclid and Nichomachus and ridiculed the rhetoricians and sophists, for he knew that first one must learn 'that of which the unskilled throng of dialecticians knows nothing'.[42] After that, not before, their knowledge will be of use. Scholars who turn first to the simplicity of Christ for instruction and only later to the liberal arts have nothing to fear. In fact, christian society has nothing to fear from the academic world at all if scholars follow this path.

How did such opinions as those of Damian filter into the world at large? Society became aware of them sometimes through personal contact, but most times through the written word. Let us look at some examples of each.

However complete the eremitic founders intended their withdrawal to be, relationships between and among them, the general public, and scholars continued to flourish. This happened often to the chagrin óf the monks. Both Bruno and Peter Damian were not permitted to remain in their solitude but were called forth by popes to become active participants

in the reform movement.[43] Peter was made cardinal-bishop of
the prestigious see of Ostia and also served as papal legate to
Milan, Cluny, Florence, Ravenna, and the royal court in
Germany. Bruno was asked by his former student, Urban II,
to act as papal advisor in Rome and reformer in southern
Italy. It is clear that both exercised significant influence upon
their worlds and that their opinions were sought and respected, not least their idea of knowledge and its place within
the Christian's life.

The communities founded by these former scholars also
maintained contacts of sorts with the academic world. First,
there was their witness.[44] The Carthusians, for example, were
an extraordinarily disciplined ascetic group, doing everything
the medieval mind could imagine to gain salvation, and here
they were fostering intellectual activity. Second, communities
like the Carthusians possessed excellent libraries that were admired, talked about, and, presumably, used by scholars. Peter
the Venerable has provided us with evidence of the Carthusians' techniques for procuring and copying books and of the
literary intercourse between the Carthusians and those outside
their community.[45] Hugh of Lincoln's biographer tells us that
Hugh was well-steeped in carthusian tradition and devoted
much labor to making, purchasing, and acquiring manuscripts
'by every possible means'.[46] Many important spiritual and
theological works were written for or at the request of the
eremitic monks. William of St Thierry, for instance, wrote his
Golden Epistle for the Carthusians, and Bernard of Clairvaux
wrote two important works at their request: *Of Loving God*
for Prior Guy; and *Sermon on the Song of Songs* for Bernard,
monk of the Chartreuse-des-Portes-en-Bugey.[47] And we have
much evidence that the more cenobitic and visible new Orders,
such as the Cistercians, were influenced by or followed in the
tradition articulated by the eremitic monks. For example,
Damian wrote: 'Whoever devoted to the study of pagan letters
or any worldly matter that concern which belongs primarily to
that scrupulous inner examination of ourselves . . . merits

perdition'. One need not ignore pagan letters if one is at all times sure 'to give to it in all events only a secondary place'.[48] In a similar vein Gilbert of Hoyland wrote: 'Not that I disparage erudition in the arts, and a ready memory in liberal studies . . . for skill in the arts is valuable, provided one uses them rightly, that is, as a step and foothold . . . to rise to higher and holier and more interior mysteries of wisdom.'[49] Even Bernard's attitude was consistent with this tradition: 'Perhaps you consider me unduly severe and narrow in my views on human knowledge, and suppose that I am censuring the learned and condemning the study of letters. God forbid that I should do that! I am well aware how much her learned members have benefitted and still benefit the church . . . .'[50] Significantly, the canons, who were influential in the early stages of the schools and among whom Damian was highly revered,[51] reiterated this theme as well. Richard of St Victor wrote: 'What is knowledge alone which does not produce holiness and love of goodness . . . ' .[52] Hugh of St Victor tells us that 'the spirit of study sharpens the mental powers, begets a love of learning, preserves knowledge acquired, turns the mind away from vain and useless things, fosters a hatred of sin, seeks quiet and peace'.[53] This statement was made without fear that study distracts the Christian, because truth and Christ are one and the pursuit of knowledge leads ultimately to Christ the Truth. 'It follows', Hugh continues, 'that all the natural arts serve divine science and the lower knowledge rightly ordered leads to the higher.'[54] Abelard summarizes this point succinctly: 'Truth is not opposed to truth',[55] and if Christ is indeed truth, the seeker of Christ obviously has an obligation to seek truth. This unitive vision attains its mature expression in the works of Bonaventure, particularly in his *Retracing the Arts to Theology, The Soul's Journey into God*, and *The Mind's Road to God*. Here truth and God are seen as one, because 'truth, assuming human nature in Christ, had become a ladder' with which the soul could rise completely

from the things of sense 'to see itself and the Eternal Truth
in Itself'.[56] Knowledge outside Christ is impossible, for 'all
kinds of knowledge are perfected in the knowledge of sacred
scripture',[57] which directs us to God, within whom truth
resides.

We must, of course, remember what motivated these early
discussions of truth in order to appreciate their contributions
and their limitations. They were not formal inquiries into the
nature of truth, for, again, society had not yet experienced
the need for such a critical philosophy. The eremitic founders
were interested not in epistomology, not in illuminationism as
an explanation of knowledge, but in integrating man's intellectual life with his spiritual. In the early eleventh century the
Christian was still hesitant and almost apologetic about his
increasing interest in intellectual matters; by the thirteenth
century he was convinced that 'the accumulation of speculative wisdom was one of the primary ends of man'.[58] To make
this transition man had first to resolve his ambivalence towards
intellectual pursuits, and it was this issue that the eremitic
monks addressed. Their contribution to the medieval intellectual tradition lies in the articulation of a unitive vision of
knowledge and the sacred, a vision capable of resolving man's
ambivalence. The monks did not 'create' this vision, for it
has enjoyed a long tradition in Christianity and in many
world religions, but they did, metaphorically, resurrect it
at a time when it answered a pressing need. By discussing
truth and expanding its symbolic content to include this
vision, christian society relaxed and proceeded onward in
its pursuit of knowledge.

By identifying the eremitic founders' role in the development of the medieval intellectual tradition, then, we gain
a clearer perception of the early stages of the transition
from cloister to classroom; we acknowledge the inter-
relationship between these monks and the schools they
left behind; we acquire insight into the broader question
of social change; and, lastly, we depart with a better

appreciation of the eremitic Orders themselves.

Central Michigan University

NOTES

1. For Bruno's life, see *Acta SS,* VI Oct., PL 152:555-606; PL 153: 11-568; A. Wilmart, 'La Chronique des premiers chartreux', *Revue Mabillon* 16 (1926) 77-142. For specific points on chronology, see John R. Williams, 'Archbishop Manasses I and Pope Gregory VII', *American Historical Review* 54 (1948-49) 804-24; *idem,* 'Godfrey of Rheims', *Speculum* 22 (1947) 29-45.

2. For Robert, see *Acta SS,* III Feb.; Rene Niderst, *Robert d'Arbrissel et les Origines de l'Ordre de Fontevrault* (Rodez, 1952); Jacqueline Smith, 'Robert of Arbrissel: *Procurator Mulierium*', in Derek Baker, ed., *Medieval Women* (Oxford, 1978) 175-84; and Penny Schine Gold, 'Male/Female Cooperation: The Example of Fontevrault', in John A. Nichols and Lillian T. Shank, edd., *Distant Echoes / Medieval Religious Women,* vol. 1 (Kalamazoo, 1984) 151-68; and PL 162:1079-82.

3. John of Lodi's *vita* is in PL 144:115-44; Damian's works are in PL 144 and 145. Also see Jean Leclercq, *S. Pierre Damien* (Rome, 1960); Owen Blum, *St. Peter Damian: His Teaching on the Spiritual Life* (Washington, D.C., 1947); and John Wang, 'St. Peter Damian, the Monk', unpublished Ph.D. dissertation, Fordham University, 1957.

4. For Stephen of Muret, see PL 204:1005-46; *Acta SS* II Feb.; Jean Becquet, 'Les Institutions de l'Ordre de Grandmont au Moyen Age', *Revue Mabillon* 168 (152) 31-42; Sharon K. Elkins, 'The Emergence of a Gilbertine Identity', in *Distant Echoes,* 169-182.

5. Stephen Harding's life is found in *Acta SS,* II Apr. Also see Bernard of Clairvaux, Epp. 45 and 49; PL 182:149-52, and 157-58; and J. Marilier, *Chartes et documents concernant l'abbaye de Cîteaux, 1098-1182* (Rome, 1961) 55-65.

6. For Bernard of Tiron, see PL 172:1363-1446; *Acta SS,* II Apr; and C. Claireaux, *Saint Bernard de Thiron* (Bellême, 1913).

7. For John Gualbert, see PL 146:671-706; *Acta SS,* III July; and S. Casini, *Storia di S. Giovanni Gualberto Fiorentino* (Florence, 1934).

8. Lester K. Little, 'Intellectual Training and Attitudes toward Reform, 1005-1150', in *Pierre Abelard, Pierre Le Venerable,* Colloques Internationaux (Paris, 1975) 235-49.

9. *Ibid.,* 248.

10. See James J. Preston, *Cult of the Goddess* (New Delhi, 1980) for an excellent study of symbols and their role in history.

11. Cf. Wolfhart Pannenberg, *Theology and the Kingdom of God* (Philadelphia, 1969) 59, a contemporary opinion about the unity of

creation as a basis for knowledge.

12. For example, Gilbert of Hoyland (d. 1172), *Sermones in Canticum Salomis, Sermo* 5:33: 'For me, any teaching which employs no reference to Christ . . . is open to suspicion and certainly to be shunned'. [ET by Lawrence C. Braceland, *Sermons on the Song of Songs* I (1978) CF 14:87]

13. Preston, *Cult*, p. 92.

14. The exact dates of Bruno's career are hazy; I am adhering to the chronology established by Williams, 'Manasses I', and *idem*, 'Godfrey of Rheims', for much of what occurred at the school at Rheims. See also PL 152:52d; and H. Lobbel, *Der Stifter des Carthauser-Ordens* (Münster, 1899).

15. We do not know for sure when Bruno resigned or if he went to Rome for support while still chancellor; we do know, however, that by 1079 Godfrey is mentioned in a charter as chancellor of Rheims.

16. PL 152:48d-49a.

17. For an overview of the Berengarius controversy and the relevant dates to this paper, see C. E. Sheedy, *The Eucharistic Controversy of the Eleventh Century* (Washington, D.C., 1947).

18. PL 152:529.

19. PL 153:631-760. See also Guibert of Nogent, *Self and Society in Medieval France,* trans. C. C. S. Bland (New York, 1970) 61: ' . . . although they [the Carthusians] subject themselves to complete poverty, they are accumulating a very rich library.'

20. PL 153:384a (a commentary on Col 2:2-3).

21. Guigues de Chastel, *Meditations of Guigo, Prior of the Charterhouse,* trans. John Jolin (Milwaukee, 1951) 225; PL 153:601-63.

22. See Steven Marrone, *William of Auvergne and Robert Grosseteste* (Princeton, 1983).

23. PL 145:836c.

24. PL 145:833c.

25. PL 145:834d.

26. PL 145:883b.

27. PL 145:834a.

28. PL 145:603.

29. PL 145:541b.

30. PL 145:603.

31. PL 145:595-622. W. H. V. Reade, 'Philosophy in the Middle Ages', in *Cambridge Medieval History,* vol. 5, edd. J. R. Tanner, C. W. Previte-Orton, Z. N. Brooke (New York, 1929) 792, comments: 'Less energy, perhaps, would have been spent in remonstrance against this apparent degradation of reason if more attention had been paid to the current

usage of terms. *Philosophia* often means no more than dialectic, and dialectic no more than a display of captious arguments. That the Christian position as a whole (the Christian philosophy, in fact) was irrational, Peter Damian and his contemporaries would never have admitted. The antithesis of *ratio* and *auctoritas* was then far less comprehensive than the final problem, scarcely realized before the age of Aquinas, whether the independence of philosophy could be reconciled with the Catholic position. To assign to dialectic a merely ancillary office is not necessarily obscurantism. It often meant no more than the logical commonplace, that *ratiocinatio* presupposes the concession of premises. In a deeper sense, it meant that experience must precede the attempt to explain it, and that the testimony of many generations cannot easily be overthrown by a talent for repartee.'

32.   PL 144:359a.
33.   PL 145:233c.
34.   PL 145:560c.
35.   PL 144:541b.
36.   PL 144:373c.
37.   PL 144:345a; 353b; PL 145:98b.
38.   PL 145:126c.
39.   PL 144:828a.
40.   PL 144:476c.
41.   PL 145:603; PL 144:828a.
42.   PL 145:233b.
43.   One must not think of Bruno or Peter Damian as unique. Other lesser known monks shared similar fates. Gerard of Czanàd, for instance, was a disciple of St Romuald and was called forth from his hermitage to become the first bishop of Czanàd, establish a school for the liberal arts and serve as special confident to King Stephen of Hungary. See A. J. Macdonald, *Authority and Reason in the Early Middle Ages* (London, 1933) 98-99.
44.   See Patricia Cricco, 'Hugh Latimer and Witness', *The Sixteenth Century Journal* 10:1 (Spring, 1979) 21-34; and *idem*, 'Monasticism and Its Role as a Liminal Community in Medieval Society', unpublished Ph.D. dissertation, West Virginia University, 1981, pp. 199-225, 266-72, for a discussion on monastic witness and its contributions to society.
45.   Peter the Venerable, Epp. 24,132,169 and 170; *The Letters of Peter the Venerable* ed. Giles Constable, (Cambridge, Mass., 1967) I : 44-47, 333-34, 402 and 402-404.
46.   Adam of Eynsham, *Magna Vita Sancti Hugonis,* II:xiii; trans. Decima Douie and Hugh Farmer (London, 1961) 85. His reasoning is

interesting: 'It was a favorite saying of [Hugh's] that these books were useful to all monks, but especially to those leading an eremitical life, for they provided riches and delights in times of tranquillity, weapons and armor in times of temptation, food for the hungry, and medicine for the sick.'

47.   William of St Thierry, *The Golden Epistle* trans. Theodore Berkeley (Cistercian Publications, 1971); and *Sancti Bernardi opera*, edd. Jean Leclercq, C. H. Talbot and H. M. Rochais (Rome, 1963-73).

48.   PL 145:835a.

49.   Gilbert of Hoyland, *Treatises* 2:2; trans. Lawrence C. Braceland *Gilbert of Hoyland: Treatises, Epistles and Sermons* (Kalamazoo, 1981) 94.

50.   PL 183:967.

51.   A. Fliche calls Peter Damian the veritable founder of the canons. See A. Fliche, *La reforme gregorienne* (Paris, 1924-37) I:337. J. C. Dickinson, *The Origins of the Austin Canons and their Introduction into England* (London, 1950) 27, says Peter Damian and Hildebrand share credit for sponsoring the regular canons. It is Damian's theology that is at the root of the canonical life. See *Opusc.* 27 (PL 145:503-12) and *Opusc.* 24 (PL 145:479-90), and Pierre Mandonnet, *St. Dominic and His Work*, trans. M. Larkin (London and St Louis, 1948) 268: 'The reformed canons embraced with their whole soul the fulness of this heritage as proclaimed in the words of Peter Damian.'

52.   PL 196:1292.

53.   PL 177:161.

54.   PL 176:183-85.

55.   Quoted in H. O. Taylor, *The Medieval Mind*, 4th ed. (London, 1925) I:349.

56.   Bonaventure, *Soul's Journey into God*, trans. Evert Cousins (Ramsey, N.J., 1978) 4.2.

57.   Bonaventure, *On Retracing the Arts to Theology*, 7; *The Works of Bonaventure*, trans. Jose de Vinck (Paterson, N.J., 1966) 20-21.

58.   Marrone, *William and Robert*, p. 13.

THE IDEA OF JERUSALEM:
MONASTIC TO SCHOLASTIC*
Thomas Renna

ONASTIC AND SCHOLASTIC. The former way to truth attained its highest development in the eleventh and twelfth centuries. The latter, in the next two centuries. While no two historians agree on definitions of monastic and scholastic—their chronology, content, or procedure—this typology can be useful in detecting shifts in fundamental attitudes in christian Europe, including its ecclesiology. What were some of the monastic views of the church? How did the schoolmen assimilate the then-current monastic concepts of the *ecclesia?* There was, of course, no 'scholastic' idea of the church, any more than there was a 'monastic' one. Monks often wrote on purely monastic concerns. But scholastic writing is often harder to classify because of its wider diversity of purpose: polemics, theology, philosophy, and pastoral affairs.

As a test case this study will examine one of the traditional synonyms for the church: Jerusalem. Did the success of the first crusade result in a new attitude towards Jerusalem, as

has been recently claimed?[1] Possession of the earthly Jerusalem, runs this argument, was deemed indispensable for
salvation.

Monks summoned the heavenly Jerusalem to designate the
end of the *vita monastica,* and even to describe the *vita* itself.
It is this notion of Jerusalem as the monastic life that became
clarified during the period 1050–1200. Before that time
Jerusalem most often meant, simply, heaven, the object of
the monk's aspirations. In this desire monastic discipline is implied, but the connection was left vague. Even Gregory the
Great, who associated *contemplatio* with the *celestis patria,*
did not make Jerusalem a salient trait of the monastic experience. He confined the idea of Jerusalem to the *vera pax*
enjoyed by the elect and the angels.[2] Greek patristic views
of Jerusalem as the goal of the ascent from the material to
the immaterial had little direct impact on monastic concepts
of Jerusalem in the early medieval West. The desert fathers
refer infrequently to the celestial city.[3] In carolingian exegesis,
Jerusalem was often used as a metaphor of divine grace descending to the holy soul, with minimal reference to the ascent
of the *anima.*[4]

In the eleventh, and especially the twelfth, century monastic writers described the progress of the contemplative soul
toward the heavenly city. Monks are already citizens of the
civitas because 1) they originated there, and will eventually
return to replace the voids left by the reprobate angels,
2) their whole way of life is an anticipation of the future life,
3) the life of God (as the angelic life) exists within the pious
soul. Jerusalem as the church triumphant consists of the elect
(or the elect and the angels). Monastic authors sometimes
implied that they were the *electi,* or at least part of this pre-
destined group.[5] They alluded frequently to Jerusalem as
both soul and church.[6] It is not always clear, however,
whether the city as church refers to the visible body, a particular group within this body, the celestial *ecclesia,* or the
church in its earthly and heavenly parts, as in the augustinian

tradition. Monks suggested that they were more fully citizens
of the church triumphant insofar as they contemplated, practised virtue, and followed the Rule of St Benedict. The holy
soul, by this argument, participates in the life of heaven
through contemplation.[7]

Twelfth-century monastic writings emphasized Jerusalem as
a metaphor of the heavenly elect. While true monks were
someday to join this elect, these authors were reticent to designate monks as the elect. Little was said, moreover, about how
the cloistered fit into the church universal. The image of Jerusalem connoted the resemblance of the holy soul to God and
his court of his city. Jerusalem signified the infusion of grace
into the soul. Crusade chronicles and *itineraria* often had the
terrestrial city prefigure the heavenly one,[8] while monastic
spiritual works rarely did. But monks did stress their own immediate participation in the life of the angels.[9] A few authors
developed the analogy of the cenobitic life and Jerusalem
on high.[10]

The early scholastics showed no particular interest in Jerusalem as an ecclesial image, although they echoed commonplaces about this city. In his *Cur Deus Homo,* Anselm of Canterbury addressed the question of whether the number of the
elect exceeds the gaps left by the fallen angels. In his defense
Anselm frequently alluded to heaven as the city which includes
both the elect—the children of Israel—and the angels.[11] When
the city is finally completed or perfected, the world will be
renewed and the bodies of the elect resurrected. But Anselm
drew no ecclesiological conclusions, despite the implications
for eschatology and apocalypticism of his treatment of the
city as increasing in number towards completion.

In Anselm of Laon's commentary on the *Apocalypse*—
which followed Walafrid Strabo—the language of the schools
is more evident. The church is holy because it is founded on
quies.[12] The church is Jerusalem because the elect see Christ,
the true peace. Jerusalem is *nova* and the corporeal body will
be renewed in heaven. The city comes down to earth in the

form of grace to the humble. Jerusalem is adorned as a bride, that is, the church accepts faith and the theological virtues by means of baptism. The spouse of the Lamb elevates the soul to the knowledge of Christ, whose church shines in all the virtues.

These interpretations of Jerusalem as church, to be sure, can be found in most previous commentaries of the *Apocalypse.* But a change of emphasis is discernible in twelfth-century works. Anselm of Laon related the structure and population of the terrestrial church to corresponding elements in the celestial city. Jerusalem's watchmen are those who refute heresy.[13] The church possesses the heavenly virtues of faith, hope, and charity. The sacraments bring the church to its fulfillment in the heavenly Jerusalem.

Similar theses were expanded by Martin of León (d. 1221), who stressed the central place of Christ in the present church. The Incarnation is a daily drama in the *ecclesia* through his sacraments and his example of humility.[14] Christ sustains the faith, virtues, and good works of his church, and in this way the saints in the celestial Jerusalem are glorified. Finally, the precious stones of the heavenly city represent the various *ordines* in the church, particularly the *vita activa* and *vita contemplativa.*[15]

A convenient transition from monastic to scholastic views of Jerusalem can be viewed in the *De claustro animae* of Hugh Fouilloy (d.c. 1174). This important tract was the first systematic attempt to coordinate two traditional images of Jerusalem: soul and church. Hugh's synthesis anticipated the solutions of later schoolmen. In the lengthy conclusion of the *De claustro animae,* Hugh unexpectedly discusses the reflections of the celestial Jerusalem in the visible church: these can be seen in the four meanings of the city: material, mystical, moral, anagogical. Throughout his work he drew parallels between the streets and squares of the heavenly city and their analogues in the contemplative soul.[16] Hugh's descriptions of the soul's peregrinations are as eloquent as any found in the writings of

Peter Damian[17] or Peter of Celle.[18] Jerusalem is the full *visio pacis* reserved for this world's worthy monks. The whole of Book Four builds to a crescendo—much like the finale of Augustine's *De civitate Dei*—in which the souls of the just are united with God after the second resurrection. Hugh is in harmony with some cistercian trends to model the monastic life on the court of heaven. The man-made cloister resembles the God-made 'cloister' in Jerusalem. God the Father is the great Abbot, and Christ the great Prior.[19] Pure souls and angels converse with each other and with God, according to Hugh.

The *De claustro animae*—despite its title—gives a large role to the terrestrial church. Indeed, the treatments of the mystical Jerusalem and the tropological Jerusalem are mostly about how the church maintains the *pax ecclesiae*. The *custodes murorum* are the doctors who refute heretics and restore peace to the church.[20] The various streets and squares of Jerusalem correspond to the continent and the married, the active and the contemplative. Since the earthly Jerusalem contains both the good and the bad, catholic leaders must ward off attacks from the wicked. The priests defend the faithful by works, sacraments, and even physical force.[21] The pacific soul is one who, like Solomon, guards the earthly *pax* of the church universal. Whereas previous monastic commentaries on the *Apocalypse* juxtaposed the images of soul and church haphazardly, Hugh's parallels were consciously and deliberately drawn. He followed the contemporary reformist trend of relating the church to the apostolic Jerusalem. The celestial Jerusalem appears as a type of both *anima* and *ecclesia*, a salient characteristic of the scholastic Jerusalem.

In his commentary on the *Apocalypse*, Albert the Great relied on Augustine's *De civitate Dei* and Haymo of Auxerre's commentary.[22] Albert's exegesis is conventional enough, although the image of Jerusalem as soul is largely absent. The usual effects on the descending city refer to the church, not to the soul. The holy city is the glory of the church *in futuro*,

but antecedents exist in the church *in praesenti:* unanimity
(or conformity), the harmony of the *cives,* security, *pax et
quies,* newness, renewal, immortality[23] —attributes which are
not associated with the soul. Albert's church is markedly
ecclesiastical, founded on unity and the sacraments, and emphasizes the duties of prelates and Dominicans. To toil on
behalf of the *visio pacis* is to advance the church's unity,
faith, and good works. Prelates and doctors imitate the
apostles in both action and contemplation. The twelve gates
of Jerusalem represent the twelve ways by which Christ enters
the church through preaching. The walls signify the temporal
and spiritual *defensores ecclesiae.* The name of Jerusalem is
written on the elect, who enjoy the *visio pacis hic* through
faith.[24] The city is *nova* because the elect aspire to spiritual
realities.

In his *Expositio in Apocalypsim,* Pseudo-Aquinas made a
distinction between the assembly of the just in Jerusalem who
see *maxime quantum ad esse,* and those *ad ipsam quantum ad
bene esse.*[25] The first form the city *in generali;* the second, *in
speciali.* Neither group, however, is named. Pseudo-Thomas
classified the various elements of the new heaven and
the new earth. Jerusalem is a type of the city of the
just because it symbolizes the way humankind ascends
from mundane, visible things to celestial, invisible things. Those
who go down with the city are the virtuous who will live with
God happily in eternity and in full knowledge of him. God
prepares his bride, the church, by heavenly gifts and works.
The just souls have love (*dilectio*), understanding (*tentio*),
and vision (*visio*); their bodies have impassibility, agility, subtlety,
and clarity.[26] All celestial virtues have some degree of fulfillment here below. Pseudo-Thomas carefully arranged these virtues to elevate the status of the doctors and preachers, who
educate others for citizenship in Jerusalem. These teachers of
virtue and doctrine he likened to the apostles, the *typi* of the
city's gates. Jerusalem's walls connoted for him faith, hope,
charity, and works, as well as prudence, temperance, fortitude,

and justice.

The Franciscan schoolmen did not hesitate to designate the *defensores* of the walls as the Friars Minor. Alexander of Bremen (d. 1271) singled out the mendicants (most notably Francis and Dominic) as the *viri boni* who come down with Jerusalem to restore the *ecclesia primitiva.*[27] Holy souls constantly ascend to the celestial Jerusalem, while, simultaneously, the *viri perfecti* (who renew the church) descend to the terrestrial Jerusalem. Going beyond any twelfth-century monastic author, Alexander made the antique Jerusalem of the apostles a figure of the rebuilt Jerusalem at this moment. The new elect, the Friars Minor, had 'returned' to regain the vision of peace to the church, a type of the heavenly *visio pacis.* The new citizens had been sent to usher in the third age of the church.

James of Viterbo distinguished between the kingdoms of Jerusalem and Babylon.[28] Christ's *regnum* on earth prefigures that in heaven. Hence the church militant must be organized according to the structure of the church triumphant. James made Augustine's peregrinating church more ecclesiastical and juridical. Whereas Augustine's church incorporated the saints of the past, present, and the future, James, stating that the *regnum ecclesiae est unum,* intimated that the present church includes the entire *corpus Christi;* it is this body which will be completed and perfected in the heavenly Jerusalem. As a final illustration of the church's *unitas* James argued that this unity produces peace. Peace now results from a harmony of citizens within the city of God—Augustine's *pax est tranquillitas ordinis.*[29] The church is one because it is pacific, albeit the pilgrim church must endure discord and violence. Alluding to Isidore of Seville, James identified the present church with Sion because it watches (or contemplates) the celestial kingdom. Jerusalem, the *visio pacis,* is the *patrie celestis pace* and this peace is Christ. Therefore, the ecclesiastical kingdom is *unitas.* But Augustine, in fact, had distinguished between Sion and Jerusalem in order to emphasize the *lack* of peace

and order in the mournful church.[30] He had used Sion to
offer hope to those now in exile and captivity. Sion suggests
imperfection. James summoned the Sion/Jerusalem polarity,
however, as a proof that the present church is a unit precisely
because it is becoming the completed peace of heaven.

The Franciscan master Peter Aureoli used biblical prophecies
to explain the course of Christian history. The allegories of the
Apocalypse forecast recent events, such as the coming of the
Cistercians and the Friars Minor.[31] By means of somewhat
contrive analogies Peter interpreted specific occurrences in
the church militant as images of the ultimate realities of the
church triumphant.

The ecclesiology of Bonaventure was grounded on a
reasoned ontology. He united soul and church into a symbio-
tic relationship, each within its own hierarchy. In the prologue
to the *Itinerarium mentis in Deum,* he had Francis sigh for
ecstatic vision 'like a citizen of Jerusalem'.[32] The experience
of Jerusalem can be attained in this life, once the soul is
hierarchically shaped according to purgation, illumination,
and perfection. By means of the theological virtues the soul is
reformed into a certain condition, when the heavenly Jerusalem
can descend into it. Each level in the soul's hierarchy (announc-
ing, declaring, leading, ordering, strengthening, commanding,
receiving, revealing, anointing) corresponds to an angelic level
in the celestial city.[33] Within the soul the first three levels
relate to human nature. The next three to effort. The last
three to grace. Upon reaching the final rank, the soul enters
into itself and enters Jerusalem. Bonaventure described at
length the various kinds of angels and their correlative realities
in the contemplative soul. The choirs of thrones, cherubim, and
seraphim match the stages of contemplation.

Bonaventure believed that his analogies, however poetic,
expressed objective reality. Often expressed in dionysian and
numerological language, the hierarchy within the contemplative *anima* is a real image of the angelic hierarchy of the
heavenly Jerusalem. Indeed, this interior arrangement in the

soul mirrors the life of the Trinity itself. Bonaventure's complex system of analogies with Jerusalem is admittedly difficult to untangle, since Jerusalem represents both the composition of the soul as well as its progress towards the goal
(Jerusalem). Then, too, Jerusalem is the soul's peace here and
also the peace to be possessed in heaven. At any rate, Bonaventure applied the idea of Jerusalem to the soul in its present
endeavors.

Just as the soul is like the church triumphant, the church
is like the soul:

> the image of our soul . . . should be clothed
> with the three theological virtues, by which
> the soul is purified, illuminated, and perfected.
> And so the image is reformed and made like the
> heavenly Jerusalem and a part of the church
> militant which, according to Paul, is the off-
> spring of the heavenly Jerusalem. For he says:
> that Jerusalem which is above is free, which
> is our mother.[34]

In some mysterious way the contemplative mind, as it moves
towards the image of the heavenly Jerusalem, becomes a pattern of the proportionate conformation between the church
militant and the church triumphant. The contemplative soul
conforms to the enlightened hierarchy (that is, the angelic)
and to the enlightening hierarchy (the Trinity). Just as the
soul contemplates, so too does the church. It is meaningless
to talk of a soul contemplating outside the church. Indeed, a
prerequisite for contemplation is an understanding of the
hierarchies of the visible church.[35] The moon, as the contemplative soul, receives its light and heat from the sun (the
heavenly Jerusalem). Hence, the church militant receives its
light (its hierarchies) from the celestial city, our mother: 'The
heavenly hierarchy is a model of the church militant.'[36] The
orders of the latter are divided into the ways of procession,

ascent, and exercise. Bonaventure then presented an elaborate sequence of equivalents between the levels of angels and divine Persons on the one hand, and the earthly church on the other. Using several series of threes (*e.g.,* prelates, masters, regulars), he assigned all orders their proper niche in the ecclesiastical framework.

As a concrete example of these exemplars, the Seraphic Doctor built his *Legenda Maior* of Francis around these interlocking archetypes. God sent Francis to reinstate his hierarchies in the human soul and the church. Francis is the hierarchic man whose manner of contemplation most resembled angelic worship.[37] His example and preaching inaugurated a new age of the church, during which time the church will more closely resemble the heavenly Jerusalem. In Bonaventure's scheme, those who live the mixed life—the mendicants—rank high in the renewed church because their lifestyle closely parallels the hierarchy of the celestial city. So too, the mendicants have re-created the life lived by Jesus and his disciples. But Bonaventure's ideal of the hierarchic soul applies to other church leaders (such as bishops) as well, and eventually to all Christians.

It should be emphasized that Bonaventure's ecclesiology rests on the holy soul's likeness to the *ecclesia contemplativa.* The final section of his *Conferences on the Hexaemeron* presents a grand vision of the soul's repose in God. The soul is hiearchized according to twelve illustrations, like twelve stars. The measurements of Jerusalem (144 cubits, etc.) correspond to the operations of the soul, which sees the city in three ways: standing, descending, and ascending. As there are six seals, so there are six ages of the world, the sixth (Christ's *ecclesia contemplativa*) being imminent. 'The contemplative church and the contemplative soul do not differ', he posited.[38] Bonaventure's definition of 'contemplation', broad enough to include worship, knowledge, and, above all, charity, is clearly more elastic and more extensive than that of contemporary monastic writers.

CONCLUSION

Jerusalem has been a powerful symbol in christian thought
since the beginning of the church. Old Testament prophecies,
the psalms, and jewish apocalyptic works gave the holy city a
unique place in the new faith. Jesus' public life and death occurred here. The Romans' dual destruction of Jerusalem permitted a gradual christian takeover of the holy places. The
myth of the church of Jerusalem, with its famed liturgy, was
well established by the third century, as was its symbolic association with heaven. After Constantine the city became a pil-
grimage center where the pious Christian could 'touch' the
divine—as a sort of sacrament—and revive memories of the
historical Jesus and his intimates. The latin Fathers liked to
equate Jerusalem with the full vision of God and the celestial
church. After Jerusalem fell to the Arabs in 638, it remained
for the most part closed to the West until the eleventh century.
But the symbolic Jerusalem persisted because of its important
role in Scripture (and biblical commentaries), in the liturgy and
in various monastic works. To some degree the recapture of the
city in 1099 intensified monastic attention to the traditional
metaphors. Monks were particularly attracted to Jerusalem as
a sign of contemplation and as a connection to the *vita monastica*. They expanded the symbolic links of Jerusalem with
angelic citizenship, the *visio pacis* in heaven, and the church
of the elect. In the thirteenth century the idea of Jerusalem
as the contemplative state was further intensified and interior-
ized.

Many schoolmen of the thirteenth century felt uneasy
about the traditional symbols of Jerusalem as the church. How
does one reconcile the images of church universal, beatific
vision, and the heavenly elect? Some mendicants focused on
Jerusalem, not in order to reject the conventional monastic
perspective of the city, but on the contrary to afix the idea
to their own assumptions about the primitive church, contemplation, celestial elect, apocalyptic new men, evangelical
poverty, and the mixed life. They employed the language of

the schools to delinate the church in its myriad functions. Their ecclesiastical model is slanted, to be sure, in favor of the church's teachers and preachers. And much of their analysis does seem abstract and detached, largely devoid of the emotive and poetic force of monastic literature. Yet while these scholars retained something of the eschatological heritage of Jerusalem, they often used the metaphor of the city to describe the church as it in fact is. They harnessed the heavenly city and brought it to earth. They tried to modernize the symbol and make it correspond to the reality of the organizational church.

But the mendicant synthesis of Jerusalem as the clerical church and as an elite within this church soon crumbled. The daughters of Jerusalem quickly tired of the classroom disputes, and returned to the peace of the cloister, if only the cloister of the heart.

Saginaw Valley [Michigan] State College

108

NOTES

*The author wishes to thank Saginaw Valley State College for generously providing him with a research grant for this study.

1. J. Prawer, 'Jerusalem in the Christian and Jewish Perspectives of the early Middle Ages', *Settimane di Studio del Centro Italiano di Studi Sull'Alto Medioevo* 26 (Spoleto 1980) 739-95.
2. M. Adriaen, ed., *Homiliae in Hiezechihelem,* CC 142 (Turnholt 1971) I; 8, 3-6; 10,23-25; II: 1, 5-7; 5,2.
3. E.g., Eucherius of Lyon, CSEL 31: 51, 188-94; W. Frankenberg, ed., Evagrius Ponticus, *Abhandlungen der königlichen Gesellschaft* der Wissenschaften zu Göttingen, Phil-hist. Klasse, N.S. 13 (Berlin 1912) 321, 361.
4. Ambrose Autpert, *Expositionis in Apocalypsim,* ed., R. Weber, CC 27A (Turnhold 1975) 776-80; Haymo of Auxerre, *In Apocalypsim,* PL 117:993f., 1192f.; Pseudo-Alcuin, PL 100:1113f. The evolution of these pre-twelfth-century monastic ideas of Jerusalem is beyond the scope of this paper. I am currently writing a book on this whole subject.
5. Berengar, *In Apocalypsin,* PL 17:790, 871. *Confessio Theologica,* 3:11-32; J. Leclercq, *Un maître de la vie spirituelle au ix^es.: Jean de Fécamp* (Paris: Vrin, 1946).
6. E.g., Bernard of Clairvaux, SC 27, edd. J. Leclercq et al, *SBOp* (Rome 1957) 1: 181-92; Godfrey of Admont, *Homiliae,* PL 174: 22, 26, 74, 95-7, 159, 809; Aelred of Rievaulx, *Sermones,* PL 195: 228-32, 265-70, 315.
7. Richard of St. Victor, *In Apocalypsim,* PL 196:857-88, (cf. cols. 412-16, 508).
8. E.g., Ekkehard, *Recueil des historiens des croisades, Historiens Occidentaux* (Paris, 1895) 5:38.
9. See G. Colombás, *Paraíso y vida angélica* (Abadía de Montserrat 1958) 245-96.
10. Baldwin of Ford, *De vita coenobitica,* PL 204:545-62.
11. F. Schmitt, ed., *Sancti Anselmi Opera Omnia 1* (Seckau, 1938) cc. 18-19; 2, 6, 16. Cf. PL 159:587-606.
12. PL 162:1575.
13. PL 162:1577.
14. PL 209:63, 404-06.
15. PL 209:410.
16. PL 176:1148-60.

17. PL 145:861-64.
18. *Sermones* 18-19; PL 202:694-98.
19. PL 176:1180-81.
20. PL 176:1144.
21. PL 176:1149 ff.
22. PL 117:937-1220.
23. A. Borgent ed., *Omnia Opera* (Paris 1890) 38: 764.
24. *Ibid.,* 539.
25. L. Vives, ed., *Opera Omnia* (1871) 31:404.
26. *Ibid.,* 405.
27. A. Wachtel, ed., *Expositio in Apocalypsim, Quellen zur Geistes-geschichte des Mittelaltes,* (Weimar: Hermann Böhlaus Nachfolger, 1955) 1: 469ff.
28. H. Arquillière, ed., *De regimine christiano* (Paris: Gabriel Beauchesne, 1926) 99.
29. *Ibid.,* 120, citing *De civitate Dei* 19. 13. Cf. pp. 132 f.
30. Cf. *Enarrationes in psalmos* 64. 3 (CC 38:824-25); *In ps.* 77. 42, (CC 39:49; *In ps.* 134. 26 (CC 40:1956f).
31. A. Seekboeck, ed., *Compendium sensus litteralis totius divinae scripturae* (Quaracchi 1896) 543-48.
32. Prol., *Omnia Opera* (Quaracchi: 1891) 5:295.
33. *Itinerarium* 4. 4 See J. Bissen, *L'exemplarisme divin selon S. Bonaventure* (Paris, 1929) 188-244.
34. *Itin.,* 4:3.
35. *Collationes in Hexaemeron* 20; *Opera* (Quaracchi, 1882) 5:612-47.
36. *Coll.* 22. 2: 'Caelestis hierarchia est illustrativa militantis Ecclesiae'.
37. Prol., *Opera* (Quaracchi 1898) 8: 504f.
38. *Coll. in Hex.* 23. 4: 'Ecclesia enim contemplativa et anima non differunt ... '.

SCIENTIA AND SAPIENTIA:
READING SACRED SCRIPTURE AT THE PARACLETE
Eileen Kearney

I N THE CONCLUSION of the *Sic et non* Prologue, Peter
Abelard encourages his students to pursue wisdom and
truth by inquiry, and he claims that the first key to wisdom
—the *prima clavis sapientiae*—is continual questioning.[1] At
several other times during his teaching career, Master Peter
considered wisdom, with Christ as revealer, in a language that
links the divine Logos with Truth (*Veritas*), with Wisdom
(*Sophia*), and with vigorous questioning.[2] But what did Peter
mean when he claimed that the first key to wisdom is an
understanding that is rooted in discursive inquiry? With
reference to the *Sic et non*, Beryl Smalley demonstrated that
Abelard is original in this stance on two counts: his alteration
of the lukan phrase, *clavis scientiae,* and his departure from
Augustine's teaching on the use of questioning in relation to
Truth.[3]

It is not my intention here to repeat the pioneering work
of Cottiaux, whose analysis of Abelard's theology includes an
illustration of the terms used by Peter to describe human

understanding of the Divine Mystery.[4] Nor do I wish to
present the doctrine of Peter Abelard within the usual context
of his defense of dialectics for the theological investigation of
truth. All too often this approach overlooks the complexity of
Abelard's thought and the way that Peter's argument transformed key ideas in the development of christian doctrine.
Inevitably, too, any inquiry into Abelard's theology that
focuses on Master Peter's skill and appreciation for logic
stresses only those texts written for the schools.[5]

I hope to show that despite the increasing debate over the
various issues of theological method and doctrine that marked
Peter Abelard's public career, Abelard continuously explored
the relationship between human understanding and God's self
disclosure.[6] Most of this writing is part of what we now call
the monastic literature, that is, Abelard's writing for Heloise,
for the monks of St Gildas, and for other nonscholastic
audiences.[7] With reference to *scientia* and *sapientia,* it was
to Heloise in particular that Master Peter expressed not only
the primacy of human understanding, with its set of twelfth-
century pedagogical tools and techniques, but also and especially his doctrine that such understanding of the mystery of
God is integral to human sanctification. The most important
text for this discussion is Letter 8, Abelard's Rule for the
Paraclete, in which he responds to questions posed by Heloise
in reference to implementing the benedictine Rule for a religious community of women.[8] Master Peter offered Heloise
what he considered to be a *summa* of monastic religion, a
systematic treatment of continence, poverty, and silence.[9]
The clear and explicit statement of purpose is somewhat misleading, however, since a rather lengthy instruction on *lectio
divina* appears at the end of this discussion of the threefold
schema. This portion of the Rule is a clear departure from
the intended scope of the letter. It stands on its own in a
literary manner, with only minimal stylistic and conceptual
links to the original theme.[10] But it is in this brief appendage,
or perhaps afterthought, that Peter Abelard explained his idea

to Heloise: to know God is an act of the human spirit in which the mind apprehends saving truth, and in that apprehension one is healed. To do this, Peter first expounded the biblical source of his insight; then, he extended Pauline teaching in the development of a new doctrine, and ultimately he corrected or altered the traditional significance of texts from the *sacra pagina*.

THE BIBLICAL SOURCE

It is Abelard's exegesis of the fourteenth chapter of Paul's *First Letter to the Corinthians* that provides the key focus for Peter's doctrine on the primacy of understanding in relation to Scripture. Paul distinguished two modes of language: one which is proper for communication with God (*quid enim loquitur lingua non hominibus loquitur sed Deo*), and one which is proper for human discourse (*qui autem prophetat, hominibus loquitur aedificationem et exhortationem et consolationes,* 1 Co 14:2-3, 14).

This latter gift is the greater, according to St Paul who explained that whoever receives the first gift should pray for the second in order to build the Church (*et ideo, qui loquitur linqua, oret, ut interpretetur,* 1 Co 14:13). Throughout his exposition of Paul, Abelard was careful not to undermine the value of the first gift. Instead, he insisted upon its ineffable character. This nonprophetic prayer, Peter wrote, is with the lips only (*qui ore tantum verba format*), and not to be expounded for understanding (*non intelligentia exponenda ministrat,* Rule, 286, 16). Abelard reiterated this noncommunicable dimension of the first spiritual gift when he explained to Heloise that if such a person prays or sings, words are formed only by the breath, the air (*orat ille spiritu sive psallit qui solo prolationis flatu verba format*), and in such cases, the understanding of the mind is not considered (*non mentis intelligentiam accomodat,* Rule 286, 19-20).

On the other hand, prophetic grace operates in relation to understanding and is not given for the gift of tongues. The prophet does what others cannot do; the prophet sees *and* understands . The very role that identifies the prophet is that understanding of the Divine that can be expressed in human language (*qui videntes dicuntur id est intelligentes ea quae dicit intelligit*). This distinctive character of the prophetic gift was made even more precise by Master Peter, who emphasized that the purpose of this power is exposition (*ut ipsa exponere possit,* Rule 286, 16-17). With Paul, Abelard taught that the gift of prophecy is preferable to other spiritual gifts: the apostle, Peter wrote, 'urges us to seek the fullness, the sense of meaning . . . ,'[11] or again, 'we need to understand the meaning of *amen* . . . . '[12] Finally, Peter reminded Heloise of the teaching of Benedict in the Rule which calls for understanding the meaning of the psalms for chant (Rule 286, 26-27). Thus, to read and to pray require the full attention of the human spirit.

ABELARD REFINES THE PAULINE TEACHING

This exegesis of Paul's teaching about the perfection intrinsic to the prophetic form of communication served only as a prelude for Master Peter, however. Abelard elaborated at length upon the value of understanding scriptural doctrine this way by instructing Heloise on the relationship of that comprehension to the purpose of prayer. Peter delineated what this means by implementing one of his favored pedagogical techniques. In a step-by-step fashion Abelard built his teaching, not by defining the nature of this understanding, but by indicating why the failure to understand doctrine is unacceptable for the spiritual life.[13] Thus: without understanding, the illiterate may pray for the wrong thing,[14] and, without understanding, the nuns can neither instruct by word, nor explain the rule, nor correct false texts.[15] Again, 'where monks do not study Scripture, where they train in chant without understanding, then they hunger and thirst for the wrong food and this leads to wrongdoing.'[16] Finally, the further one is from understanding Scripture, the less one *can* serve God, the less can one become inflamed with love for God.[17] To Master Peter, such inadequacy was not merely unacceptable; it was a negligence for which one is reprehensible.[18] Peter, in fact, was even more forceful: 'unwillingness to learn the doctrine of Scripture is a form of madness.'[19]

The climax of this argument is almost unnoticed by the modern reader; Peter tells Heloise: 'Boredom with doctrine is the beginning of withdrawal from God . . . . How can anyone love God when that person does not seek that for which the soul hungers?'[20] To express this teaching in a positive formulation is to see Peter's insistence on the primacy of understanding even more clearly: we do understand the teaching of Scripture; we can pray for the right thing; we can expound, teach, correct; we can act rightly; and ultimately, we are fixed on God, in fact we are one with God. This concern with the components of *lectio divina* and this desire to explain how the human mind participates in this encounter with God is a recurrent theme in Abelard's writing. As he presents his doctrine to Heloise though, his exposition moves beyond Scripture and alters traditional exegesis of the pauline text. Peter does two things: first, he shifts the meaning of *intelligo* so that it applies only to the second mode of communication. Human understanding operates within the domain of language and doctrinal analysis. Then, when this occurs, Peter substitutes *verba in ore* for the *loquitur lingua* of Paul's letter. These *verba in ore* have nothing to do with the special gift of the spirit that is reserved for ecstacy, for inspiration or for the inadequacy of human language to describe the ineffable. Rather, they are empty words and refer to the reprehensible failure of the individual to grasp meaning within the prophetic *cadre* of spiritual gifts.[21]

Although this ambivalence in the use of the term *intelligo* is misleading, it is clear when taken in context. In the rest of this discussion, Peter used the notion of understanding to refer to intellectual apprehension of scriptural doctrine that results from analysis and discursive reasoning.

Peter's comments on this same chapter of Saint Paul in the *Theologia scholarium* and in his Sermon on the Lord's Prayer confirm this interpretation.[22] On both occasions, Master Peter weaves the same argument as he presented to the women of the Paraclete: first of all, the word to prophesy means to expound, to interpret, to disclose meaning and, in fact, to minister; secondly, it is unacceptable to hear the words as if they were empty sounds, i.e., without understanding; thirdly, the danger of praying for the wrong thing occurs when the one who prays does not understand; and finally, the gift of prophecy has primacy over the gift of tongues.

In the *Sermon Collection,* Peter also examined the same two forms of communication as he celebrated the conversion of St Paul.[23] Here, his comments both endorse and clarify the position he took in the Rule. The sermon, number 24 in the present editions, is designed to contrast Paul with Benjamin. Peter singled out one phrase from Ps 67:28: Benjamin, the youngest, is in the lead (*Ibi Beniamin adolescentulus, in mentis excessu*).[24] Abelard explains that Paul, like Benjamin, experiences ecstasy, *in mentis excessu, i.e. in exstasi mentis factus.* Master Peter favored the apostolic character of Paul's gift, however, and observed that ultimately Paul steps from the experience which is outside the structures of rational discourse to a form of communication which explains meaning in human language. Paul describes what he knows to others.

This distinction between nondiscursive communion with God and the expression/explanation of insight into the divine mystery through the construct of human language is clearer in this sermon than in the Rule. Perhaps this is because Peter explicitly treats the grace of nondiscursive prayer with more specific, more traditional and, in a sense, more appropriate language. His exposition of *in mentis extasi* clearly distinguishes this aspect of human experience from the communion with the holy that is mediated within the understanding and knowing of God that occurs within rational discourse. But in

the sermon as well as in the Rule the second form of communication is wholly ordained toward exposition and comprehension. It is given real priority. Furthermore, by reinforcing Paul's own hierarchy as expressed in the *Letter to
the Corinthians*, Peter Abelard again established the primacy
of the prophet/teaching role in the church.[25] His stand here
cannot be taken too lightly. We do not have here the expected
pattern of *oratio, meditatio, contemplatio.* In the rather complex network of ideas that flesh out the elements essential to
lectio divina, this consistent, insistent call for exposition/
interpretation as primary is critical.[26]

ABELARD MOVES BEYOND THE TRADITION

In teaching *lectio divina* to the Paraclete, Abelard described
human understanding of the Divine with an emphasis that
takes such knowing out of the context of illumination. There is
no apparent separation between *scientia* and *sapientia* in Abelard's language; somehow, these two notions, so clearly dis-
parate for Augustine, are interwoven into a single experience
by Peter.[27] Interestingly enough, Abelard avoids reference to
Augustine in the text. Instead, Rufinus, Jerome, Bede and
Gregory provide Abelard and Heloise models of intellectual
life.[28] And then, Peter singles out Mary as the finest exemplar
of this scrutiny of the word for Mary had 'pondered the Word
in her heart'.[29] Peter explains what this means: Mary considered each word; she compared them; and she observed the
harmony of Scripture.[30] Peter describes Mary as one who,
because of her understanding, not only obeyed but also acted
with right intention:

> She knew that according to the revelation of the
> Law every animal is called unclean unless it chews
> the cud and divides the hoof. And so no soul is
> clean and pure unless by meditating to the best
> of its ability it chews the cud of God's teachings
> and shows understanding in obeying them, so that

it not only does good things but does them well,
that is, with the right intention. For the division
of the hoof is the mind's ability to distinguish,
about which it is written: 'If you offer rightly
but do not divide rightly, you have sinned.'[31]

Nothing is taken for granted in the attention one ought to
pay to Scripture. Abelard's exposition and discussion demands
a care in reading that is structured by the techniques of
twelfth-century pedagogy: to examine and to compare, to
observe and to distinguish.

We can be deceived by Abelard's lengthy citation from
Origen at the end of this instruction. Within these passages is
present much of the vocabulary that characterizes Abelard's
understanding of theology—*apprehendo, ingenium, sine dubio,
discutiendo, doceamus, scientia divina, sapientia divina.*[32] In
the passages Origen, too, cites the lukan reference to the
clavis scientiae,[33] but Origen has just finished explaining the
futility of secular knowledge to his audience, and his exegesis
of Genesis is meant to foster contemplative insight. Abelard
has, deliberately, I think, lifted the text out of context and
allowed Origen to support his own view for the primacy of
human understanding via inquiry.[34] Quietly, but dramatically,
Peter Abelard shifts the notion of pondering from a meditative, contemplative experience to discursive activity.

While the reader is struck by the shift and emphasis that
Abelard makes in his doctrine about the role of human understanding, he is apt to lose sight of Peter's concern for the moral
context he expects to find in a treatise on scriptural reading
designed for a monastic community. Peter was, of course,
sensitive to the experience of *lectio divina* as an exercise of
religious discipline. And his consideration of the relationship
between understanding and moral perfection is a constant
theme that weaves its way in and out of his argument for the
primacy of understanding. But we see in this case that when
Peter does so, he also highlights the way that moral integrity

acts both as a necessary prelude to and as the expected
fruition of such understanding. He urges the nuns to
' . . . refrain altogether from idle talk, while those of you
who have been given the grace of learning must work to be
instructed in the things which are God's . . . ' (Rule 291,
39-42).[35] For Peter, the unity of word and deed demands
that the activity of the mind parallel appropriate behavioral
patterns.[36] For example, twice in the Rule, he refers to
Gregory's comparison of Scripture to a mirror: in its reflection the soul perceives its ugliness or its beauty.[37] This experience has practical results: first, by perceiving one's moral
status, one can adjust patterns of behavior;[38] then, the mind
itself benefits from prayer, that is, it is moved/fixed toward
God by understanding the words;[39] understanding also allows
the nuns to instruct each other;[40] and when we meditate and
understand Scripture, he explains, we learn to avoid sin;[41]
finally, the further we are from understanding, the further we
are from the service and love (Rule 290, 19-21).

There is an element of growth in moral life as well, for the
more we understand, the more we grow in ardor and the better
we come to serve (Rule 291, 42-292, 10). But, ultimately and
perhaps most significantly, understanding Scripture is a protec-
tion against sin. Abelard expressed this emphatically when
he claimed that because Mary understood Scripture, she, and
subsequently all Christians, obey with the right intention
(Rule 292, 15-19). The perusal of that Word involves each
reader in a self-analysis that examines human behavior in
terms of a principle which is normative for self-awareness,
development, and sanctification. This argument, of course,
encloses Peter's teaching within the structure of his formal
doctrine on sin as consent/intent[42] and also provides a frame
of reference for the ordering of all one's life with the pursuit
of the holy as a pursuit for truth revealed in Scripture. The
notion of interiority as right intention is thus drawn into what
is essential for the reading and understanding of Scripture at
the Paraclete.

This teaching does not sound like the expected exhortation for a change of heart. Instead, Master Peter succinctly draws out a systematic schema which treats of conversion in analytic terms primarily designed for instruction. Abelard's concern for moral behavior is set in a new context—that of textual exposition. In every way, this doctrine is of the schools, and if it had been written by Peter for his students, one would not be surprised.[43] But finding it directed to the Paraclete, one is struck that the life of prayer should be explicitly explained in direct reference to grasping the sense of a text through study patterned after twelfth-century scholastic methods of textual exposition and doctrinal analysis. As texts for such reflection, we know, the community of the Paraclete read the opening chapters of Genesis, with some difficulty.[44] Heloise sought a commentary from Peter that would set forth the historical sense with clarity. Peter's *Expositio in Hexaemeron* is a rigorous and careful examination that expounds the text in detail. Then, by menas of a careful interplay of literal and spiritual exegesis, Peter furthers *sacra doctrina* for the community.[45] The *Problems of Heloise* also give witness to a careful reading of Scripture by the women of the Paraclete.[46] In particular, the text of Matthew was brought forward for scrutiny, a portion of Scripture that with the other Gospels had become a favorite in the twelfth-century schools.[47] Again, Peter's response to her forty-two questions provided not only the desired solutions but also guidelines and models for interpretation, reminding the nuns to read with care, to look for context and harmony, to distinguyish carefully.

CONCLUSION

No doubt Peter Abelard often reminded his students that 'by doubting, we come to inquiry and by inquiry we come to truth'.[48] But many of Abelard's writings were not addressed to students at the cathedral centers. Much was specifically composed for Heloise and the nuns of the Paraclete. This literature shaped the whole life of that community: letters, prayers, hymns, sermons, a breviary, a treatise on the origin of Nuns, and a Rule of monastic observance which includes a brief *excursus* on the art of *lectio divina*. This instruction on scriptural reading is framed by the pedagogical techniques of the century's most renowned teacher and informed by his insight and passion for truth.

In describing *lectio divina* for the Paraclete community, Peter Abelard explored the relationship of the soul to God in terms of human understanding. Comprehension of Scriptural doctrine is a dynamic process of the human spirit in its encounter with the Word. Peter chose a pauline text as the starting point for his discussion; but he went far beyond St Paul. If to describe personal sanctification as the search for God *in corde* was indeed not new, certainly to discuss and to evaluate understanding the meaning of Scripture *in mente* as a positive, sanctifying act of the spirit was a focus relatively unexplored. And, despite the pauline hierarchy, to set this scrutiny above mystical experience was to break with the monastic tradition and its focus on the contemplative, illuminative experience of divine wisdom.[49]

To do this Peter, of necessity, could not divorce *sapientia* from *scientia*. Wisdom is not restricted to the gift of tongues, nor is *scientia* simply a method for approaching the Divine. Rather, the apprehension of religious truth is a 'divine science' (*divina scientia*), a term Peter used to describe the understanding which saves because one encounters the truth as a word and as the Word. As he told Heloise in the *Problemata Heloissae,* to know (*scio*) what it means to be in Christ is to experience (*experior*) God.[50] And in the *Dialogue,* as well as in Letter Thirteen, Peter taught that to know the truth is to grasp the meaning of the *Verbum Dei* in Scripture and in the person of Christ as divine Logos.[51]

In the *Dialectics,* Abelard explicitly aligned *sapientia* with *scientia*. The Prologue of Book IV narrows this discussion of the relationship between insight and religious understanding by Abelard's intent to establish the validity of dialectics for theology.[52] In this passage, Abelard referred to dialectics in terms both of content and method: it is both the object/ subject of study and the means by which understanding is accomplished. In relation to theology, dialectics—as method— is not an arbitrary choice for the theologian then. Dialectics is essential to the discernment of religious truth.

Furthermore, Peter claimed for *scientia,* described as under- standing the truth of things (469, 15-16), not only its inherent good as a creation of God (469, 32-34),[53] but also an identifi- cation with *sapientia:* "There are few to whom divine grace deigns to reveal the secret of this science (*scientia*), or better to say, the treasure of wisdom (*sapientia*)'.[54] Thus, dialectics, conceived as activated within human experience as grace, becomes the most subtle, rare, precious and valuable of the arts (470, 28-30). Abelard went one step further as well by pointing to the link between natural talent and understanding. Although one cannot create talent by means of any practice or discipline of the arts, since it is a divine grace (471, 2-6), the more one is natively gifted, the more one perceives and under- stands (471, 6-10).

This discussion of *sapientia/scientia* in the *Dialectics,* when seen in conjunction with Abelard's presentation of *lectio divina* for the Paraclete community confirms that for Peter, as for Heloise, *sapientia* and *scientia* were inextricably inter- woven. The foundational insight which allowed this to happen was not only Abelard's shifting of language but also his belief that in Christ and in the Scriptures, God's word is revealed, heard, and grasped by the human spirit.

Notre Dame University

NOTES

1. Abelard, 'Prologue,' *Sic et non,* in B. Boyer and R. McKeon, edd., Peter Abelard, *Sic et non, A Critical Edition* (Chicago: University of Chicago Press, 1974) 103.
2. E.g. Christ is called the Wisdom of God in the *Dialogus inter Philosphum, Judaeum et Christianum* (ed. R. Thomas [Stuggard-Bad: Freidrich: Fromman, 1970] 87; 1. 1129-30). ET: Pierre Payer, *Abelard, Dialogue of a Philosopher with a Jew and a Christian* (Toronto: Pontifical Institute of Mediaeval Studies, 1979) 74. Cf. Letter Thirteen (PL 178: 355A-56A); a critical edition is now available by E. R. Smits: *Peter Abelard, Letters IX–XIV,* (Groningen: Bouma's Boekhaus BV, 1983).
3. B. Smalley, *Prima clavis sapientiae:* Augustine and Abelard' in D. J. Gorden, ed., *Fritz Saxl, 1890–1948, A Volume of Memorial Essays from His Friends in England,* (New York: Thomas Nelson and Sons, 1957) 93-100. The biblical text is Lk 11:52: 'Alas for you lawyers who have taken away the key of knowledge *(clavis scientiae).* You have not gone in yourselves and have prevented others going in who wanted to.'
4. J. Cottiaux, 'La conception de théologie chez Abélard', RHE 28 (1932) 247-95, 533-51, 788-828.
5. E.g. J. Jolivet, *Arts du langage et théologie chez Abélard,* Etudes de philosophie médiévale, 57 (Paris: J. Vrin, 1969). Even very recent studies limit the focus to Abelard's teaching in the schools and hence emphasize the question of dialectics, e.g. C. Lohr, 'Peter Abalard und die scholastischen Exegese', *Freiburg Zeitschrift für Philosophie und Theologie* 28 (1981) 95-110.
6. Abelard's condemnations both at Soissons (1121) and Sens (1140), for example, culminated two periods of intense negative reaction to his theology. An essay on the nature of the conflict by J. Châtillon sets this antagonism toward Abelard in the context of the tension between advocates of either monastic or scholastic approaches to truth: 'Guillaume de Saint-Thierry, Le monachisme et les écoles: A propos de Rupert de Deutz, d'Abélard et de Guillaume de Conches', in M. Bur, ed., *Saint Thierry, Une Abbaye du VIe aux XXe siècles,* Actes du Colloque International de l'Histoire Monastique, Reims-Saint-Thierry, 11 au 14 octobre 1976 (Saint-Thierry: Association des Amis de l'Abbaye de Saint-Thierry, 1977) 375-394 (ET to appear from Cistercian Publications).
7. E.g. Letters 12 (PL 178: 343-52) and 13 (PL 178: 351-56) or

Abelard's sermons for the feast of Pentecost (PL 178: 505D-524C). For an appreciation of Abelard's contribution to monastic audiences, see J. Leclercq, ' "*Ad ipsam sophiam Christum*": Le témoinage monastique d'Abélard', RAM 46 (1970) 161-81. A more recent comparison of the polarities between monastic and scholastic tensions is the study of J. Verget and J. Jolivet: *Bernard–Abélard, ou le cloître et l'école,* Deux Hommes dans l'Histoire de l'Eglise (Paris: Fayard Mame, 1982). A precise analysis of the issue from the point of view of language and themes treated in writings of twelfth-century canons by C. W. Bynum is especially helpful: 'The Spirituality of Regular Canons in the Twelfth Century', in *Jesus as Mother, Studies in the Spirituality of the High Middle Ages* (Los Angeles: University of California Press, 1982) 22-58.

8.   The numbering of the letters varies. In the earlier editions such as Migne, Abelard's *Historia calamitatum* is numbered as the first of the letters; hence Abelard's Rule is Letter Eight (PL 178: 255-314). However, recent editions do not always include the *Historia calamitatum* within the letter collection. Thus, Heloise's letter which requests the Rule from Peter, (number six in Migne, PL 178: 213-26), is edited by J. T. Muckle as Letter five, 'The Letter of Heloise on Religious Life and Abelard's First Reply', MS 17 (1955) 240-81. Abelard's reply includes two letters: the first is his treatise on the origin of nuns and the second is the Rule itself..This Rule is numbered as Letter Seven in the edition of T. P. McLaughlin, 'Abelard's Rule for Religious Women', MS 18 (1956) 241-92.

9.   Peter writes: 'Tripertitum instructionis nostrae tractatum fieri decrevimus in describenda atque munienda religione vestra et divini obsequii celebratione disponenda in quibus religionis monasticae summam arbitror consistere, ut videlicet continenter et sine proprietate vivatur, silentio maxime studeatur', Rule, 243, 24-27. All latin citations from the Rule are from McLaughlin, with both page and line numbers indicated. ET: B. Radice, *The Letters of Abelard and Heloise* (New York: Penguin Books, 1979) here p. 184.

10.   E.g. Abelard alludes to the *Moralia* of Gregory the Great which compares Scripture to a mirror for the soul, (Rule, 243, 6; ET 184). Later in the letter, the image is repeated in Abelard's treatment of *lectio divina* (285, 23-30; ET: 257). Another metaphor from the *Moralia* included in the earlier part of the letter is Gregory's exposition of Job 39:5. which compares the wild ass who freely roams in the wilderness to the monk in solitude and contemplation (Rule, 247, 22-36; ET 191). The image of an ass returns in the section on *lectio divina* but here Abelard draws a great contrast to Gregory with one of the sayings of Cato concerning the ass who sits upon the lyre, signifying a reprehensible

lack of understanding by the reader (Rule, 285, 33-34 and 289, 7; ET 257). Cf. Abelard's lengthy citations and exposition of the same gregorian text in his sermon for the Feast of John the Baptist, S 33 (PL 178: 582-607); also, note J. Leclercq's discussion, 'Études sur le vocabulaire monastique', *Studia Anselmiana* 48 (1961) 39 and 159.

11.   Rule, 286, 24-26: 'Unde hanc in verbis perfectionem nos admonet habere, ut non more puerorum verba tantum sciamus proferre, verum etiam intelligentiae sensum in iis habere atque aliter nos orare vel psallere infructuose protestatur.' ET 259.

12.   Rule, 286, 35-287, 5; ET 259-60. Abelard's teaching on the importance of understanding in prayer is a theme that appears in other texts, e.g. his *Commentary on the Apostles Creed* (PL 178: 617-23, here 620D-21B) and his sermon On the Lord's Prayer, S 14 (PL 178: 489-95, here 489C-490C).

13.   The method which characterizes twelfth-century pedagogy is also used by Abelard in his *Ethics,* where he describes sin by distinguishing sin from lust, from concupiscence, from desire, and from the will, D. E. Luscombe, ed., *Peter Abelard's Ethics* (Oxford: Clarendon, 1971) 2-37.

14.   Rule, 286, 35-37: 'Qua etiam ratione, inquit Apostolos, cum benedictiones in ecclesia fiunt respondebitur amen, si quod oratur in illa benedictione non intelligitur?' ET 259.

15.   Rule, 287, 3-5: 'Denique quae scripturae non habet intelligentiam, quomodo sermonis aedificationem sibi ministrabunt, aut etiam regulam exponere vel intelligere, aut vitiose prolata corrigere valebunt?' ET 260.

16.   Rule, 287, 6-10: 'Unde non mediocriter miramur quae inimici suggestio in monasteriis hoc egit ut nulla ibi de intelligendis scripturis sint studia, sed de cantu tantum vel de verbis solummodo formandis, non intelligendis, habeatur disciplina, quasi ovium balatus plus utilitatis habeat quam pastus, Cibus quippe est animae et spiritualis refectio ipsi divina intelligentia Scripturae.' ET 260.

17.   Rule, 290, 19-21: 'Qui profecto tanto minus Deum amare et in eum accendi possunt, quanto amplius ab intelligentia ejus et a sensu scripturae de ipso nos erudientis absistunt.' ET 265.

18.   Rule, 287, 34-36: 'Quae quidem negligentia tanto amplius in monachis qui ad perfectionem aspirant est arguenda . . . . ' ET 261. Cf. Abelard's discussion in the *Theologia scholarium,* PL 178: 1054 BC.

19.   Rule, 288, 1: 'Si autem utrumque cum possit non vult, insaniae morbo laborat' ET 261. The same idea appears with reference to Herod's sin in his sermon for the Holy Innocents, S 34 (PL 178: 608A) and the account of the fate of Jephtha's daughter in his planctus: 'O mentum judicis / O zelum insanum, principis . . . ' (PL 178: 1820). For a dis-

cussion of the *planctus* in light of the tradition, see M. Alexiou and P. Dronke, in the *Note e discussioni:* 'The Lament of Jephtha's daughter: Themes, Traditions, Originality', *Studi Medievali* 12 (1971) 819-63.

20.   Rule, 288, 1-3: 'Initium enim recedendi a Deo fastidium doctrinae est et cum non appetit illud quod semper anima esurit, quomodo diligit Deum?' ET 261-62.

21.   Abelard's language is clear: ' . . . qui ore tantum verba format . . . ' , Rule, 286, 16; and, ' . . . qui solo prolationis flatu verba format . . . ' and also, ' . . . nostrae prolationis flatus solummodo verba format . . . ' , Rule, 286, 19-21. ET 259.

22.   Consult *Theologia Scholarium* in Migne (PL 178, here 1052C-56A) and as previously noted, Abelard's Sermon On the Lord's Prayer (PL 178: 489C-90C.)

23.   Cf. S 24 (PL 178: 531-36). An examination of the manuscript tradition of these sermons by D. van den Eynde appears in 'Le Recueil des Sermons de Pierre Abélard', *Antonianum* 37 (1962) 17-54.

24.   The meaning of this passage is considered doubtful by contemporary exegetes. Abelard avoids any attempt to interpret the passage in a literal manner (PL 178: 534C-35B).

25.   Abelard's interest in this ordering of the states of life is not unusual although he does vary the hierarchy. E.g., in the fourteenth *Problemata Heloissae,* he places the *continentes* at the highest echelon of the hierarchy (PL 178: 696D-702). Most often, however, Abelard teaches the primacy of the preaching/teaching role in the Church (PL 178: 465A, 502C, and 523C). In these cases Abelard is expounding the words of Christ from Mt 5:19: ' . . . the man who keeps them [the commandments] and teaches them will be considered great in the kingdom of heaven'.

26.   See B. Smalley's discussion in *The Study of the Bible in the Middle Ages* (University of Notre Dame Press, 1964) 26-36. The elements of *lectio divina* are discussed at length by J. Rousse in 'Lectio divin et lecture spirituelle', DSp 9 (1975) 470-87. Cf. J. Leclercq's essay, 'Les caractères traditionnels de la *"lectio divina"*, in *La Liturgie et les paradoxes chrétiens,* Lex orandi 36 (Paris: Les Editions du Cerf, 1963) 243-57.

27.   Cf. R. Nash, *The Light of the Mind, St. Augustine's Theory of Knowledge* (Lexington: University Press of Kentucky, 1969). Although this is a very brief study, the hierarchy and relationship of *sapientia* and *scientia* is especially clear.

28.   E.g. the choice of citing Rufinus' *Historia monachorum,* 21, is especially significant because of the terms used there to discuss *lectio:* 'As for meditation on and understanding of the divine Scriptures and

also of the divine science (*scientia*), never have we seen such a degree of training (*exercita*) so that you might suppose every one of them to be orators for divine wisdom (*sapientia*)', Rule, 290, 7-9. ET 265. This is my own translation.

29.   Lk 2:19 cited in the Rule, 292, 11-12: 'As for Mary, she treasured all these things and pondered them in her heart'. Abelard did not mean to imply that Mary's pondering of the Word is akin to the gift of tongues, however. Rather, he idealized the mother of Jesus as one who listened to the words of Jesus 'with the ears of understanding', Rule, 292, 24-26. ET 269.

30.   Rule, 292, 14-15: ' . . . quia studiose singula discutiebat et invicem sibi ea conferebat, quam congrue scilicet inter se convenirent omnia'. ET 268.

31.   Rule, 292, 15-21. ET 268-69.

32.   Origen, *Homilia XII in Genesim* 5 (PG 12: 229, 231, 232, 235) cited in the Rule, 291, 5-38. ET 266-68.

33.   Rule, 291, 22-23. ET 267.

34.   Abelard does the same thing when he quotes Jerome in Letter Nine (PL 178: 325-36). What appears to be a patchwork of lengthy citations is a careful clipping away of sections in Jerome's teaching that would modify Abelard's intense focus on the excellence of the mind in the pursuit of wisdom. Cf. Smits, pp. 219-37.

35.   Rule, 291, 39-40: 'Vos autem non sic, sed vaniloquio penitus supersedentes quaecumque discendi gratiam assecutae sunt, de iis quae ad Deum pertinent erudiri studeant . . . . ' ET 268.

36.   Abelard's writings reflect an interest in the relationship between discovering (learning) and teaching characteristic of Augustine's *De doctrina christiana,* especially Book IV, 1 and 6. Other examples in the Rule include Abelard's citation of Abba Palladius (Rule, 287, 45-46; ET 261) and his comment that Jerome learned not only from the words of Scripture but also from the example of the others, Rule, 290, 32-36, ET 265. C. Bynum's study, *Docere Verbo et Exemplo: An Aspect of Twelfth-Century Spirituality,* incisively examines one way in which the shift from a monastic/contemplative sense of the apostolic life to a more evangelical concern for the neighbor can be discerned (Missoula, Montana: Scholars Press, 1979).

37.   Rule, 285, 26-36. Cf. the study of R. Bradley on the history and significance of this analogy in the tradition, 'Backgrounds of the Title *Speculum* in Medieval Literature', *Speculum* 29 (1954) 100-115.

38.   Rule, 285, 23-25: 'Speculum animae scripturam sacram constat esse in quam quilibet legendo vivens, intelligendo proficiens, morum suorum pulchritudinem cognoscit vel deformitatem deprehendit, ut

illam videlicet augere, hanc studeat removere.' ET 257. Cf. 287,3-5.

39.   Rule, 286, 20-23: 'Cum vero spiritus noster orat, id est nostrae prolationis flatus solummodo verba format, nec quod ore profertur corde concipitur, mens nostra sine fructu est quem in oratione videlicet habere debet, ut ipsa scilicet ex intelligentia verborum in Deum compungatur atque accendatur'. ET 258-259. Cf. 287, 3-5.

40.   Rule, 287, 3-5: 'Denique quae scripturae non habent intelligentiam, quomodo sermonis aedificationem sibi ministrabunt, aut etiam regulam exponere vel intelligere, aut vitiose prolata corrigere valebunt?' ET 260.

41.   Rule, 287, 25-29: 'Cuius quidem intelligentiae quae sit utilitas non praetermisit, subjugens . . . . Multae quippe iniquitatis viae ita per se sunt apertae ut facile omnibus in odium vel contemptum veniant, sed omnem iniquitatis viam nonnisi per eloquia divina cognoscimus, ut omnes evitare possimus.' ET 261.

42.   *Ethics* (ed., Luscombe, p. 4: 'Nunc vero consensum proprie peccatum nominamus . . . '

43.   See chapters five and six of the *Didascalicon* in which Hugh of St Victor addresses his students on the art of reading Scripture. However, even though Hugh's text was written for an academic audience, its doctrine is more traditional than Abelard's. Hugh never confronts the problem of reconciling *sapientia* understood within its augustinian frame of reference and his exhortation to embrace *scientia* as essential to understanding Scripture. ET J. Taylor, *The Didascalicon of Hugh of St Victor,* Records of Civilization, Sources and Studies, 64 (New York: Columbia University Press, 1962) 120-51. In the next generation of school masters, Peter Lombard would confront the issues in the Book of Sentences, where he distinguished three kinds of understanding: *sapientia, intellectus* and *scientia,* cf. Book III, Dist. 25: 'Quomodo differant sapientia et scientia'; 'In quo differat sapientia ab intellectu'; and, 'Quod sapientia ista Dei est, nec illa quae Deus est', cf. *Magistri Petri Lombardi, Sententiae in IV Libris,* editio tertia (Rome: Editores Collegii S. Bonaventurae, Ad claras aquas, 1971).

44.   Abelard's Letter–Preface makes note of Heloise's request, PL 178: 731C-32A.

45.   Abelard's commentary, though, is structured both by the scriptural word and by the doctrinal focus of a creation/redemption parallel. Cf. *Expositio in Hexameron,* in PL 178:731-784 and the additional fragment edited by E. M. Buytaert in 'Abelard's *Expositio in Hexaemeron*', *Antonianum* 43 (1968) 174-79. Cf. E. Kearney, 'Peter Abelard as Biblical Commentator: A Study of the Expositio in Hexaemeron', in R. Thomas *et al.,* edd., *Petrus Abaelardus, 1079-1142, Person, Werk und Wirkung,* Trier Theologische Studien, 38 (Trier: Paulinus-Verlag, 1982)

199-210.

46. *Problemata Heloissae,* PL 178: 677-730.

47. B. Smalley's research continued to offer significant resources for our understanding of the teaching of Scriptures in the Schools. Cf. *The Gospels in the Schools c. 1100- c. 1280* (London: Hambledon, 1985). Published posthumously, the study contains essays published in *Franciscan Studies* (1979 and 1980) and RTAM (1978 and 1979) in addition to an additional chapter as an overview. Note also an earlier collection of previously published essays that cover the vast scope of medieval commentaries: *Studies in Medieval Thought and Learning from Abelard to Wyclif* (London: Hambledon, 1982).

48. 'Prologue', *Sic et non,* p. 103. E.g. Heloise reflects her awareness of this principle in the third question of the *Problemata Heloissae:* 'Quae profecto responsiones non immerito dubitationem exicitare videntur. Qui enim quaerit utrum hoc sit vel illud, nequaquam enuntiando dicit quod hoc sit, vel illud, sed quasi dubitando quaerit utrum ita sit', PL 178: 680BC.

49. See J. Leclercq's essay 'Lecture priante', in *La Liturgie,* pp. 243-69, or his presentation of the monastic ideal in his major work *The Love of Learning and the Desire for God* (New York: Fordham University Press, 1961).

50. Question 29 of the *Problemata Heloissae,* PL 178: 713-14.

51. Letter 13, PL 178: 355, and a parallel passage in the *Dialogue,* Thomas, ed., pp. 95-97. ET 80.

52. *Petrus Abaelardus, Dialectica,* ed., M. L. de Rijk (Assen: Royal Van Gorcum, 1956). References to the Prologue of Book IV will be indicated by page and line number within the essay. Cf. Abelard's parallel discussion in both the Theologies: Theologia Christiana III, 7-8, ed. E. M. Buytaert, *Petri Abaelardi, Opera Theologica II, Theologia Christiana,* Corpus Christianorum, Continuatio medievalis, XII (Turnholt: Brepols, 1969) pp. 196-97, and the *Theologia scholarium,* PL 178: 1044-46.

53. *Theologia Christiana,* III. 6; p. 196.

54. *Dialectica,* 470, 27-28: 'At vero perpauci sunt quibus huius scientiae secretum, immo sapientiae thesaurum, divina revelare gratia dignetur ... '.

ANSELM AND AQUINAS:
CENTER AND EPICENTERS
Michael W. Strasser

IN THE OPENING CHAPTER of his dialogue *On the Teacher*, St Augustine made it clear to Adeodatus that all speech and, in fact, all thought is a form of teaching. This is to say that we formulate things in words only to remind ourselves or others of something.[1] If this is true, then the words of a monk are the words of a teacher every bit as much as are the words of a university professor. It is the purpose of teaching in each case that distinguishes them. From this difference there arises a difference of principles as well as a difference in presentation.

If we take Saints Anselm of Canterbury and Thomas Aquinas as guides to the monastic and the scholastic approaches to the truth, we shall find that they both revolve about the same absolute center but that Aquinas circles about numerous epicenters as well.

THE PROBLEM
The facts are well known: the explanation for them is not.

Here are the facts. When Anselm asks himself if there is one truth in all true things his answer is a resounding yes: ' . . . the highest truth subsisting through itself is the truth of no thing; but when something is in accord with it, then truth or rightness is said of it.'[2] Or, as he put it earlier in the same Chapter Thirteen: 'Truth therefore is one in all things.'[3] When Aquinas asks this same question, on the other hand, he answers both yes and no. 'It ought to be said that in one way there is one truth by which all things are true and in another way not.'[4]

We ask ourselves, how could these two doctors of the Church, these two philosophers of the medieval West, answer the same question in such very different ways? The answer may be that Anselm is proceeding in the pre-aristotelian manner characteristic of the Fathers of the Church and especially St Augustine,[5] while Aquinas, having learned from Aristotle to distinguish theoretical truth from practical truth, is constructing a sacred theology that is primarily theoretical. What follows is an attempt to explain these different ways of teaching.

Having outlined the problem presented by these two authors and its possible solution, we would like to insist on the fact that the similarities uniting them are greater than the differences dividing them. We give some examples of their similarities first and then pay tribute to the scholar who first suggested our solution.

An example of their similarity is seen in the speculative power of the two writers. We shall see an instance of Anselm's speculative genius in a moment. And anyone familiar with the Fathers of the Church who reads the Prologue to Aquinas' first theological synthesis, *The Commentary on Peter Lombard's Sentences,* must be moved by the very first sentence, which points out that among the various views of wisdom that have been presented, 'One singularly strong and true was given by the Apostle who said that "Christ is the power and wisdom of God".'[6] In fact, says Aquinas, if reason allows itself to be led by the hand by faith, it grows in its ability to understand the articles of faith; 'Thus it is said in one translation of Isaiah 7:9,

"unless you believe you will not understand".'[7] This fidelity
to the augustinian tradition as developed by Anselm is not
surprising when we remember that Aquinas read most, and
perhaps all, of the major treatises of Anselm and quotes him
hundreds of times, usually with approval.

But, returning to our problem, I would like to acknowledge
that I have seen nothing that so clearly suggests a solution to
it as the work of Dom Jean Leclercq.[8] He shows that monastic
theology was intended for those who were cloistered; scholastic
theology was not thus restricted; its aim was knowledge, and its
style impersonal and as clear as possible. The former was personal; it was intended to give 'a certain appreciation, of savoring
and clinging to the truth and, what is everything, to the love of
God'; in short it led to an experience of divine things rather
than a knowledge of them.[9] 'The monastery was . . . a "school
of charity", a school for the service of God.'[10] Therefore,
Leclercq describes monastic writings as having a 'literary character' and a 'mystical orientation'.[11] In the words of St Gregory,
they point toward a 'knowledge through love'.[12] Even the conclusion to Anselm's *Proslogion* (cc. 25-26) exhorts the reader
to a contemplation of divine happiness as though it were the
end of all moral exhortation.[13] To put it yet another way:
'The monastic writings are directed to the practice of the
Christian life'[14] and edification.[15] Two adjectives seem especially apt: 'pastoral', as a description of monastic writing;[16]
and 'professorial' as the category for the scholastics.[17]

In evaluating these two approaches, Leclercq points out
some of the dangers associated with the scholastic milieu: it
can lead to an excess of reading to the neglect of prayer;[18] the
abuse of dialectics can produce a curiosity which is a form of
pride.[19] Nevertheless, the two approaches correspond to two
different states of life, christian life in the cloister and christian life in the world,[20] both of which are legitimate;[21] but, if
one has to choose between them, one must say: 'monastic
theology is a theology of admiration and therefore greater
than a theology of speculation'.[22]

There is no question in my mind that Thomas Aquinas would not only agree with the accuracy of Dom Leclercq's manner of distinguishing these two approaches but that he also agrees with his final evaluation of them.[23]

Anselm, however, would have been able to agree only in part. He would have applauded Dom Leclercq's account of the monastic approach to the truth. But, he could not have recognized the scholastic approach as it is found in Aquinas.

The external evidence for saying this is as follows. Since it was Aristotle who first distinguished theoretical knowledge from practical knowledge and therefore theoretical truth from practical truth, and since the relevant Aristotelian works were not available in the western world prior to the twelfth century, Anselm could not have known them.[24]

Internal evidence that Anselm was acquainted with no more of Aristotle than the Old Logic (*Categories* and *On Interpretation*) is provided by F. S. Schmitt in his *Index Auctorum* to the critical edition of Anselm's works.[25] Needless to say, the Old Logic contains no reference at all to Aristotle's division of theoretical and practical types of knowledge.

That is not to say that Anselm never used expressions that could be associated with the aristotelian distinctions. He does use the words 'speculation', and 'contemplation'. But, his merely occasional use of these terms is in accordance with general classical usage: *speculatio* is simply the knowledge (*cognitio*) that is acquired by looking at the object;[26] similarly, *contemplari* is the act of attentively looking at something, especially with the mind.[27] Neither word carries any further weight that might reflect the aristotelian distinctions. We meet the same negative result when we examine Anselm's use of *cognitio, intellectus, ratio, scientia* and *veritas*. As to the words 'theoretical' and 'practical', they do not appear at all in the 'General Index of Persons and Things' of Fr Schmitt.

Having seen, then, how much, or if you will, how little, Aristotle Anselm knew, we must point out that while Anselm was acquainted with Boethius' *Commentary on Porhyry's*

Isagoge, he knew only the first edition of this work. It is the
second edition of this commentary in which Boethius briefly
distinguished two kinds of philosophy as *speculativa* and
activa.[28] In short, Anselm did not have even a second-hand
knowledge of the aristotelian distinction.

ANSELM'S APPROACH TO THE TRUTH

What, then, was Anselm's argument for saying that there is
only one truth for all things? Here is a paraphrase of the thirteenth and last chapter of Anselm's *De veritate.*

Anselm refers first to the definition of truth which he had
established earlier: 'truth is rightness perceptible to the mind
alone (*veritas est rectitudo mente sola perceptibilis*)'.[29] Now,
if there is a diversity of rightnesses dependent on the diversity
of things, then these rightnesses depend upon the being of the
things themselves. Therefore, as the things in which they are
could vary so could the rightnesses. So too will the color of a
body change when the body that has it changes.

But, Anselm points out, rightness is not related to signification in the same way that color is related to body. After all, if
no one wishes to signify what ought to be signified, there will
be no signification; is it not yet right that such a signification
be made? Therefore, when the signification does not exist the
rightness does not perish. Consequently, rightness does not
depend on the being of any signification. It is clear now that
rightness is not related to signification as color is related to
body. It is also apparent that the rightness of a will or indeed
any other rightness is dependent not so much on the will or
any other changing thing but on a rightness that remains
immutable.[30] 'There is consequently only one truth in all
things.'[31]

Truth is improperly said to belong to a will or an action or
anything else

> because it does not have its being in the things
> in which it is said to be, nor does it have its

being from them or through them. But, when
things themselves are in accord with that which
is always present to things which are as they
should be, then it is called 'the truth of this or
that thing' . . . in the same way as one speaks of
'the time of this or that thing' when there is one
and the same time for all the things that are
simultaneously in it; and if this or that thing were
not, nevertheless the same time would be. And
just as time considered by itself (*per se consideratum*)
is not called the time of anything, but when we
consider the things which are in it we speak of
'the time of this or that thing' so too the highest
truth subsisting through itself belongs to no
thing; but when some thing is in accord with it,
then we speak of 'its truth or its rightness'.[32]

Let us now examine the context of Anselm's argument. The
'highest truth' to which Anselm refers in the last sentence
above he had earlier described (Chapter Ten) as a unique
rightness.[33] While all other rightnesses are such 'because
the things to which they belong either are or do what they
ought, the highest truth is not rightness because it ought to be
or ought to do anything. For all are owing to it but it owes
nothing to anyone; there is no other reason by which it is
what it is except that it is.'

The starkness of this last description can leave us cold if
we have not read the preceding chapter (Chapter Nine), in
which Anselm tells us about 'the truth which is in the
essence of things'. He had pointed out there that while everyone knows that truth and falsity are found in signs, people
easily forget that truth and falsity are found in everything.
'For, since no one must do anything except what he ought
to do, from the very fact that someone does something, he
says and signifies that this is what he ought to do. If he does
what he ought to do, he speaks a truth. But, if he does not he

lies.'[34] Therefore, 'from the very fact that a thing is, it says
that it ought to be'.[35] This is why we believe that actions
speak louder than words. This reiterates the divine exem-
plarism Anselm had referred to still earlier (Chapter Seven):
'truth is in the essence of all the things which are, because
they are that which they are in the highest truth'.[36] And,
prior to this (Chapter Five) Anselm had quoted the Lord who
said: 'he who does evil hates the light'; and 'whoever does the
truth comes to the light'.[37] If doing evil and doing truth are
opposites, Anselm reasons, then to do the truth is to do well;
and, of course, to do as one ought is the meaning of doing
well and truly. No wonder, then, that Anselm can say: 'truth
and rightness and justice define each other'.[38]

It is against this biblical background[39] that sees all being
and action both as originating from goodness and as oriented
toward goodness that Anselm can say: 'from the very fact that
a thing is, it says that it ought to be'. In this light, to say that
the nature of the highest truth (what it is) is accounted for
simply by its own being (that it is) is to identify that nature
with subsisting rightness and subsisting justice.

In summary, Anselm's argument for the unity of the truth
whereby all things are true, when taken in the context of the
entire dialogue, appears as an earlier version of what will be
called by Thomas Aquinas his fourth 'way' of demonstrating
the existence of God. We recall that Aquinas there argues
from the various grades of goodness, truth, nobility and the like
to the existence of a maximum. For things are named good,
true and noble inasmuch as they resemble that which is best,
most true and most noble. We must conclude that that maximum exists because the maximum in any class of things is
the cause of all the things in that class. 'Therefore there must
also be something which is to all beings the cause of their being, goodness and every other perfection; and this we call
God.'[40]

If we are correct in likening Aquinas' fourth way, in spite
of its use of Aristotle, to Anselm's argument for the unity of

truth are we not contradicting our earlier assertion that it is
the speculative approach that characterizes the former and
the practical the latter? After all, are not valid demonstrations of God's existence at the very pinnacle of philosophic
speculation? In Aquinas' judgment they most certainly are.[41]
How then could Anselm present his eloquent version of this
most subtle argument?

But this difficulty is based on the false premise that the
practical approach to truth must exclude all speculative arguments. Nothing could be more false; all we need do is turn to
the works of Augustine or Plato before him. The writings of
both of them are studded with the most brilliant of speculative arguments. The question of a general approach to the
truth is not: can our author employ speculative reasoning?
The question rather is this: what is our author's primary purpose in writing?

The answer to this question in the case of Anselm is not
easy to find if only because, as we saw earlier, he never had
presented to him the alternatives Aquinas did. On the other
hand, we do know that nowhere in his works does he speak
about the truth in such a way as to contradict what he has
said in the *De veritate*. 'There is only one truth in all things.'
Truth is improperly said of anything else; that is, to the extent that a thing is as it ought to be we speak of 'the truth of
this or that thing'. Now, it is this single-minded concern with
the goal of human life that characterizes what Aristotle called
practical knowledge.[42] Still, it must be added: Aristotle might
have had some difficulty in recognizing Anselm's goal. For to
say that the goal of life is the first truth is to speak the language of faith.[43]

Language of faith though it be, it is a language that includes
speculative arguments. Assuming that Anselm knew what he
was doing in constructing such arguments, just as surely as
Augustine and Plato did, must we not admit that the distinct-
tion of theoretical and practical reasoning was known prior
to Aristotle?

No doubt about it. If Plato saw the difference, and he did,[44] the same was most likely true of Augustine and Anselm. A knowledge of this difference is probably as old as the knowledge of reasoning itself. Mankind often judged correctly before logic was a science, said John Stuart Mill.[45] Most certainly. Yet, the human family did not have a scientific or explicit knowledge of the various forms of reasoning until Aristotle spelled them out. Similarly, although Archimedes did 'modern science' in antiquity, mankind waited for Galileo reflectively to articulate the method peculiar to that type of knowing. So too, it was only when Aristotle clearly differentiated the subject matter, principles, procedures and ends of theoretical and practical knowledge that his students could exploit them with consistency. Thomas Aquinas was one of those students.

AQUINAS' APPROACH TO THE TRUTH

If Anselm's language is the language of faith, so is that of Aquinas. We have seen that from the very beginning of his career Aquinas was convinced: unless you believe you will not understand. But at the beginning of his writings Aquinas is equally convinced that his work ought to be pursued primarily as a speculative one:

> Although this science is one still it is complete
> and sufficient for every human perfection because
> of the efficacy of the divine light . . . Thus it perfects
> man both in right action and in regard to contempla-
> tion of the truth; that is, both as to what is practical
> and also speculative. But, because every thing ought
> to be considered principally from its end and the end
> of this teaching is the contemplation of the first truth
> in our fatherland, therefore, it is principally specula-
> tive. And since there are three speculative habits
> according to Aristotle [*Ethic.* VI, c. 7] namely wisdom,
> science and understanding; we say that it is wisdom in

> that it considers the highest causes and is, as it
> were, the chief and principal and orderer of all
> sciences; also it ought to be called wisdom even
> more than metaphysics because it considers the
> highest causes after the manner of those causes
> themselves because it is received directly from
> God through inspiration.[46]

There is nothing in Aquinas' last word on the subject that
differs from what he had said above.[47] Sacred teaching
includes both speculative and practical knowledge; just as God
—who provides the origin of this knowledge—'by one and the
same knowledge knows both himself and his works. But it is
more speculative than it is practical because it treats of divine
things more especially than it does of human actions; even of
those it treats inasmuch as man is ordered by them to the perfect knowledge of God in which eternal blessedness consists.'[48]

But, if one were to argue with Aquinas by saying that the
teaching of which he speaks is acquired by study whereas wisdom is had by an infusion from above since it is included
among the gifts of the Holy Spirit, how would he reply?

After reading Pseudo-Dionysius' *De divinis nominibus* II.9,
he had one basic response:

> Since judgement belongs to wisdom, there is a
> two-fold wisdom in accordance with a two-fold
> manner of judging. For a man may judge in one
> way by way of inclination, just as someone who
> has the habit of a virtue judges rightly of what
> ought to be done according to that virtue inas-
> much as he is inclined toward it; thus it is said in
> *Ethics X* [1176 a 17] that the virtuous man is
> the measure and rule of human acts. In another
> way a man may judge by knowledge, just as a
> man instructed in moral science may judge of
> virtuous acts even if he lacks virtue.

Therefore, the first way of judging of divine
things belongs to the wisdom which is called a
gift of the Holy Spirit: 'the spiritual man judges
all things (1 Cor 2:15). And Dionysius says:
'Hierotheus is taught not only as one learning
but as experiencing divine things'. But the
second way of judging belongs to this teaching
inasmuch as it is acquired by study, although its
principles are received through revelation.[49]

The first form of wise judgement may itself be of two
sorts. That is, it may follow upon a right inclination resulting from an acquired habit. This judgement, as Aristotle
observed, must depend on knowledge, on the choice of right
action for its own sake and on a firm and unchangeable
character; nevertheless 'as a condition of the possession of
the virtues knowledge has little or no weight, while the other
conditions count not for a little but for everything'.[50] The
other sort of wise judgement follows on a right inclination
that issues from a habit that is taught by 'a more divine inspiration than is given to most people' (*ex quadam inspiratione
diviniore', quam communiter fit multis*); that is, such a
person

> not only receives knowledge of divine things in
> his intellect but by loving also he is united to
> them by affection (*per affectum*). For passion
> seems to belong to appetite rather than to
> knowledge; because known things are in the
> knower according to the mode of the knower
> and not according to the mode of the things
> known; but appetite moves toward things
> according to the mode with which they are in
> themselves and thus is in some manner con-
> nected to those very things.[51]

Elsewhere Aquinas contrasts his speculative teaching with the kind outlined in Pseudo-Dionysius by referring to the latter as 'experiential'[52] or as an 'affective knowledge of the truth'.[53] Now 'affective knowledge' is the same as 'practical knowledge'.[54] One fundamental difference seems to be that the former is 'acquired by human study'; the latter belongs to the gift of wisdom which presupposes faith which is an assent 'to the divine truth for its own sake'.[55]

Another clear contrast between the two is found in the fact that the profit (*fructus*) of practical knowledge cannot be in itself because it is 'not known for its own sake but for the sake of something else; but speculative knowledge has its profit in itself, namely its certitude of the things of which it is'.[56]

Aquinas even saw these two modes of knowing as corresponding to different graces. Thus, one person will have 'the work and grace of teaching; he uses doctrine so that he can studiously and faithfully teach . . . but regarding practical knowledge he [the Apostle Paul] adds: "he who exhorts", that is he who has the work or grace of encouraging men to the good, uses it in exhortation.'[57]

We now have most of the ingredients of our solution. For Aquinas, sacred teaching is primarily speculative and only secondarily practical, since its primary purpose is knowledge; practical knowledge, however, 'is not for its own sake but for the sake of something else'. Secondly, speculative knowledge has as its subject matter things that already exist, in this case divine things; on the other hand, human actions that ought to be done in the future are the proper concern of practical knowledge. Thirdly, the procedure of acquiring speculative knowledge is by study, while practical knowledge results from an inclination either acquired by habituation or received as a gift of God. Fourthly, 'teaching', as Aquinas understood it, must be distinguished from exhortation according to their different modes of presentation. Teaching in the strict sense is for the sake of 'instructing the intellect"; but the words of a sermon, for example, can also have the purpose of 'moving affection' as when someone speaks in a way that delights his audience so that they listen willingly; or, words may be spoken so that the listener loves the things that the words signify and wants to fulfill them—in this case, the speaker actually changes (*flectat*) the listener.[58]

But, there is a fifth difference distinguishing these two kinds of knowledge. In speculative knowledge, the principle or origin of the knowing is the form of the thing known or 'that which the thing is'; in practical knowledge the principle is the end.[59] Needless to say, the end of practical knowledge must be within the knowing subject, either in his art, in the case of the artist, or in his choosing in accordance with 'right desire', in the case of the moral agent.[60] It is this affective character of practical knowledge expressed, for example, in counsels, encouragements, commands and prohibitions that calls for passionate language in order to affect the choice of the hearer.

But this distinction which places the first principles or starting points of speculative knowledge outside the knower and *in the things known* clearly accounts for Aquinas' giving an answer to our initial question that is so different from that of Anselm.

It is this dispassionate and objective manner of speaking that Aquinas found most appropriate to a speculative kind of knowledge. Occasionally he described it by saying that he was speaking 'formally'.[61] At other times, when speaking of the kind of predicate that is used according to the analogy of attribution, he will say that its 'complete intelligible structure' (*ratio completa*) is found first of all in its primary analogate as, for example, health is found first of all in an animal and only in relation to this is it also said of the art of healing.[62]

When he goes on to discuss the question with which we are immediately concerned he tells us: 'it is clear from what has been said that truth is properly (*proprie*) found in the intellect, whether human or divine, just as health is in the animal.'[63]

And, when he gives us his final treatment of our question he tells us that he is speaking of the truth according to 'its own intelligible structure' (*propria ratio*).[64]

From this comparison we can learn that when we speak in the manner appropriate to speculative knowledge we should speak of things in terms of 'their own intelligible structures' or 'properly' or according to their 'complete intelligible structures' or 'formally'. To speak in any other way in this context is presumably to speak 'improperly'. We say this because when Aquinas was asked about the virtue of truth 'by which a man shows himself in statements and actions as he is', he said that

> the truth of life is spoken of in a particular way
> inasmuch as a man fulfills in his life that to
> which the divine intellect orders him; just as it
> has been said that truth is also in other things.
> But, the truth of justice is found where a man
> gives to the other what he ought according to
> law. Thus, one ought not to proceed toward
> truth in general from these particular truths.[65]

Yet, is this not Anselm's procedure? We make a special point of quoting these passages concerned with vital human activities in order to underline the fact that from the point of view of a speculative approach to the truth one is interested in it as it is 'in general', not as it is found in particular truths; according to its 'complete intelligible structure' then, truth is located in an intellect and not as it is found 'also in other things'.

Then, in the same context, Aquinas raises the anselmian objection:[66]

> Anselm says in the book *De veritate* that just
> as time is to temporal things so is truth to true
> things. But there is one time for all temporal

things. Therefore there is one truth by which
all things are true.

Aquinas briefly replies: 'the statement of Anselm is true
inasmuch as things are called true in relation to the divine
intellect'. But, we now know that it is only 'in relation to
the divine intellect' that truth is found 'also in other things'.[67]
But the clearest expression of our authors' differing approaches to the truth is apparent in Aquinas' following comparison: 'Thus, therefore, truth is originally in an intellect but
secondarily in things inasmuch as they are related to an intellect as to their origin.' To illustrate the first notion of truth
he presents definitions provided by Augustine and Hilary. To
exemplify the second he finds definitions again in Augustine
but also in Avicenna and Anselm: 'The following definition of
Anselm [belongs to the truth of the thing in its relation to an
intellect] – "truth is rightness perceptible to the mind alone";
for that is right which agrees with its origin.'[68]
What is Aquinas doing here? He has acknowledged the value
of Anselm's testimony and at the same time he has shown its
limits. From Aquinas' perspective Anselm's view of the truth
is that of things insofar as they are related to an intellect; that
is, it is proper to practical knowledge.
Confronted with such a juxtaposition, a contemporary
historian would say that to apply an aristotelian distinction
to a pre-aristotelian author is to read history backwards.[69] As
an interpreter of history in today's sense of the word he is
perfectly correct. But if Aquinas is making use of the *pia
expositio* mode of interpretation he, too, may be correct.
From this atemporal point of view in which all of one's predecessors are treated as contemporaries, one takes it for
granted that had they known the things we know they would
have acknowledged them at least as promptly as we do. Starting from the author's own words, one draws a line in the direction of the truth, both as known to him and as now known to
us. In this way we discover 'Anselm's intention'.[70] The quo-

tation from his commentary on St Paul that we saw earlier was another example of Aquinas' use of this method of 'respectful interpretation'.

We have said that when Aquinas cited Anselm it was usually with approval. The qualified approval that he here gives to the anselmian view according to which there is only one truth by which all things are true amounts, however, to his saying that from a speculative perspective Anselm is speaking improperly. And there are times when he felt forced to put it that bluntly.[71] In the present case he does not use the expression *improprie;* he simply tells us where truth is properly located and then he points to its location in the thought of Anselm.

Is there no place then for speech which is not proper to the speculative mode but is 'figurative' or 'metaphorical' or 'symbolical' or 'parabolical'? In fact, it is both 'necessary and useful' that Holy Scripture use metaphors. First, because it is natural to man to arrive at intellectual truths through sensible things, since all our knowledge originates from the senses. It is fitting, secondly, that spiritual truths be presented by means of figures taken from bodily things so that even the uneducated who are not suited to intelligible things might grasp them.[72]

It was no less fitting, then, that monastic writers should proceed in the patristic tradition and speak in biblical language. This does not mean that these same sources were not the primary springs from which Aquinas himself drew his teaching. For him, as for Anselm, the chief condition for achieving union with the first truth is still that perfection of desire which is charity.[73] Aquinas was not a monk; but, as a dominican friar, he led a life that was in many respects the same as that of Anselm.[74]

The reason for the difference is that Aquinas was teaching at a different time and in a different place. He had at his disposal sources that had not been available two centuries earlier. Also, the milieu in which he worked was not the cloister but

a graduate classroom of theology. Not only were his listeners
people from every sort of background,[75] but as graduate
students they could be assumed to be already committed to
an in-depth study of their discipline;[76] that is, it could be
presumed that they no longer needed to be persuaded of its
value. All that was needed was that everything be explained
according to its own intelligible structure. This is no longer
the 'school for christian living' whose sole purpose is to educate men for citizenship in the kingdom of God.[77] It is a
university. Therefore, it has a two-fold purpose. Its ultimate
end, in the case of theology, is the same as Anselm's. But its
immediate and specific end is new: the transmission of a kind
of knowledge that is acquired by studying each thing in terms
of 'that which the thing is' or its own form.

CONCLUSION

We have not attempted to explore the activity of teaching
so much as the purposes and principles of two kinds of teaching. In any case, for Aquinas the performance of teaching
seems always to belong more to the active life than to the
contemplative.[78]

What we have sketched are the two kinds of knowledge
that these different sorts of teaching attempt to convey. One
is a knowledge whose ultimate end is beyond itself, divine
happiness; but its immediate end is not knowing but doing
the truth, that is, willing as one should. For the achievement
of both these ends it regularly uses exhortation. Aquinas calls
this 'practical knowledge'; for it circles around a single center:
the one efficient, exemplary and final cause of all things, the
'primal truth'.

Another is a kind of knowledge whose ultimate end also lies
beyond itself, in heaven; meanwhile, however, its immediate
end is obtainable within itself. This immediate end is the
knowledge of God that reason can derive from creatures.
Nevertheless, because this knowledge is speculative it must
begin from the 'intelligible structures' peculiar to those

creatures. Therefore, in the course of orbiting about the same 'primal truth' circled by Anselm, it also revolves around as many creaturely truths as come under the intelligible structure of its formal object;[79] these may be as varied as 'truth in general', 'being in general',[80] 'the essence of law'[81] or the nature of Platonism.[82] The list is long but in every case the theologian is to be attentive to the thing's 'complete intelligible structure'. Since these are the principles of a scientific kind of knowledge,[83] then, if the sacred theologian must 'studiously and faithfully teach' the doctrine he has received, it follows that he must first of all studiously and faithfully study these principles. *Contemplare et contemplata aliis tradere.*

If Aquinas' accomplishment is not the first in the Middle Ages,[84] it is surely among the first instances of what is now accepted as the norm among scholars and all those involved in graduate education. Although he has nowhere spelled out 'the complete intelligible structure' of scholarship or university teaching, by his own example Aquinas has shown us what it is. More than that, he has shown us that he knew very well the ways in which he was both similar to and different from his revered predecessor, Anselm. He even knew why.

If it is not an oversimplification to characterize the monk, Anselm, with Newman's motto, *cor ad cor loquitur,* it is then no less fitting to characterize the scholastic, Aquinas, with a paraphrase of that same motto: *intellectus ad intellectus loquitur.*

Duquesne University

NOTES

1. Saint Augustine, *De magistro* c. 1; ed. Guenther Weigel, *Sancti Aureli Augustini Opera* Sect. VI Pars IV; CSEL 77 (Vienna: Hoelder-Pichler-Tempsky, 1961) p. 3, 1-13.

2. St Anselm of Canterbury, *De veritate* c. 13; ed. Franciscus Salesius Schmitt, *Sancti Anselmi Opera Omnia*, 6 vols. (Edinburgh: Th. Nelson & Sons, 1961) p. 199, ll. 27-29. Hereafter this edition will be referred to simply by the initial letter the editor uses to indicate an anselmian work, followed by the page and line numbers; in the case of this reference, for example, it would be V 199, 27-29. Similarly, references to other works of Anselm will be, for example, M 77, 21-24, an allusion to the *Monologion;* and I 10,1-4, a reference to *Epistola de incarnatione verbi.*

3. V 199, 11.

4. St Thomas Aquinas, *Summa theologiae,* (Ottawa: Prima Pars, 1941) q. 16, a. 6. This edition, which contains the corrections provided by the leonine critical edition, will subsequently be referred to simply as *ST* plus the part of the *Summa* and the question and article; for example *ST* I, 16, 6.

5. Jasper Hopkins, *A Companion to the Study of St. Anselm,* (Minneapolis: University of Minnesota, 1972) 16-36.

6. St Thomas Aquinas, *Scriptum super libros Sententiarum,* ed. R. P. Mandonnet, (Paris: Lethielleux, 1929) Vol. 1, Prologue.

7. *Ibid.,* q. 1, a. 3.

8. *The Love of Learning and the Desire for God: A Study of Monastic Culture,* trans. Catharine Misrahi, 2nd rev. ed., (New York: Fordham University Press, 1974); also cf. M.D. Chenu, *Toward Understanding St. Thomas,* trans. A.M. Landry and D. Hughes, (Chicago: Henry Regnery Co., 1964) 72.

9. *The Love of Learning,* pp. 6, 7; cf. pp. 2-9, cf. also p. 182, 188, 263-264.

10. *Ibid.,* p. 251.

11. *Ibid.,* p. 9.

12. *Ibid.,* p. 42.

13. *Ibid.,* p. 86; cf. *Epist.* 112 (1946) 246. For this notion of contemplation as intending 'to foster the desire for the heavenly life', cf. pp. 108-109.

14. *Ibid.,* p. 188.

15. *Ibid.,* p. 199.

16. *Ibid.,* p. 188, 207.
17. *Ibid.,* p. 216; cf. M.D. Chenu, *Toward Understanding St. Thomas,*
p. 61.
18. *The Love of Learning,* p. 244.
19. *Ibid.,* p. 253.
20. *Ibid.,* p. 240; cf. p. 310.
21. *Ibid.,* p. 270.
22. *Ibid.,* p. 283.
23. *ST* II-II, 45, 3, ad 1.
24. Armand A. Maurer, *Medieval Philosophy,* (New York: Random
House, 1962) 86; Jasper Hopkins, *A Companion to the Study of
St. Anselm,* (Minneapolis: University of Minnesota, 1972) 28-29.
Granted, Anselm died in the first decade of the twelfth century—1109.
But James of Venice did not translate the New Logic (*Topics, Prior &
Posterior Analytics* and *Sophistical Refutations*) until 1128. In fact,
none of the works of Aristotle apart from the Old Logic (*Categories &
On Interpretation*) had been translated until after Anselm's death; see
Maurer, *Medieval Philosophy,* pp. 86-87.
25. Franciscus Salesius Schmitt, *Sancti Anselmi Opera Omnia,* Vol. VI,
p. 21.
26. M 77, 21-24.
27. I 10, 1-4; V 191, 11-18.
28. See Boethius, *In Isagoge Porphyrii commentarium editio secundae,*
lib. I, c. 3 (CSEL 48:140-141). For the citations of Boethius in Anselm
see Schmitt, Vol. VI, 22.
29. V 191, 19.
30. V 197, 28-198, 10:
   M. Non similiter se habent color ad corpus et rectitudo ad
significationem.
   D. Ostende dissimilitudinem.
   M. Si nullus aliquo significare velit signo quod significandum
est: erit ulla per signa significatio?
   D. Nulla.
   M. An ideo non erit rectum, ut significetur quod significari
debet?
   D. Non idcirco minus erit rectum, aut minus hoc exiget rectitudo.
   M. Ergo non existente significatione non perit rectitudo qua
rectum est et qua exigitur, ut quod significandum est significetur.
   D. Si interisset, non esset hoc rectum, nec ipsa hoc exigeret.
   M. Putasne cum significatur quod significari debet, significa-
tionem tunc esse rectam propter hanc et secundum hanc ipsam

rectitudinem?

D. Immo non possum aliter putare. Si enim alia rectitudine recta est significatio, pereunte ista nihil prohibet rectam esse significationem. Sed nulla est recta significatio, quae significat quod non est rectum significari, aut quod non exigit rectitudo.

M. Nulla igitur significatio est recta alia rectitudine quam illa, quae permanet pereunte significatione.

D. Palam est.

31. V 199, 11.
32. V 199, 17-29.
33. V 190, 1-4.
34. V 189, 3-7.
35. V 189, 25.
36. V 185, 18.
37. V 181, 12-14; Jn 3:20.
38. V 192, 8.
39. Anselm had said in his Preface (V 173, 2) that this is one of his three works which 'belong to the study of sacred scripture'. The other two are *De libertate arbitrii* and *De casu diaboli.*
40. *ST,* I, 2, 3. For an analysis of the 'fourth way' as it appears in Aquinas' commentary *Super librum de causis expositio* see Michael W. Strasser, *Saint Thomas' Critique of Platonism in the* Liber de Causis, (dissertation, University of Toronto, 1962) pp. 190-206. While I have found no explicit acknowledgement of Anselm in Aquinas' various presentations of the fourth way, he does use the distinction of the degrees of more and less with regard to color from the degrees of more and less of specifically different natural gifts. Did he borrow this from Anselm or did both derive it from some common source?
41. *ST* I, 1, 1.
42. *Nicomachean Ethics,* VII, 8 (1151 a16) 'in actions the final cause is the first principle'. See *Metaph.* II, 1 (993b21) 'the end of practical knowledge is action'., and *Nicomachean Ethics,* VI, 2. 'the good state [of the practical intellect] is truth in agreement with right desire'.
43. Aquinas, *ST,* I, 1, 1 & II-II, 4, 2, ad 3 & I-II, 3, 5.
44. See Plato, *Statesman* 258 DE. For the addition of this nuance I am indebted to the generous suggestion of the distinguished scholar-in-residence at the Institute for Cistercian Studies in 1983, Professor Edward A. Synan.
45. John Stuart Mill, *A System of Logic,* London (1895) 6.
46. *Scriptum super libros Sententiarium Prologus,* Q[a]III.
47. *ST,* I, 1, 4.
48. Aquinas' concept of *sacra doctrina* as primarily speculative is

parallel to his notion of faith. Since the primary object of faith is the first truth, faith is in the speculative intellect as in a subject. But, because the first truth is the end of all our desires and actions it operates by love; just as Aristotle observed, the speculative intellect becomes practical by extension; *ST,* II-II, 4, 2, ad 3 m; See Aristotle, *De anima* III, 10 (433 a 15-20).

49.   *ST,* I, 1, 6, ad 3 m.

50.   *Nicomachean Ethics,* II, 4 (1105 a31-1105 b4).

51.   St Thomas Aquinas, *In librum beati Dionysii De divinis nominibus expositio* (Turin, Rome: Marietti, 1950) c. II, l. 4.

52.   *ST,* II-II, 97, 2, ad 2.

53.   *ST,* II-II, 162, 3, ad 1.

54.   Aquinas, *De malo,* 16, 6, ad 8; ed. P. Bazzi, M. Calcaterra, T.S. Centi, E. Odetto, P.M. Pession *Questiones disputatae,* vol. 2 (Turin, Rome: Marietti, 1949).

55.   *ST,* II-II, 45, 1, ad 2.

56.   *ST,* II-II, 8, 8, ad 3.

57.   *In omnes s. Pauli apostoli Epistolas commentaria,* Vol. I, *Ad Romanos* c. XII, (Marietti: Turin, Rome, 1929) p. 173-4.

58.   *ST,* II-II, 177, 1.

59.   Aquinas, *Summa contra gentiles* III, 97; ed. Leonina Manualis (Rome: Desclée, Herder, 1934).

60.   *ST,* I-II, 1, 1, ad lm & 1, 4. See Aristotle, *Nic. Ethics* VI, 2 (1139 a26-69); *Metaph.* E, 1 (1025b 18-26); K7 (1064 a 10-18); *PA* I, 1 (640 a3-4).

61.   Aquinas, *De veritate,* 1, 1; ed. R. Spiazzi, *Questiones disputatae.* vol. 1 (Turin, Rome: Marietti, 1949).

62.   *De ver.,* 1. 2. This is what Aristotle called *pros hen* equivocation; see J. Owens, *The Doctrine of Being in the Aristotelian Metaphysics,* (Toronto, 1951) 54-57.

63.   *De ver.,* 1, 4.

64.   *ST,* I, 16, 6: 'Respondeo. Dicendum quod quodammodo una est veritas, qua omnia sunt vera, et quodammodo non. Ad cuius evidentiam, sciendum est quod, quando aliquid praedicatur univoce de multis, illud in quolibet eorum secundum propriam rationem invenitur, sicut animal in qualibet specie animalis. Sed quando aliquid dicitur analogice de multis, illud invenitur secundum propriam rationem in uno eorum tantum, a quo alia denominantur. Sicut sanum dicitur de animali et urina et medicina, non quod sanitas sit nisi in animali tantum, sed a sanitate animalis denominatur medicina sana, inquantum est illius sanitatis effectiva, et urina, inquantum est illius sanitatis significativa. Et quamvis sanitas non sit in medicina neque in urina, tamen in utroque est aliquid per quod

hoc quidem facit, illud autem significat sanitatem.

Dictum est autem quod veritas per prius est in intellectu, et per posterius in rebus, secundum quod ordinantur ad intellectum divinum. Si ergo loquamur de veritate prout existit in intellectu, secundum propriam rationem, sic in multis intellectibus creatis sunt multae veritates; etiam in uno et eodem intellectu, secundum plura cognita . . . Si vero loquamur de veritate secundum quod est in rebus, sic omnes sunt verae una prima veritate, cui unumquodque assimilatur secundum suam entitatem. Et sic, licet plures sint essentiae vel formae rerum, tamen una est veritas divini intellectus, secundum quam omnes res denominantur verae.'

65.   *ST,* I, 16, 4, ad 3; cf. Anselm, footnote 30.

66.   *ST,* I, 16, 6, ob. 2.

67.   See foonote 64.

68.   *ST,* I, 16, 1: 'Sic ergo veritas principaliter est in intellectu; secundario vero in rebus, secundum quod comparantur ad intellectum ut ad principium.

'Et secundum hoc, veritas diversimode notificatur. Nam Augustinus, in libro *De vera relig.,* dicit quod "veritas est, qua ostenditur id quod est". Et Hilarius dicit quod "verum est declarativum aut manifestativum esse". Et hoc pertinet ad veritatem secundum quod est in intellectu. —Ad veritatem autem rei secundum ordinem ad intellectum pertinet definitio Augustini in libro *De vera relig.* talis: "Veritas est summa similitudo principii, quae sine ulla dissimilitudine est". Et quaedam definitio Anselmi talis: "Veritas est rectitudo sola mente perceptibilis"; nam rectum est quod principio concordat.'

69.   See the paper of Dr Raymond DiLorenzo in this same conference which considers the application of 'practical' to Plato's philosophy as inappropriate.

70.   *De veritate,* 3, 1. A good account of the *pia expositio* is given by Chenu, *Toward Understanding St. Thomas,* pp. 145-149. A reconstruction of the likely remote sources of this method of interpretation is given by M.W. Strasser, *St. Thomas Critique of Platonism in the* Liber de Causis, pp. 25-26.

71.   *ST,* I, 34, 1 c. and ad 3m.

72.   *ST,* I, 1, 9; cf. *ST,* I, 10, ad 3.

73.   *ST,* I, 12, 6.

74.   James A. Weisheipl, *Friar Thomas D'Aquino: His Life, Thought and Works* (Garden City, NY: Doubleday & Co., 1974) 24-25.

75.   M.W. Strasser, 'The Educational Philosophy of the First Universities' in Douglas Radcliff–Umstead, ed., *The University World: A Synoptic View of Higher Education in the Middle Ages and the Renaissance*

(Pittsburgh: University of Pittsburgh Press, 1973) 4.

76.   Mastery of a discipline seems to have been the aim of medieval university education. See M.W. Strasser, 'The Educational Philosophy of the First Universities', p. 14.

77.   M.W. Strasser, 'Aquinas and the Community of Human Persons', *The University of Dayton Review,* Vol. 12, no. 1 (Dayton: University of Dayton, 1975) 6.

78.   *De veritate,* 11, 4.

79.   *ST,* I, 1, 3.

80.   St Thomas Aquinas, *In duodecim libros Metaphysicorum Aristotelis expositio,* ed. M.R. Cathala & R.M. Spiazzi, (Turin & Rome, 1950) Prooemium, pp. 1, 2.

81.   *ST,* I-II, 90; see M.W. Strasser, 'St. Thomas Aquinas on Natural Law', Elwyn A. Smith, ed., *Church–State Relations in Ecumenical Perspective* (Louvain, 1966) pp. 153-4.

82.   R.J. Henle, *Saint Thomas and Platonism,* (The Hague, 1956).

83.   *ST,* I, 1, 2.

84.   The first may have been St Albert the Great; see M.D. Chenu, *Toward Understanding St. Thomas,* p. 43.

A DISPUTED QUESTION:
WHETHER WHATEVER IS KNOWN
IS KNOWN IN THE DIVINE IDEAS
15 June 1983

Participants:
Timothy Noone, bachelor
John McCall, bachelor
Edward Synan, Master
of
The University of Toronto

PROLOGUE

Edward Synan, Master:

TODAY WE HAVE A PROBLEM that Shakespeare faced and solved. Since we do not have his talent, let us borrow his solution.

In a medieval university, to conduct a proper disputed question took two days. On the first day young scholars, 'bachelors', perhaps with support from the university

audience, wrangled over any and all arguments that might
be adduced, pro or con, concerning a puzzle that the presid-
ing Master was bound in honor to settle.

My pre-Vatican II biretta and cassock, lineal descendants
of the medieval Doctor's cap and gown, will remind you of
who is in charge here.

Two young scholars, gowned but not capped, will bring in
a selection of arguments they have found in the actual text of
a published thirteenth-century disputation—which, of course,
may be far removed from the form in which it was actually
disputed. Here and there, they may feel free to slip in a point
or two from elsewhere. In any case, the text beneath our presentation is the Fourth Question on the knowledge of Christ
by John Fidenza, whom we know as 'Bonaventure', 'Good
Fortune', Doctor of Theology in the University of Paris as of
1257.[1] The English translation used is that by Canon Eugene
Fairweather, priest of the Anglican Church in Canada and
Professor in the University of Toronto.[2] My 'magistral determination' stands to Bonaventure's *solutio* as do our bachelors'
arguments to those that Bonaventure's text preserves.

The Quaracchi Latin text and Fairweather's English translation, along with the historical reality of a university disputed
question, impose upon us the same necessity that prompted
Shakespeare to write a marvelous Prologue for his play on
Henry V of England: too many people, too much time
elapsed, too little space to include everything. The play, after
all, presents the battle of Agincourt; it involves England,
France, and the narrow seas between. How could all that he
crammed inside the tiny circle, in Shakespeare's happy phrase,
'this wooden O' that was the Globe Theatre? His solution was
to ask the audience to use their imagination. Here is the way
that Shakespeare put his request (*with* some omissions, or,
ought I rather to say 'without') some of his glorious language;
a few lines of blank verse, a rhyming couplet to cap his case:

> . . . can this cockpit hold
> The vasty field of France? or may we cram
> Within this wooden O the very casques
> That did affright the air at Agincourt?
> O pardon! since a crooked figure may
> Attest in little space a million;
> And let us, ciphers to this great accompt,
> On your imaginary forces work . . .
> Piece out our imperfections with your thoughts;
> Into a thousand parts divide one man, . . .
> . . . many years
> Into an hour-glass . . .
> Admit me Chorus to this history;
> Who prologue-like your humble patience pray,
> Gently to hear, kindly to judge, our play.

What of our project? What can be said in the spirit of Shakespeare to ease our way into your minds and hearts? Here is
my best effort:

> O for a Muse of thought that would ascend
> The brightest heaven of invention,
> Old Paris for a stage, scholars to act . . .
> But pardon, friends,
> The banal brash spirits who will try
> On this familiar platform to evoke
> So great a business . . .
> Extend our boundaries with your boundless thought;
> Into a series do divide each argument;
> Turn minutes into hours, even days—
> We, Shakespeare-like do ask that you deploy
> Fantasy—that this disputed question you enjoy!

One of our bachelors will speak to the negative, the other to
the affirmative. At one moment what they say will echo the

citation of 'authorities', those great figures from the past
who were manipulated with subtle skill by medieval Masters;
it was a Cistercian who said of his scholastic contemporaries'
methods that 'Authority has a nose of wax—it can be turned
in different directions'![3] to which, of course, the scholastics
might well have rejoined that Alan of Lille himself brought
in all the gods and goddesses of Olympus and made them
stand for sound grammar and sound christian morals. Do
please remember that we (in the most literal sense) do not
have all day for their exchange; one authority must do for
many.

Beside 'authority' you will hear the voice of 'reason', arguments explicitly or implicitly syllogistic. Here too your ima-
ginations must multiply the restricted sampling they will
proffer.

If the 'pro/con' format is disturbing, it must be held in
mind that Aristotle himself is at the fountain head of that
technique for settling philosophical (or any other!) problems. On his authority every question raised was formulated
in such a way that a 'yes/no' answer is possible; each issue
was put into the form of a question beginning with the word
'whether', in Latin, *utrum* or *an*. Normally the Master who
would preside formulated the question as a teaching device.
At times he might be daring enough to post his name with
the invitation to challenge him on a *quaestio quodlibetalis,* a
question on 'anything you like'. At the end of the middle
ages Thomas More did just that in Brussels at the court of
the Emperor, Charles V.[4] In a move much misunderstood, it
seems, he wrote up the problem: *An averia capta in wither-
namo sint irreplegibilia*? If we can believe legal historians,
this asks, more or less, whether animals, taken in reprisal
owing to some injustice, real or fancied, and removed from
the jurisdiction where taken, might provoke an equivalent
reprisal with respect to the property of the one who had so
taken them, or even from some one else who might be
expected to put pressure on that person and those animals

be brought into the original jurisdiction. According to the historian to whom we owe the anecdote, the Master who had put up his name for a *quaestio de quolibet* elected not to debate this one.

No matter; Bonventure did put his name to the question we shall present. In John McCall and Timothy Noone, graduate students of the University of Toronto, please imagine medieval bachelors, perhaps seconded by members of the audience; in me please imagine the prestige and glory of a medieval Doctor whose solution, somewhat like that of a civil judge, will enter into the tradition of precedent that will guide, but not totally bind, future generations.

His question Bonaventure formulated as:

WHETHER WHATEVER IS KNOWN BY US WITH CERTITUDE IS KNOWN IN THE ETERNAL REASONS THEMSELVES?
UTRUM QUIDQUID A NOBIS CERTITUDINALITER COGNOSCITUR COGNOSCATUR IN IPSIS RATIO-NIBUS AETERNIS?

John McCall, Bachelor:

It is presupposed in the question disputed today that the Divine Ideas are the Ideas in God's mind by which he knows his creation. These Ideas represent creation to God, and since God's knowledge is perfect, the Ideas represent all creatures perfectly: not only as they are, but as they should be. Therefore, the Ideas can be said to be the truth of creatures, all truth, or truth itself which is the foundation of the Divine Wisdom. The question before us is whether they are also the foundation of *human* knowledge. To ask this is to ask whether whatever is known by us with certitude is known in the Divine Ideas. And that this is the case can be proved from many great authorities.

St Augustine, who is not merely a Doctor of the Church or a Master of Theology but is the greatest of the great Fathers of the Church, says in his work *On Free Will*[5] that since truth itself does not change with time or place, nor is subject to the bodily senses, but is present to anyone, anywhere, and at any time, it is obvious that truth, in which we know all things that are true, is greater than our own minds which can be known only to ourselves alone, in time, and in space. Augustine has asserted many times, moreover, that we know, not in the truth of the changing world or in the truth of our own fallible minds, but in the eternal, unchanging, omnipresent truth in God. These are his words: 'It is clear that there exists above our minds a basis of judging, or a law, which is called truth and it is incontestable that this immutable law, which is above the human mind, is God.' That is from his work, *On True Religion,*[6] and he says just as much again in the twelfth book of his *Confessions* when he states: 'Suppose that two men see that what one of them says is true. Where, I ask you, do they see it? They do not see it in the one or the other, but both of them see it in the same omnipresent truth which is above both their minds.'[7] In his work, *On the Trinity,* he puts it this way: 'When the impious see the rules according to which each ought to live, where do they see them? Not in their own impious minds surely, but in the book of that light which is called truth.'[8] Again, speaking of the philosophers in the eighth book of the *City of God,*[9] he says: 'Those whom we rightly prefer to all . . . say that the light of our minds by which we learn all things is the very God Himself by whom all things were made.' And again, in the ninth book of the *On the Trinity,* 'It is proved that we either accept . . . or reject, when we rightly accept or reject anything, by other rules which remain altogether unchangeable above our minds.'[10]

From these authoritative texts, therefore, it is clear, on the authority of St Augustine himself, that when we know we know in the Divine Ideas. But other authorities may be cited to prove this as well.

St Ambrose himself, the great Bishop of Milan and Father of the Church, says: 'By myself I see nothing but the empty, the fleeting, the perishable.'[11] Those are Ambrose's own words. So if it is true that we have any certain knowledge, we must see it through something which is above ourselves, unless we wish to contradict holy Ambrose and say that we see something that is absolute and permanent either in ourselves or in the world. Also, St Gregory, that great Bishop of Rome and Father of the Universal Church, says that in man there is an inward teacher that guides man to truth.[12] But if we were to claim that our intellects are self-sufficient for understanding through the light of created reason alone, then we would not need an inward teacher of the kind that holy Gregory says that we do. Since, on the authority of St Gregory, we do in fact need an inward teacher, then it is established that we know in the Divine Ideas.

And to the authority of the Fathers we may add the testimony of our monastic brethren, those monks who are the heart of the mystical body of the Church. St Anselm himself says in his *Proslogion:* 'How great is that light from which shines every truth that gives light to the rational mind! How full is that truth in which is to be found everything that is true!'[13] Now, since everything that is seen to be true is seen where it is true, then on the authority of St Anselm we must say that we see truth in the Divine Ideas. Also, Isaac, that holy monk and Abbot of Stella, testifies to this being true when he deals with the text of the Psalm, (13:10): 'In thy light we shall see light.' Isaac says: 'As that by which the sun can be seen goes out from the sun, so with God light, which goes out from God, irradiates the mind.'[14] According to this holy authority, therefore, all truth is seen in the Divine Ideas.

The same conclusion can be shown to be true by human reason also, and not only by authority. We may turn to the holy reasoning of St Augustine who is the most astute of all our christian philosophers, or we may even turn to the reason of Aristotle who is the greatest of the pagan philosophers who lacked the light of Revelation.

From Augustine's works we may construct the following proofs:[15]

It is certain that everything changeable is higher than the changeable. Now, that by which we know when we are certain of our knowledge must be unchangeable, because if it was changeable, we could never be certain that our knowledge was true or not. But our mind is changeable. Therefore, that by which we know is above our minds. But there is nothing above our minds save God and eternal truth. Therefore God and the eternal truth in God, which are the Divine Ideas, are that by which our knowledge exists. This reason alone can prove.

I have another argument: Everyone concedes that everything that is not subject to judgement is higher than that which *is* subject to judgement. Thus the norm by which we do judge our knowledge to be true must be higher than our own knowledge and therefore be higher than our own minds in which our knowledge exists. But what is higher than our mind can only be the Divine Ideas themselves. Therefore, when we know, and judge our knowledge to be true, we do so in the Divine Ideas.

I have another argument drawn from the works of St Augustine: Now, it is evident to all that the rule by which all men judge their knowledge to be true must be available to all men, anywhere, any time, and without limit. For instance, when the ancient Greeks judged that the proposition 2+2=4 is true, they did it according to the same rule which we use today since we also find it to be true, and in the same way. This rule therefore transcends time and place and individual minds. And it does so without any limit to this transcendence. But this illimitable rule cannot be created, but can only be uncreated, since everything created is limited. Therefore, this rule must necessarily be uncreated, and thus must be God himself who alone is uncreated. Therefore, when we know by this rule, we know in the light of the Divine Mind.

I have another argument in which St Augustine makes use of the thought of Aristotle:[16] Augustine points out that every created thing is comprehensible in itself. Then he points out that according to Aristotle, (*Physics* 1.4), the laws of numbers and mathematical figures and of demonstration, when they are increased to infinity, are incomprehensible to the human intellect. Therefore, he concludes, when man understands these laws to be true, he must understand them in the light of something which exceeds everything created. but there is nothing of this sort but God Himself and his eternal reason. Therefore, when we know these laws to be true in their infinity, we know them in the light of the Divine Ideas in God.

This can be shown in another argument.[17] It is a common experience to find that even impious men can know what piety is. Now, when such men know piety, they must know it either by its presence, or by a likeness received from without, or from something which is above them. There are no other alternatives. But such a man or men cannot know piety from its presence because it is not present to them since they are impious. And they cannot know piety through a likeness received from without because only the senses are the doors to the soul from without and piety cannot be sensed. Therefore they must know piety through something above their intellects, which, as we have seen, can only be the Divine Ideas in God.

All of these arguments come from the writings of St Augustine. Therefore, not only his great authority, but also his purely rational insights prove that when man knows, he knows in the Divine Ideas themselves.

Timothy Noone, Bachelor:

You, sir, have referred to these lines of argument or *rationes* from St Augustine. But surely these views are susceptible of refutation.

The first argument begins from the superiority of the immutable to the changeable and infers that our minds somehow reach an immutable entity in knowledge; but, if this is conceded, various absurdities follow. For example, the train of every scientific principle is unchangeable—'the whole is greater than its parts' to name one such principle. Now if every principle is immutable and every immutable truth is God, then every principle and all knowledge is really God. This, however, is untenable and so likewise is the assumption.

Another argument against this view is that if all truth is one, and it has been granted that Eternal Reason is one in the highest degree, and every unchanging truth is derived from the Eternal Reason, then we are left with a monistic universe and all things will be one. For surely it is clear we have knowledge about a wide diversity of things and there is some 'truth' to be found in them. But according to the view put forth, all truth is one and so all beings, in which there is truth, are one.

But there are other arguments that we can bring to bear against this view. For everything which is God must be adored and everything that is immutable is God. It follows, then, that every immutable truth must be adored and the truth of a proposition such as 2+2=4 must be adored!

Every unchangeable truth is God Himself, according to the thesis. Hence, whosoever grasps clearly and certainly any truth, sees God. But even the damned and the devils perceive some truth and must, accordingly, see God. Beatitude itself consists, moreover, in seeing God and whoever sees God is blessed. Therefore the damned are blessed!

You, sir, cited authorities which corroborate the thesis of the Master. Authorities can be adduced, however, to prove the contrary. Let us take Scripture, to begin with. In the first letter of the Apostle to Timothy (1 Tim 6:16) it says about God that 'He is one who alone has immortality and resides in inaccessible light whom no man has seen nor is able to see'. But everything by which or in which we understand is accessible to the one understanding. Hence that by which or in which we understand cannot be the light of Eternal Reason.

Augustine can also be used to support the contrary for he says in the first book *On The Trinity* that, 'the sharpest point of the human mind is not fastened in such a heavenly light (as the Divine Light) unless it is cleansed through the righteousness of faith'. If the Light of the Eternal Reason were the cause of the knowledge of all truth then no soul would understand truth except a soul cleansed and sanctified. But clearly even the pagans attained to some truth and since the conclusion is false, so is the assumption.

Again Augustine, the great Doctor of the Church, in the ninth book *On the Trinity* says that 'the [human] mind gathers knowledge of incorporeal realities through itself just as it acquires knowledge of corporeal realities through the senses of the body'. Therefore it does not seem that whatever the mind knows, is known through the Eternal Reasons.

Augustine also states in the ninth book *On the Trinity* that 'We must hold that the nature of the human intelligence has been so created that, as something subject to intelligible reality by the will of the Creator, it sees these [intelligible] realities in a certain incorporeal light *sui generis,* just as the body's eye sees things in this corporeal light'. Hence it seems that just as the created light of corporeal reality is adequate for knowing sensible things so, likewise, a spiritual light of this same kind has been created with the cognitive power and this cognitive power is adequate for grasping intelligible reality.

Dionysius the Areopagite, the great author of the most sublime treatises on spiritual things, and one mentioned by the Apostle, speaks against the thesis of the master in his *Letter to Caius,* 'If anyone seeing God understood what he saw, he did not see Him, but some other being or truth. For God Himself is above intelligence and even above substance.' Hence in knowing our mind, at least in the present life, does not reach Uncreated Truth.

The Master's thesis is, last of all, contrary to the expressed opinion of the Philosopher. For the Philosopher says in the third book of his treatise *On the Soul* that 'our understanding is with the continuum and time', but these Eternal Reasons are above time and our intellect, therefore, does not reach these Reasons in its knowledge. The Philosopher in the same book states that 'in every nature there is something that makes all things and something else that becomes all things and thus we must posit, with regard to intelligence, that there is an agent intellect and a possible intellect'. But these intellectual processes are sufficient for perfect cognition and thus there is no need of the Divine Reason's aid.

John McCall:

There are two things which must be answered in what you have just said. The objections against St Augustine's reasoning must be answered and the authorities which you cited in your defense. The second of these are the more serious because the first are so simple that they hardly deserve to be answered.

To the objection that if the immutable truth is God, then the truth of a demonstrative principle would be God, and that all truths would be one, and that truths such as 2+2=4 would have to be adored: to all of these one reply can be made because all these objections are based on a single error. They fail to distinguish between truth that is immutable absolutely and truth that is immutable in relation to something higher. Now, when it is said that immutable truth is above the human mind, and is therefore God, this refers to absolutely changeless truth itself. But when it is said that the truth of a principle or a proposition about something created is immutable, it is evident that it is immutable only in relation to truth itself. For example, the proposition 2+2=4 is true, but it is not all truth nor is it truth itself. It is judged to be true in the light of truth itself, and so it cannot be God but is judged in the light of truth which is God.

And if it is objected that true propositions such as 2+2=4 are judged to be true in the human mind itself by itself, it must be said that since the mind itself is created and may err, it cannot derive absolute truth from itself. It draws truth from itself and from the world, but this is created truth which must be measured against truth itself to be known as true since created truths are not true *per se* but must be judged to be true. Such truths are not God, not one, nor to be adored. You are right to say that they are accessible even to demons. But do not mistake them for the absolute truth which can be clearly seen only by those who can enter into the innermost silence of their heart, and to this no sinner attains but he alone who is a supreme lover of God.

Proceeding now to the authorities which you advanced against the Master's thesis that whatever is known is known in the Divine Ideas can be answered one by one in this way.

To the first objection, drawn from St Paul's first letter to Timothy, to the effect that God dwells in light inaccessible, and thus man cannot attain to this light when he knows; this can be said: this text refers to access to the light of God in its fulness. In this sense it is true that no creature can see it except after death and in the glory of beatitude. But the Master does not maintain that our knowledge is in the light of God seen fully and in its entirety. And so your objection does not contradict his thesis.

This is made more clear in the consideration of your second objection drawn from St Augustine's *On the Trinity,* to the effect that 'the sight of the human mind is too weak to be focussed on so excellent a light', etc. To answer this we must distinguish between the way in which a man of wisdom attains to the Divine Ideas, and the way in which a man of science attains to them. For the man of wisdom attains to them as through contemplation by which he 'reposes' in them. And to this wisdom no one fully comes unless he first is fully 'cleansed by the righteousness of faith'. The man of science, however, attains to the ideas as things that draw him to them from afar. Augustine is right in saying that only the pure can see the Divine Light, but this refers to the way they are seen in wisdom, not to the way in which they are seen in science. And it is science that is being discussed here. The same answer can be made to your objection drawn from St Dionysius who does not deny that 'the true light which enlightens every man who comes into the world' is reached by our minds, but only in this life it is not fully seen.

In answer to your objections drawn from St Augustine's *On the Trinity,* chapters 9 and 12, to the effect that the soul acquires the truth of things through its own power of sensation, and that the soul acquires truth through a light which is the soul's own, I readily concede that what Augustine says here is true. But to say that the soul has its own powers does not exclude the possibility that these powers work only in cooperation with the power of God. The Master's thesis does not deny that each man draws his knowledge from the world through sensation, and uses the light of his own soul. But what is in question here is the ability of these powers *alone* to account for man's knowledge. Your objections do not touch on this issue, and so they do not contradict the master's thesis. They leave open the possibility, which we claim is a fact, that man's powers require the aid of a further light from God in order that it attain certain knowledge.

From this understanding, the answer to your objections drawn from the writings of Aristotle can be seen. We too can say with the Philosopher that man's understanding relates to time and place, and that man has an active and potential intellect. But this does not mean that man has his knowledge only from the world, nor does it mean that the active and potential intellects suffice to attain knowledge. As was said before, man's own personal powers are not excluded when we say that whatever we know we know in God's own light. These powers are simply held to be insufficient to attain certain knowledge without the aid of this divine light.

This can be made more clear by the following proofs drawn from reason alone:

To begin the first argument, we point to the fact that the soul can in fact turn toward truth outside of itself in the world by its own power, and by its own power it can also turn toward truth in itself which are our ideas. Now, we must recall that our ideas are more general in their nature than the truths which are outside the soul which are the particular things of the world. But above the general ideas within itself the soul can also consider truth itself, which is the highest most general idea because it contains all truths, not as a bag contains stones, but as an idea unifying all particular truths in the world or in the soul into a simple unity. Now, having called this to mind, we must also remember that Aristotle says in the tenth book of his *Metaphysics* that the simpler something is, the greater priority it has.[18] Therefore, the turning of the soul toward truth itself is naturally prior to its turning toward the less general truths in itself, or the even less general truths in the world. To say this does no injury to the soul's ability to turn toward itself or the world, but it means that it is impossible for the soul to know anything unless it first knows the highest truth of all, which is God's wisdom.

There is another argument to be made. As Aristotle teaches, man's intellect is a potency which must be reduced to act by means of an agent.[19] Thus man is said by Aristotle to have a 'potential' intellect and, since every being in potentiality must be reduced to act by means of something existing already in act in the same genus of being, man must also have an 'agent' intellect. The question is whether this agent intellect suffices to explain man's knowledge. That it is not can be proven in the following way: Either the agent intellect already understands what it learns, or it does not. If it does not, then it has not the power to reduce the potential intellect to act, and thus there would be no knowledge because man would totally lack the power to attain it. But if it is true that the agent intellect already understands what it learns, and thus is in act what is to be acquired, then there is in reality no such thing as learning because man would then already know everything. But this is patently absurd. Therefore, we cannot say that the potential and agent intellects suffice to explain the reality of man's knowledge.

I have another argument to prove this is so. Now, according to all the saints, God is said to be the teacher of all knowledge. This can only mean one of the following cases: either God cooperates in a general way with every intellect, as he does with all other creatures; or, secondly, God teaches by infusing knowledge as a gift of grace; or, thirdly, that the human intellect actually does attain to God when it knows truth. But if God teaches by cooperating with the creature in a general way only, then it would follow that he teaches the human senses in just the same way as he would teach the human intellect and therefore there would be no difference in the truth known by each of them. But this is clearly false, since the intellect knows universal truths such as the truths of mathematics, and the senses know particulars of the world in their truths. On the other hand, if it is held that God teaches because he infuses knowledge as a gift of grace, then all knowledge would be gratuitous and open only to the holy. But the evil of this world do, alas!, have knowledge, and so it cannot be said that God gives knowledge as he gives grace. This leaves us with the last alternative: that God is to be called our teacher because our intellect attains to him as to the light of our minds and the principle by which we know every truth.

T. Noone:

Now let us consider the matter from the viewpoint of reason. Firstly, experience teaches that as Aristotle states in the *Posterior Analytics* 'a memory is produced from repeated sensation of the same thing, and from many memories, one experience, and from repeated experiences, a universal

[notion]. The universal is the principle of arts and science'.
This dependence of intellection or sensation is equally clear
from the fact that those who lack one of the senses are
entirely ignorant of those things that are known through that
sense. A man who is blind from birth has no notion of blue or
anything else that comes through the sense of sight. It is obvious, then, that certain cognition in the present life comes
from the inferior, that is, the realm of sensation, and not from
the superior where the Eternal Reasons reside. Therefore, we
do not know things, as long as we are in our present condition,
in the Light of the Eternal Reasons.

Another argument from reason is that the imaginative cognition does not need a superior light or power. The power of
imagination is entirely adequate for producing images. If intellection is a higher power than imagination, then intellection
a fortiori will be adequate for understanding truth and the
Eternal Reasons are, thus, superfluous. The same argument
moreover can be made with regard to sensation.

J. McCall:

The answer to this argument of yours requires that I repeat
once more: To assert with Aristotle that knowledge comes
from experience simply means that the light of God is not the
only cause of our knowledge, but that the light of the soul
and the world also contribute to our acts of knowing. But it
does not follow from what you have said that the light of our
soul or the world or a combination of these suffice as the
foundation of our knowing. This argument of yours to this
effect is once again answered by pointing this out, as it was
answered some time ago by pointing out the same thing.

In this argument, you have supposed that imaginative
knowledge is the same as intellectual knowledge. Your argument depends on these two being the same. But this is not the
case, because imaginative cognition does not possess certitude,

and therefore it has no need of the divine light in which to
see the immutable. Only the immutable can serve as the base
of certitude, as was said before. Therefore, since only intellectual knowledge has certitude, only it has need of recourse
to God's light. Your argument is therefore false.

T. Noone:

The principles of being and knowing are the same, for as
the Philosopher states in the *Metaphysics,* 'in whatever way
something is related to being in that same way it is related to
truth'. If, therefore, the proper principles of being are *created*
principles, then whatever understanding we gain about them
must also be through created, and not uncreated, principles.
The *ratio* of our understanding corresponds proportionally to
each knowable thing with the result that certain knowledge is
obtained about that thing. The Eternal Reasons (if they are
the reasons by which we know) are not themselves distinctly
perceived by the intellect of the wayfarer; and so all knowledge that comes from them will be as unclear and confused
as our perception of these Eternal Reasons is.

According to the thesis of the Master whatever is understood with certitude is known in the Eternal Reasons. But just
as the Philosopher says in his *Posterior Analytics,* 'the cause
of an attribute's inherence in a subject always itself inheres in
the subject more firmly than the attribute', e.g., the cause of
our loving anything we hold dear is itself more dear to us than
the thing loved. If we apply this principle to the question, it
follows that the Eternal Reasons should be better known to
us than the things which we know through them. This position, however, is clearly incorrect.

Let us now follow out the simile given in support of the
Master's thesis. If we do know all things in the Eternal Reasons
do we know them in the way that we see objects in a mirror? This
cannot be an adequate question, however, because when we see

objects in a mirror we also see the mirror and if we should
know in the light of the Eternal Reasons we would also perceive the Eternal Reasons but this is clearly absurd.

Another problem with this view is that the Eternal Reasons
are always the same and are equally certain for things that are
contingent, necessary, present, future, etc. If we know in the
light of these Reasons, then, our knowledge should bear a like
certitude with regard to these diverse matters. It is clear, however, that our knowledge of what will occur tomorrow is not
anywhere near as certain as our knowledge of present things.
To use the Philosopher's example, the sea battle tomorrow
may or may not occur. Therefore our knowledge is not derived from the Eternal Reasons since it does not entail the
same certitude.

There are two final problems with the Master's thesis.
Firstly, the Eternal Reasons are the ultimate causes of things
and knowledge of them is wisdom. According to the Master's
thesis whatever is known is known in light of these Reasons,
hence, whoever knows or understands with certitude is wise
since he perceives the Eternal Reasons, the ultimate causes.

The second problem is similar to the first. If we do grant
that whatever is understood is known in the Eternal Reasons,
these Reasons would have to be known either as it were,
through a veil or without a veil. If through a veil, then all
knowledge is unclear and unstable. If without a veil then all
men see God, the Eternal exemplar, *absque omni aenigmitate*
which is clearly absurd.

J. McCall:

Your argument here is ingenious because surely I do not
want to deny that the principles of being are the same as the
principles of knowledge. To deny this is to deny that what we
know when we know is being or reality. But I can make the
reply to your argument that the principles of being are not

sufficient for full knowledge any more than they are sufficient for being. For if you say that they are sufficient for being, then you deny that God is needed as the creative principle of the being of the world. Therefore, although the principles of being are in fact the principles of knowledge also, they do not on that account exclude the primary ground of knowing from our knowledge any more than they exclude creation as the primary ground of the act of being. And so your argument does not contradict the Master's thesis that the primary ground of human knowledge is the Divine Wisdom.

It is a pleasure for me to say that for once I agree with you. You are right to say that each and every knowable object has its own proper principle of knowledge. But, alas, you are wrong to maintain that these principles are the whole ground of our knowledge. We do not see them with full distinctness in themselves, but along with them we require a created light of principles and likenesses of known objects from which we derive the proper principle of our knowledge of each and every thing that is known. Your argument, then, does not stand against the Master's thesis.

This argument of yours is useful only in pointing out how important it is to affirm that it is in conjunction with the created truth of principles, and not by itself alone, that the eternal truth moves us to knowledge. Thus it does not follow that truth itself is known to us in itself, but rather it is known to us as it shines forth in its created principles. Thus it is in a way most certain to us because our intellect simply cannot think that it does not exist. For instance, if we were to think that truth does not exist, then our thought 'truth does not exist' would be true. But then truth would exist. Now, this assuredly cannot be said of any created truth, but only of truth in itself. And so your argument fails.

This argument fails because it uses incorrectly the analogy drawn from a mirror. The point you draw from the analogy requires that the mirror represent something properly and distinctly, and this is evident only in a material mirror. But

these conditions do not apply to the eternal mirror as far as
those who have the vision of God are concerned. They see
God face to face and without a mirror. And we do not see the
Divine Ideas clearly and distinctly here on earth, but only, as
St Paul says: 'through a glass, darkly'. Therefore your argument does not invalidate the master's thesis because the 'mirror' meant by St Paul was not meant in a material way.

The answer to this objection is already obvious from what
we have said before: namely, that there is a great difference
between knowledge of the Ideas which the saints have in glory
and the knowledge which we have of the Ideas here below.
There we will see them clearly and distinctly (if we see our way
to God in his glory); here we see them 'through a glass, darkly'.
The Master's thesis does not require that the Ideas be seen in
their clarity here below, but only that we attain to them as a
regulating and motivating force in our knowledge.

This argument goes to the opposite extreme of the error in
your last two objections. You are right to insist on man's
inability in his present state to know anything in the eternal
reasons without a veil and without obscurity, but we must point
out that the reason for this weakness on man's part lies in
the obscurity of the image of God in man owing to sin. It does
not follow, however, that nothing is known with certitude or
clarity because the created principles of knowledge which are
the co-agents of human knowledge together with the Divine
Ideas can be seen by our mind clearly and without a veil. We
can only see the Divine Ideas through a veil and 'in a dark
manner', but this does not apply to our seeing the created
principles of things within our own souls and in the world
because our soul is on the same level as these. To draw an argument from our ability to see the Divine Ideas themselves only
through a veil, therefore, does not disprove the Master's thesis.
The master does not say that we see the Divine Ideas themselves, but only that we see them through our knowledge,
because it is true that whatever we know with certitude we
know in the Divine Ideas, which is not to say that we know

the Divine Ideas themselves.

E. Synan:

SOLUTIO

I answer that knowledge 'in the eternal reasons' can be understood in three ways.

A *first* way is to understand that the eternal reasons are the entire and only light in human knowing. This was the error of the first Academy—and where did it lead? Because we do not see directly those reasons, they fell into the scepticism of the new Academy (against whom Augustine wrote) and decided that we know nothing with certitude.

A *second* way is to say we do not attain to them at all, but are under their influence. This is as much as to say that Augustine was deceived! His authoritative texts cannot easily be dragged in that direction! How absurd to say this about so great a Father of the Church and, among all the expositors of sacred Scripture, the most authoritative. Besides, that 'influence': if 'general', then God ought no more to be called the 'Giver of Wisdom' than 'Giver of good crops' nor would knowledge be said to come from him any more than does money! If 'special', (as is grace) then all knowledge would be infused, poured into us—none acquired, none innate. Every point of this is false.

A *third* and the right way is to say that eternal reason is required as regulating and motivating our created rationality, not as the sole reason, nor in all its own proper clarity, but *with* created reason and partially contuited by us in accord with our wayfaring state. Augustine insinuated as much in his *On the Trinity* 14.14.

Two considerations compel this solution: the nobility of knowledge and the dignity of the human knower.

The *nobility of knowledge* implies immutability from the side of what can be known and, from the side of the one who

knows, infallibility. Created truth fails the first requirement,
for nothing created is of itself immutable; the light of created
reason fails the second requirement, for nothing created is of
itself infallible. Recourse must be had, therefore, to the Truth
that is immutable and to the Light that is infallible—to the
transcendent 'Art', that is, to the divine Being as containing
the intelligibility of what is to be created in all its multiplicity
and variety.

The *dignity of the one who knows:* A human is possessed
of a higher and lower reason; the superior of these is the
'image' of God and by this we adhere to the eternal reasons;
thanks to this we judge with certitude. For creatures are
images and footprints and similitudes of God; image as related
to God as to one's Object; footprint as compared to God as
to the Principle of all that is; similitude if one in whom God
dwells, be united to Him by an infused gift, that is, by grace.

In this state of wayfarer a human does truly know, but not
clearly, not fully, not distinctly—one knows in proportion to
one's similitude to God, in proportion to one's innocence; in a
state of sin, then in a darksome way. In the glory of the
world to come, however, when truly deiform, we shall know
with fullness and with clarity.

Finally, the whole soul does not 'know' and so it is that
one must abstract from fantasy in knowing things . . . .

NOTES

1. *Doctoris seraphici s. Bonaventurae . . . opera omnia.* (Quaracchi: Collegium s. Bonaventurae, 1891) t. 5: pp. 17-27.
2. *A Scholastic Miscellany: Anselm to Ockham,* ed. and tr. E.R. Fairweather (London: SCM Press, 1956) The Library of Christian Classics, Vol. 10: 379-401.
3. Alan of Lille, *De fide catholica* 1. 30; PL 210, 333 A: 'Auctoritas cereum habet nasum, id est, in diversum potest flecti sensum.'
4. J.D.M. Derett, ' "Withermam." A Legal Practical Joke of Sir Thomas More' *The Catholic Lawyer* 7 (1961) 211-242.
5. Augustine, *De libero arbitrio,* 2.14.38 (PL 32:1262).
6. Augustine, *De vera religione,* 30.56 to 31.57 (PL 34:147).
7. Augustine, *Confessiones,* 12.25.35 (CSEL 33:336).
8. Augustine, *De trinitate,* 14.15.21 (PL 42:1052).
9. Augustine, *De civitate Dei,* 8.7 (CSEL 40:336).
10. Augustine, *De trinitate,* 9.6.10 (PL 42:966).
11. As Father Fairweather points out, this fragment is described by Migne (PL 42:1150) as coming from the *Soliloquies* of Augustine. Cf. *A Scholastic Miscellany,* p. 381, n. 19.
12. Gregory, *Homil. in evang.,* 2.30.3 (PL 76:1222).
13. Anselm, *Proslogion,* 14.
14. Isaac of Stella, *De anima,* (PL 194:1888).
15. The sources of these arguments can be found respectively in: *De lib. arb.,* 2.9.25 to 2.15.39 (PL 32:1253-62): *De vera religione,* 30.54 to 32.59 (PL 34:145-49); *De musica* 6.12.35 (PL 32:1182f).
16. Augustine, *De libero arbitrio,* 2.8.20ff. (PL 32:1251-53), and *De trin.,* 9.8.12ff (PL 42:994-97).
17. *De trin.,* 8.6.9 (PL 42:953-56).
18. Aristotle, *Metaphysics,* 10.1, 1059b34-36.
19. Aristotle, *Metaphysics,* 8.8, 1049b23-27.

MONASTIC AND SCHOLASTIC THEOLOGY
IN THE REFORMERS
OF THE
FOURTEENTH TO SIXTEENTH CENTURY
Jean Leclercq OSB

T HE PROBLEM of the connections between 'cloister' and 'school', symbolising two approaches to truth, has very ancient origins: it is almost as old as monasticism itself and we even find some of its roots in St Augustine.[1] In the West, the problem was very clearly set forth in the twelfth century and has persisted ever since. It will be dealt with in this paper within certain well-defined limits. The first are chronological: the period of the fourteenth to the sixteenth century, during which there was a transition—already prepared in the thirteenth century—from one society, Church and culture, in which monastic institutions held a prominent place, to another. Within this period we shall deal only with the trends of reform which were extremely important in this evolution. And even here we shall not be able to describe all the reforms: we shall attend simply to the more typical ones. They will be dealt with in the order in which they occurred.

It is necessary to distinguish the characteristic features of each trend from both an historical and a geographical point of view and to stress the common features. They have already been studied in well-documented works, and we shall not pretend to do something new here. We are simply giving an inventory of results already reached.

A survey of this kind has more than an historical interest linked solely with knowledge of the past. There is something topical about it, for today new perspectives have been opened up in theology and from these three major points have emerged. Theologians like Lonergan, Rahner and others, first of all, have drawn our attention less to the 'essential' character of religious facts and more to the 'mysteries' which these doctrines attempt to express.[2] Furthermore, the imagination is recognized as having an important part to play along with reason as an instrument in the development of knowledge.[3] Lastly, the bond which ought to exist between 'theology' and 'spirituality' answers to a concern being felt today by many persons.[4]

Now, these three aspects of the problem were already present in the twelfth century. They are intricate, difficult to define, and even more difficult to express. Today, as yesterday, the first problem which crops up has to do with vocabulary. In order to characterize the specific and relative tendencies of both cloister and school, writers use words like *philosophia christiana*,[5] 'kerygmatic' or 'contemplative' theology for the cloister and 'active' or 'pastoral' theology for the school.[6] Or again, a distinction is made between *sentio* and *disco*. It is almost impossible to sum up in a few words these different frames of mind, each of which is very rich. About the first, and its difference from the second, the expression 'monastic theology', proposed several years ago, has been largely accepted. It has suggested the title of a book[7] and has become a bibliographic heading.[8] It has also been the subject matter of successive chronicles and publications the most recent of which dates from 1982.[9] It has also been confirmed by several research projects conducted independently of one another about purgatory,[10] marriage,[11] and man's attitude to the feminine.[12]

In the thirteenth century, the problem became more complex to the extent that it was asked whether or not theology is a science and, if it is, in what way.[13] The great Doctors of the mid-thirteenth century and the following decades were able to maintain an enviable balance between monastic theology and the scholastic method. The application of the aristotelian notion of science made by St Thomas and his contemporaries to theology is inspiring more and more new interpretations.[14] One of the most recent of these acknowledges that Hervé Natalis, a disciple of St Thomas, adhered to the opinion expressed by his master in his Prologue to the Sentences: 'Theology is not a science, *simpliciter* and strictly speaking, nor even properly speaking, a subsidieary science'.[15] This was also the position defended by several thomists of the same period.[16] However that may be, the prevailing temptation at that time was to gratify oneself with 'useless questions affectioned by the doctors' of the day. The study of law, that is to say, canon law, also held an attraction considered by some to be harmful.[17] And it was in order to ward off such dangers, from monks and others, that reformers were forever popping up.

THE FOURTEENTH CENTURY

New facts.

In the first half of the fourteenth century, two new facts orient all subsequent evolution: one is on the level of ideas, the other concerns legislation. The former is linked up with a Franciscan from Oxford, John Duns Scotus,[18] and follows in the wake of a crisis which occurred after the zenith period of St Thomas. He and others, in particular Henry of Ghent, had drawn up a series of syntheses between the traditional teaching of the Church and a form of aristotelianism, mixed with platonism, interpreted by the Arabs and brought to Paris via Spain. This set of philosophical ideas used to be called 'averroism', but today scholars prefer to call it 'integral aristotelianism'. In 1277, the bishop of Paris, Étienne Tempier, condemned certain propositions inspired by this philosophy, some of which had been taken from St Thomas. In the next generation, until the end of the thirteenth century, admirers and adversaries of earlier syntheses clashed in what Maurice de Wulf in his teaching called 'the mêlée of the masters'. This helped give theological research a certain subtle and very controversial tone. It was from this milieu that Duns Scotus called the 'subtle doctor', emerged. His own synthesis, in its turn, lies at the origin of a set of ideas called nominalism. The most illustrious representative of this school of thought is another Franciscan, William of Occam. He too was accused and he defended himself in the course of a lawsuit held at Avignon from 1324–1329. In the process he came to attack pope John XXII and his successor, Benedict XII, in writings which touch on philosophy, theology, and politics all at once. This is not the moment to analyze the content of these writings. The important thing to notice is that discussions of this kind gave new meaning to the 'monastic–scholastic' issue: the ideas being debated came to be less and less directly concerned with the facts of revelation, and the method used in debate gave more and more place to abstraction. Both ideas and method gave rise to unceasing polemics.

The question of the connection between scholasticism and monastic studies still had some elements in common with the general problematic of the twelfth century, the century during which it had been set out very clearly for the first time. New elements had come up, however, and had to be taken into account. The doctrinal contribution made by the major syntheses of the thirteenth century could not be ignored: monastic and scholastic theology were in no greater opposition than previously: they continued to be distinct from one another as they had been in the past, but the difference between them was more marked. It became increasingly more difficult to wed them together harmoniously: monastic circles were menaced with slipping into ignorance and the schools with excessive reasoning.

It was then that, for the first time in the history of the Church, a pope intervened on the legislative level and proposed—even imposed—a *ratio studiorum,* a programme of studies for monks. With this, became what had theretofore been latent, diffused, sometimes confused, and susceptible of only practical solutions the object of clear-cut distinctions, doctrinal justifications, and well-defined norms. Benedict XII made an institutional application of what had so far been simply a difference of intellectual attitudes between monasticism and scholasticism.

The pope's short pontificate (1334–1342) was decisive in this area.[19] Already in the year following his election, in 1335, he promulgated four decretals which aimed at reforming the monastic Orders. One of these decretals, the *Summi magistri,* has been given the name of *Benedictina,* not because it was addressed to 'the Benedictines', for they had not yet been so baptized and were known simply as the 'Black monks', but in memory of its author, pope Benedict. Another text, addressed to the Cistercians, *Fulgens sicut stella,* followed on a few weeks later. The first continues to be the basic document. A Cistercian, a doctor in theology of Paris, but really better versed in canon law, Benedict XII attempted to put some order into all the institutes of claustral life. In his mind, there was no clear distinction between monks and regular canons (when he wrote for canons he went back to the text he wrote for the black monks and simply replaced the words referring to monks and their superiors by 'canons' and 'prelates').[20] Within the monastic Orders, properly speaking, an evolution had taken place which had led some monks to take on pastoral work of a priestly nature. The legislator took this into account, but it was something which had not crept in among Cistercians. Consequently, the pope reiterated the prohibition already made in the thirteenth century forbidding Cistercians to study canon law. He authorized the black monks to do so only on condition that first place be given to theology.

He laid down that abbots of all Orders should send subjects to attend university colleges, especially those in Paris. On the whole this prescription remained without effect. Why? First and foremost because the structure of monastic institutions was not centralized as was that of the mendicant Orders. Each abbey or priory was autonomous.[21] This did not favor a system which required, in particular, the pooling of financial resources.[22] There was, however, another and deeper reason: at the root of the situation we notice 'the tension between "monastic" and "scholastic".'[23] Since the thirteenth century it had been clear that there was a typology distinguishing the 'contemplative life' of the monks from the 'active life' of those—religious or others—who by profession and by vocation devoted themselves to pastoral activity. The former had to lead an inactive life, *vita inactiva,* and the latter were inclined to despise them for this: *simplicitatem claustralium deridebant.*[24]

It would be interesting to study this problem and the application of the solution laid down by Benedict XII in various regions and generations. Social, political, and economical factors intervened to a greater or lesser degree in certain situations. The black monks had been accorded the 'privilege' of a dispensation from one of the fundamental requirements of the Rule of St Benedict: equality between nobles and the poor.[25] Aptitude for studies could become a restriction for recruitment.[26] Whatever the practical results, the position of monasticism in the general typology of the religious life was now well-defined by the decretals: monks who had no pastoral activity were described as 'ascetic' and 'contemplative'; the others were described as clerical, ecclesiastical, hierarchical, and, in the field of cultural activity, intellectual. Benedict XII proposed a compromise between the two. In ordering certain monks to pursue scholastic studies, he paved the way for what has been called their 'Akademisierung' and 'Scholasticisierung', which 'represents, without any doubt, a break with the previous monastic world'.[27] History has proved that, on the whole, the monks and spiritual leaders of the two ensuing centuries had a healthy reaction in favor of their traditional identity.

Final orientations.

There is no need here to go through all the chronological stages of this on-going evolution in ideas, institutions, and texts. Many a name could be cited: this history has already been related.[28] We need only recall a few representative figures.

At the beginning of the fourteenth century there was an event which is a sort of symbol: in 1302 one of Scot's bachelors in a dispute at Paris opposed his master's ideas to those of a saxon dominican, Eckart.[29] Following this, two distinct trends of thought made their appearance and have never ceased to occupy the scene. One of them, which we may call 'spiritual', was evidenced by writers like Tauler, Suso, and Ruysbroek; the other, styled 'humanist', was promoted by Petrarch, Gerson, Ficino, and Pico de la Mirandola.[30] There may have been differences between some of these thinkers on particular points of doctrine, but they were unanimous in criticizing scholasticism. They were generally not to be found in monastic instiutions of the benedictine tradition: always in the background and sometimes to the fore is the Charterhouse. But the opposite of scholasticism is what one of their best historians has called 'monastic theology'.[31]

To sum up in a few words the reproaches they hurled against scholasticism we may mention its exclusive taste for abstraction, precision of concepts, priority given to objective knowledge; its rationalism, dryness, subtlety; its search for systematic thought, its sterile discussions between rival systems. On the other hand, a 'spiritual philosophy' they expected to consider the concrete, the historical fact, actual experience; the existential, the affective; personal relations with God. The models of this attitude were the persons who

in the patristic and monastic tradition had searched the
Scriptures—St Bernard is mentioned and stressed—and their
followers in the franciscan tradition up to and including St Bonaventure. The supporters of this opinion rejected neither
theology nor speculation: some of them taught a 'speculative
mysticism'. There dawned, however, a growing hostility to
the University, for it swayed minds and institutions, opening as it did the way to church careers.

THE FIFTEENTH AND THE SIXTEENTH CENTURIES.
Italian monastic reformers.

These are represented by Jerome Alioti, born in 1412. He
became a Benedictine at Arezzo at the age of eighteen, and
two years later wrote his first treatise *On the happy state of
the monastic life.*[32] He had a fairly eventful existence at the
time of the Councils of Basel, Ferrara, and Florence. He fell
into the temptation which seems to have been frequent, even
normal, for italian abbots, and became a bishop. In spite of
his endeavors in several towns, however, he did not have much
success. He was closely united to the milieu of Ambrose Tra-
versari and the humanist Camaldolese monks of Florence.
When he died in 1480 his most striking work was still his
treatise *On the Formation of Monks (De monachis erudiendis),*
which he composed in 1441. The teaching he sets out there is
completed by his other texts, especially his letters.

His aim was not to take up a stand against scholasticism and
university studies, but to remedy the deficiencies of monasticism in his time and country. In particular, he wanted to
remedy the ignorance, the *indocta simplicitas,* of monasticism.
On the other hand, however, he does not want monks to fall
into the 'subtleties', the 'distinctions', the 'vain curiosity'
which he combats in words very similar to the terms used by
St Bernard. He was very aware of the distinction between the
monks and the mendicant friars of his time, Dominicans and
Franciscans who, because oriented to pastoral activity, had to
go through preparatory studies. Monks were to seek union with

God, contemplative wisdom, by searching the Scriptures by a
lectio which was real study and a *meditatio* which stirred up
their faith in Christ and their knowledge of his mysteries. And,
as St Bernard had already taught, this science prepared them to
refute heresies.[33] Such studies require time. Alioti protested
against anything added on to the Divine Office; he was in
favor of shorter but more fervent services. His sources and
models were the Fathers of the Church: he quotes, among
others, St Basil, St Benedict, St Gregory, and St Bernard. In
short, he was an authentic representative of the monastic
tradition; but he belonged to his own century and no longer
to the twelfth. The fundamental convictions were the same,
but an historical evolution had taken place, and he noticed
this, not so much in the development of scholasticism as in
the progress of humanism. He did not aim at forming doctor-
monks, but educated, cultured, even well-read monks whose
theological knowledge would be in keeping with their life of
prayer.

    In the next generation, Paul Giustiniani, before becoming a
camaldolese monk in Tuscany in 1510, was, until the age of
thirty-three, imbued with ancient greek and latin literature,
especially stoic philosophy. Once converted, this humanist
repudiated his sources: he wrote:

> What need do we still have then to read Aristotle's
> *Ethics, Economics* and *Politics*? Shall we dare to com-
> pare the *Dialogues* of Plato with holy Scripture and
> the letters of Cicero with those of St Paul? In the
> Psalms all the rules of eloquence are observed. All the
> knowledge we seek, the rules of conduct we need
> are found in Holy Scripture and it is only there that
> they are fully found.

Compared with the 'ancient theology of the Fathers', 'new
theology, that of Paris, the one that proceeds by questions',
he considered very corrupt, nothing but a series of disputes

for the pleasure or the glory of discussion, a web of subtle and useless arguments. This science had become more a science of logic, physics, or metaphysics than a science of theology.

> I will now close this discourse and this notebook
> with a healthy sentence: if someone wants to love
> God, let him give up the vanities of all other disci-
> plines, and let him read attentively the true theology
> of Christians in antiquity. But, in my opinion, the
> man who gives himself to new theology and wishes
> to draw love out of it is working in vain.

The discredit that we see thrown on scholasticism here was not applied to St Thomas. On more than one occasion, Giusti-niani tells of his esteem for St Thomas and all that he had received from him. But we can notice here how a humanist accustomed to frequenting the sources, and studying Plato, Plotinius, and Aristotle in their own texts, reacted to a purely speculative theology which was no longer in touch with pa-tristic writings. The Fathers spoke to Giustiniani of sacred mysteries and in them he found more reasons for loving God than he did in abstract discussions saturated with philosophy.[34] And, like so many others, he was fond of St. Bernard.[35]

German monastic reformers.
The most illustrious of the german monastics reformers was John Trithemius and what his most recent historians call his 'monastic theology'.[36] Born in 1462 and becoming a Bene-dictine at the age of twenty, he was elected abbot a little later. Up to his death in 1516, he was one of the driving forces of the reform of the Congregation of Bursfeld. Noticing that cer-tain 'learned people' (*docti*) got lost in vice, he saw 'simpli-city'[37] as the characteristic of monks: *'Nos in simplicitate nostra . . . '*. He believed in the importance of books—both the reading and the making of them; his praise of the role of the copyist and the writer in the Church is very similar to

what Peter the Venerable said.[38] If monks are to do pastoral
work, in his opinion, they must prepare for it by suitable
studies. But more often he insisted on the importance of
lectio divina as a means of acquiring a sort of spiritual understanding of Holy Scripture. He insisted on the primacy of
love. With St Bernard he denounced 'curiosity' and advocated
the 'true philosophy' of Christians: 'affective knowledge'
which commits the whole man.[39] For Trithemius, too, the
models run from Origen to St Bernard:[40] like other reformers
he considered patristics as including more than antiquity and
extending into the middle ages: he names authors of the
seventh, eighth and ninth centuries, as well as Peter Damian
and St Anselm.[41]

In one of his treatises Trithemius makes a very clear distinction between two 'theologies' and points out differences
which he found in the writings of Ps-Dionysius the Areopagite.
One of these theologies is 'speculative, we call it scholasticisim:
it is conceptual, philosophic, useful for stirring the soul to
love'. But it can degenerate into 'battalogia'. The other is
'mystical', 'we acquire it by the workings of a purified heart
(*affectus*), it is the fire of love which teaches it'. And he adds:
'Such is your theology, you who live in the cloisters . . . *Haec
est theologia vestra, claustrales . . .* ' .[42] More than once in his
writings he described the characteristics of this theology, but
he added nothing new to what St Bernard had already said:
he is simply wordier.[43] In his writings we find no radical
opposition to scholasticism but he had a very marked preference for mystical and affective theology. What Trithemius
proposed was a biblical humanism.[44]

Other writers went further. John Keck, abbot of Tegernsee,
launched into a violent diatribe against the scholastics. This
purple passage, amusing in its excessiveness, is worth quoting
because it contains accusations found in other authors too:

> Inde tanta sectarium varietas, inde briga et contentio
> eorum, quorum hii Thomestarum, hii Albertistarum, illi

Scotistarum, alii Ochamistarum sectam profitentur.
Qui magis utique a se differe, distare seu dissonare
videntur, quam patres illi, quorum se discipulos
gloriantur aut imitatores. Non potest utique hec
eorum tam contentiosa sapientia esse desursum
descendens . . . Nec placet honorem illum scripturis
beati Thome, Alberti Magni, Scoti, Ocham et similium
impendere, qui solis scripturarum libris, qui canonici
appelantur, est exhibendus, ut scilicet eorum auctorem
nullum scibendo errasse aliquid firmissime credamus.[45]

Humanist reformers.

There were many in France and elsewhere, for 'humanism'
was not limited to Italy.[46] We cannot deal with all of them so
we shall select only a few who are representative of successive
generations, different countries and circumstances. They all
have in common a close connections with monastic institutions: with Carthusians in the case of Petrarch and others:[47]
with Cluny, which several of them entered, in France.[48] The
esteem they had for monasticism caused them a certain sorrow at seeing studies neglected; some of the monks were quite
ignorant, others were following scholasticism as it was practised at that time. What did these reformers want to put in
its place?

> Quite simply the 'monastic theology' which was
> current before the diffusion of scholasticism and
> whose most illustrious and typical representative
> is St Bernard. The advocates of this theology fought,
> in the twelfth century, against the development of
> scholasticism exactly as did the christian humanists
> and the spirituals after Petrarch and Gerson, and for
> the same reasons. The humanists found their struggles
> and aspirations in the monks of the twelfth century.
> The quarrel between St Bernard and Abelard fired
> up again, so to speak, and the humanists took sides

with the abbot of Clairvaux.[49]

The man who set the tone in France from the end of the fourteenth century on was John Gerson (1363–1429) of the University of Paris. He even became chancellor in 1395. And yet these words are considered appropriate for situating him in history: 'Gerson and St Bernard: the fifteenth century recognized itself in the twelfth. Between the two, a common enemy: scholasticism'.[50] Together with Bernard he condemned the wrong use of *curiositas*.[51] His position may be summed up in these few lines he wrote to the Celestines:

> *Linque quaestiones scholasticas quae erudiunt*
> *intellectum; satis tibi sint regulares nostrae*
> *observantiae quae accendere debent affectum.*[52]

In the same line, with shades and variations, we find Nicholas of Cusa and others.[53] Erasmus (1466–1536) was their most distinguished spokesman. His teaching has been carefully studied and historians agree in discerning in him the same dilemma between 'monastic' and 'scholastic'.[54] He is more severe than others on St Thomas.[55] His opinion on monastic studies is amply treated in his letter to the benedictine abbot Paul Volz.[56]

Jesse Clichtove, his contemporary (1472–1543), has been studied in two learned books by Jean–Pierre Massaut.[57] Clichtove was a 'humanist' theologian and another admirer of the theology of St Bernard.[58] 'A certain type of life, the monastic kind, is necessary for theological work as recommended by Clichtove'.[59] He 'combats the scholastic methods at the Faculty of arts' and, in theology he reproached them for 'abandoning the Scriptures, getting lost in uncertain commentaries, the confusion of "questions" proliferating into "quibbling" and turbulent "disputes", far from silent meditation and inner prayer, pride of the spirit and sterility of

practice, an arid, cold, bristly and off-putting style'.[60] The
work of St Thomas was not like that: Clichtove exhorted
Dominicans to prefer his 'silence' to 'the noisy discussions
which overwhelm even the ears of the walls'.[61] After that he
'calls the monks to the Universities'. For two reasons. First, he
believed 'that good scholastic theology is possible on the
condition it goes back to its golden age, and takes its inspiration from its best representatives, in the case in point,
St Thomas'.[62] Then he

> claimed to reform, or rather transform, the Univer-
> sities, especially the faculties of arts and theology,
> by introducing the ancient monastic culture, very
> precisely 'monastic theology', with its intellectual
> equipment, its spiritual climate, its mental back-
> ground and even its system of concrete living.[63]

Protestant reformers.

It is well-known that Luther held in great esteem St Bernard
and the theology he represented. An historian writes of Calvin
that he 'saw Bernard as a representative of the pure Augustinian
tradition in opposition to decadent scholasticism'. Calvin's
doctrine was not new but rather 'the doctrine which Augustine taught which was shut up in the cloisters of monks for
almost a thousand years. It was Peter Lombard who opened
the door to "pernicious error". The implication is that
Bernard is the witness of Augustinianism during the middle
ages, in opposition to scholastic error'.[64]

The Council of Trent.

Already in the Council's first session, May 28, 1546, a fairly
animated discussion arose about obliging all monks to attend
lessons on Holy Scripture. The abbot of Saint Justine of Padua
asked that the *cavillas scolasticorum cavillationes* be rejected,
'for', he said, 'scholastic lessons like that generally give rise
to discord and must be ruled out for monks'.[65] Once again the

carthusian model was proposed, for it was considered the
perfect example of the monastic attitude. The dominican
Suso reasserted that for knowing Scripture well nothing is
more useful than the 'scholastic way', so much so that if
religious were dispensed from it 'nothing could more rejoice
the very Protestants'.[66] In the debate which followed, some
maintained that Scripture could be understood and heresies
refuted without scholasticism, while others held that it was
indispensable 'on condition it remain a handmaid and not
the mistress.[67] The abbot of Cava even went so far as to
'condemn scholastic discipline'.[68] The majority of the fathers
who spoke 'praised scholasticism' but asked that it not be
imposed on monks. Thus the difference between monastic
and scholastic studies was maintained. It was not an opposition. But the abbot of Cava was able to argue the distinction
by reading 'reasons drawn from canons and councils'.[69] These
arguments pleased the 'General of the Hermits' but he asked
that mention of 'scholastic conflicts' be avoided. He added—
and with that the debate was closed—'may vain disputes be
ruled out for every religious'.[70] Thus scholasticism as such
was acknowledged to be good and necessary, but it was an
accepted thing that it gave rise to useless controversies and
these were judged to be incompatible with a monk's spiritual
life.

CONCLUSIONS

Constants and questions.
    The historical sketch which has been made here allows us
to notice certain constant elements in the past and suggests
questions about the future.
    In the period extending from the fourteenth to the
sixteenth centuries, reformers—who were never lacking—
agreed with the humanists and opposed scholasticism; thus
scholasticism would seem contrary both to reform and to
humanism.

They were opposed to scholasticism not for what it was in itself and as it had been practised in the past, but in the form it took in their own day. They advocated returning to a theology that was in keeping with ancient and medieval patristics, in particular that of the twelfth century. They were unanimous in placing St Bernard among the Fathers, the last of the Fathers.[71] Among the representatives of scholasticism in its golden age, the thirteenth century, the majority of reformers had great admiration for St Thomas and everyone admired St Bonaventure. They laid the blame on their successors, sometimes the 'thomists', more often the 'scottists' and the 'occamists'.

The reproach most frequently hurled at scholasticism, the charge of getting lost in too many subtle and futile questions, had already been very clearly stated—and not without humor— by St Thomas himself. It was, in fact, in reaction to this devia- tion that he stated writing his *Summa Theologica:*

> We have indeed noticed that in using the existing works in this matter, novices are greatly hindered now by the useless multiplication of questions, articles and proofs; now because instead of following an order of disci- pline, one is caught up in the heat of commentaries or the hazards of dispute. In both instances one is led to frequent repetition which engenders confusion and lassitude in the mind.[72]

A constant theme in this whole evolution is the criticism of *curiositas,* with reference made to what St Bernard had written in his treatise *On the Steps of Humility and Pride.* Bernard also mentioned it in various other places as well, and his very complex teaching on this point deserves to be known thoroughly.[73]

Something common to all reformers, and to humanists as a whole, was their loving commitment to Jesus Christ. The abstract discussions of a certain kind of scholasticism they considered distractions. From this point of view the 'christocentrism' of Erasmus has an exemplary value.[74]

The conflict in all this was not between knowledge and ignorance—non-knowledge, anti-knowledge—to which some people today feel attracted,[75] but arose rather over the strict application to theology of the aristotelian idea of science, as it was then thought of. In our day several people think, rightly, that theology truly is a science, not in the ancient meaning of the word, but as it is presented by Lonergan and others.

We have then two forms of religious knowledge symbolized by two traditions, that of the schools and that of the cloister. And it is there, precisely, that lies the topicality of the problem today. On the one hand, for example, a review of several books on the sacraments has been given the title *Feu la scholastique* and it ends with this epitaph *Sic transit theologia scolastica.*[76] On the other hand, other voices are being raised (not only among the monks)[77] in favor of 'monastic theology'.[78]

We must, however, be careful not to misunderstand this expression. It does not mean that we are dispensed from doing real theology, nor should it lead us to think that this is merely an easy form of affective piety. We could just as easily say that scholasticism, if the method is applied to the letter, dispenses us from personal reflection. Between these two approaches to truth we must find some way of making a synthesis. We could say that in the twelfth century the situation was neatly summed up in three words: 'monastic *and* scholastic'; far from there being an opposition between them, at that time they profited one another and yet remained distinct. In the thirteenth century, it seems that, when faced with a choice between 'monastic *or* scholastic', the greatest minds chose the latter. But because of the way things developed, there arose in the fourteenth and fifteenth centuries a clash, 'monastic *versus* scholastic'. Still later, one often gets the impression of a 'scholastic *without* monastic' theology. Perhaps the real problem is how to fit 'monastic *within* scholastic' and 'scholastic *within* monastic'.[79]

Clervaux, Luxembourg

NOTES

1. Alfonso Pompei, OFM Conv., 'I "Sermones" di s. Antonio e la teologia francescana', in Antonio Poppi, ed., *Le fonti et la teologia dei sermoni Antoniani,* Atti del Congresso internazionale di studio sui "Sermones" di S. Antonio di Padova (Padua, 1982) 765.

2. Matthias Newman, OSB, 'The religious Structure of a Spirituality', in *American Benedictine Review,* 33 (1982) 115-148.

3. William V. Dych, 'Theology and the Imagination', in *Thought. A Review of Culture and Idea,* 57 (1982) 116-127. This number of Thought is entitled Faith and Imagination Issue.

3. Thomas Franklin O'Meara, OP, 'Creative Imagination: The Aesthetic Horizon in Theology', in Luke Salm, FSC, ed., *The Catholic Theological Association of America. Proceedings of the Thirty-Sixth Annual Convention,* (Bronx, New York, 1981) 83-97. The bibliography on this subject is constantly increasing.

4. Andrew Louth, *Theology and Spirituality* (Oxford: SLG Press, 1981). See also the article quoted above, note 2. Current interest in the theme of the 'school' of Christ, of the Holy Spirit, of charity, of christian philosophy, may be seen in the fact that recently, following a program of monastic studies there is an anthology composed of eight cistercian texts of the twelfth century, in some of which what is to be learnt in this school is contrasted with the reasonings of Aristotle and syllogisms: Bernardo Olivera, OCSO, 'Plan de formacion monastico Cisterciense', in *Cuadernos monásticos* 17 (1982) 173-174: 'La escuela monastica'.

5. Michael Casey, OCSO, 'Leadership in a Benedictine Tradition. An Interrogation of Tradition', in *Ijurunga. An Australasian Benedictine Review* (March, 1982) 22, describes monastic theology.

6. Such characteristics are set out at the beginning of the important article of Jean-Pierre Massaut, 'Humanisme et spiritualité du 14e au 16e siècle, in *Dictionnaire de spiritualité,* VII 1 (Paris, 1969) col. 990.

7. Odo Brooke, OSB, *Studies in Monastic Theology,* Cistercian Publications, Kalamazoo, Mich., 1980.

8. *The Way,* 19 (1979) 164-165.

9. 'Desiderió e intelletto. La teologia monastica', in I. Biffi–C. Marabelli, *Invito al medioevo,* (Milan, 1982) 47-56. To the references given there describing 'monastic theology' as a category fitting the historical situation of the twelfth century, we may add others: Ulrich Kopf, *Die Anfänge der theologischen Wissenschaftstheologie im 13.Jahrhundert,* (Tübingen: J. C. B. Mohr, 1974) 8-15, 27-29; Joachim Ehfers, 'Monas-

tische Theologie, historischer Sinn und Dialektik', in A. Zimmerman, *Antiqui et moderni,* (Berlin, 1974) 64-69, 74-79; François Petit, *Norbert et l'origine des Prémontrés* (Paris, 1981) 71 and 92; Joachim Ehfers, 'Die hohen Schulen', in Peter Weimer, ed., *Die Renaissance der Wissenschaften im 12.Jahrhundert,* Zürcher Hochschulforum, 2, Zürich–Munich: Artemis Verlag, 1981) 67; David N. Bell, 'Baldwin of Ford and Twelfth-Century Theology', in E. R. Elder, ed., *Noble Piety and Reformed Monasticism.* Studies in Medieval Cistercian History VII, (Kalamazoo, Mich.: Cistercian Publications, 1981) 136-142; *Renaissance and Renewal in the Twelfth Century,* ed. by Robert L. Benson–Giles Constable with Carol D. Lunham, (Cambridge, Mass.: Harvard University Press, 1982) where I have dealt with 'The Renewal of Theology', p. 68-87. The concept of monastic theology is applied to Peter Damian by Giuseppte Fornasari, 'Pier Damiani e Gregorio VII: dall'ecclesiologia "monastica" all'ecclesiologia "politica",' in *Fonte Avellana nel suo millenio* I, *Le origini* (Fonte Avellana, 1982) 151-244, in particular p. 199.

10.   Jacques Le Goff, *La naissance du purgatoire* (Paris: Gallimard, 1981) p. 295.
11.   J. Leclercq, *Monks on Marriage. A Twelfth Century View* (New York: Seabury, 1982) *passim.*
12.   J. Leclercq, *S. Bernard et les femmes* (Paris, 1982), p. 113-128.
13.   A bibliography is given in *Invito al medioevo* (n. 9).
14.   Denis J.M. Bradley, 'Aristotelian Science and the Science of Thomistic Theology', in *The Heythrop Journal,* 22 (1981) 162-171; Vittorio Sainati, *Il problema della teologia nell'età di S. Tommaso,* Biblioteca di cultura contemporanea, ed., G. D. Anna, (Florence: Messina, 1977). On the problems of the "Verwissenschaftlichung' of theologies in St Thomas and today, see the bibliography in Peter Eicher *et al., Die Theologie und das Lehramt,* hg. von Walter Kern, (Freiburg im Br.: Herder, 1982) 26-28.
15.   Cited by Louis Sturlese in his review of Sainati, in *Studi medievali,* 21 (1980) 989.
16.   Under the title 'La théologie comme science dans la littérature quodlibétique', in *Recherches de théologie ancienne et médiévale,* 11 (1939) 351-374, I have published several of these texts.
17.   Among other witnesses we have these extracts of unedited monastic sermons conserved in a Dublin manuscript, Trinity College, 341 (thirteenth century), fol. 50: 'Multi claustrales qui dilatantur in intellectu et restringuntur in affectu, sublimia loquuntur et infima agunt', and fol. 62ᵛ: 'Stultas autem questiones et genealogias et contentiones et pugnas legis devita. Sunt enim inutiles et tamen hodie doctores nostri ea diligunt'.

18. The most recent set of studies, with bibliography, is in *Jean Duns Scot ou la révolution subtile. Entretiens et présentation de Christine Goémé*, (Paris: FAC Editions Radio France, 1982).

19. Laetitia Boehm, 'Papst Benedikt XII (1334-1342) als Förderer der Ordensstudien. Restaurator - Reformator - order Deformator regularer Lebensformen', in *Studien und Mittelungen zur Geschichte des Benediktinerordens*, 90 (1979) 151-213.

20. *Ibid.*, p. 287.

21. *Ibid.*, p. 308. The same structure prevented monastic Orders from becoming great 'missionary' Orders as did the Institutes founded from the thirteenth century onward, as I have shown in the article entitled 'Monachisme chrétien et missions', in *Studia missionalia*, 28 (1979).

22. That is what I had already pointed out in connection with Cluny, in 'Les études universitaires dans l'Ordre de Cluny', in *Mélanges bénédictins* (Saint-Wandrille, 1947) pp. 349-373.

23. Boehm, p. 291.

24. Text cited *ibid.*, p. 300.

25. Texts cited *ibid.*, p. 306. On the fact that benedictine Rule and tradition are entirely contrary to this privilege, I have quoted texts and facts in the article entitled 'The Problem of Social Class and Christology in Saint Benedict', in *Word and Spirit*, 2 (1980) 33-51.

26. Boehm, p. 306.

27. *Ibid.*, p. 309.

28. For example by François Vandenbroucke, in collaboration with J. Leclercq and L. Bouver, *The Spirituality of the Middle Ages* (New York: Seabury 1977).

29. Jean Duns Scot, p. 18.

30. J.P. Massaut, art. 'Humanisme et spiritualité', IV: 'Du 14e au 16e siècle', in *Dictionnaire de spiritualité*, VII (Paris, 1969) col. 990-991.

31. Albert DeBlaere, 'Humanisme chrétien et vocation monastique', *Studia Missionalia*, 28 (1979) 106.

32. Klaus Ganzer, 'Monastische Reform und Bildung. Ein Traktat des Hieronymus Aliotti (1412-1480) über die Studien der Mönsche', in R. Baümer, ed., *Reformatio Ecclesiae. Beiträge zur Kirchlichen Reformbemühungen von der Alten Kirche bis zur Neuzeit. Festgabe für Erwin Iserloh*, (Paderborn, 1980) 180-189.

33. Super Cantica, 36. 2; *S.Bernardi Opera, 2* (Rome, 1958) p. 4.

34. Quoted in J. Leclercq, *Un humaniste ermite. Le Bienheureux Paul Giustiniani (1476-1528)*, (Rome: Edizioni Camaldoli, 1951) 32-33. For other texts in the same sense, see pp. 50 and 126.

35. *Ibid.*, p. 54, and p. 177, and the Index, s.u. Bernard.

36. Klaus Ganzer, 'Zur monastischen Theologie des Johannes Trithe-mius', in *Historisches Jahrbuch,* 101 (1981) 385-421; Noel L. Brann, *The Abbot Trithemius (1462-1516). The Renaissance of Monastic Humanism* (Leiden: Brill, 1981).

37. Ganzer, 'Zur monastischen Theologie . . . ' , p. 386, n. 13.

38. *Ibid.,* p. 188. See Peter the Venerable, Epist. 20, ed. Giles Constable, *The Letters of Peter the Venerable,* I (Cambridge, Mass.: Harvard University Press, 1967) 38-39; quoted in J. Leclercq, *Pierre le Vénérable* (Saint-Wandrille, 1946) 268, and, among other witnesses in same sense, by Louis Gougaud, 'Muta praedicatio', in *Revue bénédictine,* 42 (1930) 170-171.

39. Ganzer, p. 409.

40. *Ibid.,* p. 396, 399, 400.

41. *Ibid.,* p. 407.

42. *Ibid.,* p. 400-401. Criticism of scholasticism becomes, more and more, a literary theme. In this satire of theology contrary to what it should be for monks, Trithemius writes: 'Theologiam sanctam in batto-logian perniciosam verterunt . . . ' , cited *ibid.,* p. 401, n. 104. The word *battologia* is not altogether a neologism. We find it, in latin, neither in antiquity nor in the middle ages: it is given no attention among the articles in the *Thesaurus Linguae Latinae* or in the *Mittelateinisches Wörterbuch.* But we find it once in biblical greek, in Matthew 6:7, where it is the equivalent of πολυλογία used immediately after in the same verse. In greek, it derives from a verb meaning 'mumble', 'ramble on' or 'talk drivel'. Henry George Liddell – Robert Scot, *A Greek English Lexicon* (Oxford, 1948) 1:311, translate it by 'to speak stammeringly, say the same thing over and over again'. Other equivalents given are: 'to jabble, bumble, twaddle, blab, chit-chat'.

43. *Ibid.,* p. 393.

44. *Ibid.,* p. 410.

45. *Ibid.,* p. 416-417.

46. For a general view, see J.P. Massaut – Raymond Marcel, 'Human-isme et spiritualité, DSp 7:995-1006.

47. J.P. Massaut, *Josse Clichtove. L'humanisme et la réforme du clergé,* I, (Paris: Belles Lettres, 1968) 134-136. The admiration of Petrarch for monasticism extended as well to other orders and continued constant, as has been shown by Giles Constable, 'Petrarch and Monas-ticism', in *Francesco Petrarca Citizen of the World (Studi sul Petrarca, 8)* (Padova: Antenore – State University of New York Press, Albany, 1980) 53-99. On his opposition to scholasticism, see pp. 56-57.

48. *Ibid.,* p. 145-147.

49. *Ibid.,* p. 381-382.

50. *Ibid.,* p. 127.

51. On *curiositas* in Gerson, see the bibliography in Ganzer, pp. 192–193; Heiko A. Obermann, *Contra vanam curiositatem. Ein Kapitel der Theologie zwischen Seelenwinckel und Weltall* (Zurich, 1974). Herbert Smolinsky, 'Johannes Gerson (1353–1429), Kanzler der theologischen Studien', in *Historisches Jahrbuch,* 96 (1978) 284-291, has shown how Gerson depended especially on the *De gradibus humilitatis et superbiae* of St Bernard, who, here, depends on St Gregory the Great. Wolfgang Hübener, 'Der theologisch- philosophische Konservatismus des Jean Gerson', in A. Zimmermann, ed., *Antiqui und Moderni,* Miscelanea mediaevalia, 9 (Berlin, 1974) 174-179, has insisted on the influence which Gerson had on thinkers who came after him.

52. Quoted in Gamber, Monastische Reform, p. 194.

53. W. Kölmel, 'Scholasticus literator. Die Humanisten und ihre Verhältnis zur Scholastik', in *Historisches Jahrbuch,* 93 (1973) 301-335.

54. J.-P. Massaut, 'Histoire, humanisme et théologie. Un Erasme des profondeurs', in *Revue d'histoire ecclésiastique,* 69 (1974) 457.

55. J.-P. Massaut, 'Erasme et Saint Thomas', in *Colloquia Erasmiana Turonensia,* II (Paris: Vrin, 1972) 581-611.

56. English translation with introduction in John C. Olin, ed., *Christian Humanism and the Reformation. Selected Writings of Erasmus* (New York: Fordham University Press, 1976) 106-133. In the Preface of his edition of St Jerome, on his work on the Fathers of the Church, Erasmus gave this justification: 'Let me not hesitate to proclaim that this theology is far more conducive to Christian learning and a pious life than that which is now treated far and wide in the schools, crammed so full with Aristotelian principles, contaminated by such sophistical nonsense, not to say dreams, entangled so in the labyrinths of vain and petty questions that, if Jerome himself came back to life or Paul, he would find nothing there resembling theology'. *Hieronymi opera* (Basel, 1516) II, fol. 2, cited and translated by John C. Olin, *Six Essays on Erasmus and a Translation of Erasmus' Letter to Carondelet . . . ,* (New York: Fordham University Press, 1979) p. 34. On the importance of monasticism in Erasmus, see J.-P. Massaut, art. 'Humanisme et spiritualité', DSp 7:1006-1028. On the difference which Erasmus made between 'the discourse of scholasticism' and that of real and ancient theologians, consult, Marjorie O'Rourke Boyle, *Erasmus on Language and Method in Theology* (Toronto – Buffalo: University of Toronto Press, 1977), 121-122. On the importance of great literature in all this tradition I have given indications under the title 'La tradition littéraire de l'Eglise', in *Seminarium,* (1982).

57. J.-P. Massaut, *Josse Chlichtove* (cited n. 7) vol. 2, note 47.

58.   *Ibid.,* 1, p. 379.
59.   *Ibid.,* 381.
60.   *Ibid.,* 380.
61.   *Ibid.,* 409, 414-415.
62.   *Ibid.,* 411.
63.   *Ibid.,* 384.
64.   Anthony Lane, *Calvin and St. Bernard* (A dissertation, to be published) pp. 17-18.
65.   This has been the object of a qualified account—on which I depend in what I say about Luther—by Steven Ozment. 'Humanism, Scholasticism and the Intellectual Origins of the Reformation', in *Continuity and Discontinuity in Church History: Essays Presented to George Hunston Williams,* (Leiden: Brill, 1979) 133-149. On 'the triumph of biblical humanism over scholastic theology' at the University of Wittemberg at the time of Luther, see Lewis W. Spitz, 'The Course of German Humanism', in H.A. Oberman and T.A. Brady, edd., *Itinerarium Italicum: The Profile of the Italian Renaissance in the Mirror of its European Transformations: Dedicated to Paul Oskar Kristeller on the Occasion of His 70th Birthday* (Leiden, 1975) 416-417, with bibliography.
66.   *Concilium Tridentinum,* I (Freiburg, 1901) p. 60.
67.   *Ibid.,* p. 67. On this see, Klaus Ganzer, 'Benediktineräbte auf dem Konzil von Trient' in *Studien und Mitteilunger zur Geschichte des Benediktinerordens,* 90 (1979) 157; Hubert Jedin, *Geschichte des Konzils von Trient,* II (Freiburg, 1957) 98-99.
68.   *Concilium Tridentinum,* V (1911) 150-151.
69.   *Ibid.,* p. 151, note f.
70.   *Ibid.,* p. 152 and note *a.*
71.   The idea that St. Bernard was the last but not the least of the Fathers, was suggested by Erasmus, taken up by Clichtove, handed on to Mabillon and then to Pius XII; on the history of this idea and on its significance, see Oliver Rousseau, 'S. Bernard, le dernier des Pères', in *S. Bernard théologien,* Analecta S. Ordinis Cisterciensis, IX 3-4 (Rome, 1953) 300-308.
72.   Summa theologia, Prologus. Under the title 'Lo sviluppo dell' altegiamento critico degli allievi verso i maestri dal X al XII secolo', in *Università e società nei secoli XII-XVI,* Centro italiano di studi di storia e d'arte (Pistoia, 1982). I have set this text of St. Thomas in tradition and in its historical context.
73.   Under the title 'Curiositas', I have assembled texts.
74.   J.-P. Massaut, 'Humanisme et spiritualité chez Erasme', in *Humanisme et spiritualité* (above, note 47): 'Jésus-Christ, mystère de Dieu et salut de l'homme', col. 1011-1012; 'La loi nouvelle et la philosophie

Christi', col. 1012-1013; 'Le christocentrisme', col. 1014-1015.
76.   P. de Clerck, 'Feu la scolastique. Quatre livres sur les sacrements',
in *La foi et le temps,* N.S., 3 (1981) 269-281.
77.   Claude J. Peifer, OSB, 'The Formation of Non-Clerical Junior
Monks', in *American Benedictine Review,* 33 (1982) 41.
78.   Albert Deblaere, SJ, 'Humanisme chrétien et vocation monastique',
in *Studia Missionalia,* 28 (1979) 106-107. Kenneth C. Russell, 'A Medieval Dynamic Understanding of Meditation', in *Review for Religious*
(May–June, 1982) 417.
79.   Another way of formulating the problem is taken by Fr Michel
Corbin, SJ, who concludes his presentation of one effort made in theology today by saying that it 'attempts to re-establish its theology as
wisdom, not under, but above science which is always abstract, partial
and positive': *L'inouï de Dieu. Six études christologiques,* (Desclée de
Brouwer, 1980); 'Avertissement', p. 8. It is titillating to notice to what
extent the reproaches once made by the humanists in dealing with the
scientific theology of scholasticism coincide with those formulated
today by a catholic critic speaking of theological science as it has prevailed ever since. To notice this, one need only read the pages by José M.
Castillo, SJ entitled 'Une contribution de la théologie', in *Science et
antiscience, Recherches et débats,* Nouvelle série, 1. 'Secrétariat international des questions scientifiques' (S.I.Q.S.) (of the M.I.C.: Mouve-
ment international des intellectuels catholiques) (Paris: Le Centurion,
1981) 176-179.

THE PATRISTIC HUMANISM OF SKELTON'S
PHYLLYP SPAROWE
M. J. Doherty

IN THE FIRST THREE DECADES of the sixteenth century, the poetry of an Englishman who was neither a monk
nor a scholastic theologian had much to say about the
traditions of cloister and classroom as they existed in the
early tudor period. The poet, John Skelton, was both a
scholastic cleric and a literary man; his various roles as university scholar, royal tutor to young Prince Henry, country
pastor, and spiritual advisor to ladies well suited his development as an observer of society and a satirical poet.[1] The great
humanist, Erasmus, praised Skelton as 'the light and glory of
English letters'.[2] Literary historians have subsequently disputed whether Skelton's poetic vision reveals more the mind
of an English renaissance humanist and reformer than that of
a medieval grammarian.[3] At least one of Skelton's poems
demonstrates that scholasticism and humanism together infused his wit with moral tension and influenced his expression
of social criticism. In *Phyllyp Sparowe,* a poem set in a monastery school, Skelton applied both approaches to truth in his

challenge to the abuse of reading and writing in contemporary monastic education.

When this poem is read critically as a broadly christian humanist statement—whether medieval or renaissance in its idea of human nature—it not only speaks to the issue of intellectual and moral formation of the young but also provides an image of practical spirituality and spiritual direction at the turn of the sixteenth century. Yet critical studies of Skelton have rarely investigated at any depth the theological underpinnings which motivate and guide his poetic speech. A richly theological foundation establishes the positive standards of value implied in his raillery. Many readers of *Phyllyp Sparowe* receive it as a light poem and relish its earthy humor; they fail to see that Skelton's presentation of an adolescent's experience of sensuality and of death is not only earthy and funny, but heavenly and profoundly comic at the same time.[4] The satire makes a witty poetic vehicle for the moral tenor of Skelton's analogy of the sparrow: the christian comedy of the worth of the embodied and immortal soul.

In the following essay I shall discuss the theological vision of *Phyllyp Sparowe,* arguing that patristic tradition enabled Skelton to integrate his appreciation of monastic values, of scholastic reasoning, and of humanistic love of literature into a singular poetic statement. By imagining the distortions that the influence of classical letters produces in the intellectual and moral development of a young, aristocratic Englishwoman who attends a monastery school, Skelton created a tudor recapitulation of ancient christian spirituality and of scholastic doctrine; since certain religious—namely, the benedictine nuns of Carrow Abbey where the poem is situated—taught this schoolgirl classical letters, Skelton's satire simultaneously lampooned a monastic abuse of humanist learning. Skelton's control of his christian satire allowed him to move from secular literature through theological doctrine to the Gospel in a continuum; thus he adapted the claustral ideal of virginity and the life of prayer to the spiritual needs of a young

laywoman who must learn, in her reading and writing, to live
in the world but not be of it. Patristic theology supported the
penetrating intention of his satire—moral reform—and gave it
specifically christian purpose in Skelton's coupling of an
accurate representation of fallen human nature with expressed acknowledgement of the power of divine Providence
to effect change for the better. The reading of satire constituted Skelton's proposed method for teaching the difference
between truth and falsehood: reading helps one sort out the
discrepancies between things as they seem to be and things as
they really are and between things as they are and things as
they ought to be so that, in good self-knowledge, one may
move one's life toward greater conformity with revealed
truth.[5] Since the opinions of four ancient christian writers
especially support Skelton's point of view on his heroine's
earthly *and* heavenly knowledge of love, my explication of
the poem will attend especially to their ideas. Saint Jerome
addressed several exhortations to the life of virginity and
prayer to women; Saint Augustine not only expressed the
doctrine of two kinds of love, *cupiditas* and *caritas,* but also
documented the progress of spiritual growth in his use of the
confessio; Saint Basil evaluated secular literature with regard
to the primacy of Scripture; and Saint Paulinus of Nola coined
his own poetic image of the sparrow and saw Christ himself
as the Sparrow whose death and resurrection summon human
beings to heaven. Before I discuss the poem, however, I shall
provide a working definition of patristic humanism and a
brief historical note on Jane Scroop, Skelton's *persona,* and
on Carrow Abbey, where Jane's reading and writing ought to
lead her to truth.

Knowledge of the Fathers did not in itself distinguish the
intellectual lives of monks, scholastic theologians, and humanists at the turn of the sixteenth century; they all practised
some form of 'asking the Fathers' and arrived at some sense
of a patristic idea of human nature.[6] In general, three features

of patristic thought may be said to outline its anthropology and define its humanism. First of all, although patristic ethics uniformly struggled with the shameful discrepancy between the human vocation and the human performance, patristic anthropology emphasized human dignity; the Fathers affirmed that men and women were made in the image and likeness of God.[7] Secondly, as the Fathers articulated christian doctrine and composed scriptural commentaries, they supported the primacy of Scripture as revealed truth transcending historical culture even while they used the structures of classical thought.[8] For them, theological orthodoxy on, for example, the providential nature of salvation history—the participation of the embodied soul in the divine works of creation and redemption through the incarnate person of Christ the Word—corresponded to the measure, or rule of faith, presented in the scriptural word of God.[9] Finally, patristic writers took their knowledge of classical learning and literature seriously, contending within themselves over the right and wrong ways for Christians to appropriate secular letters. A grand moral *contentio,* an expressed tension between the just practice of religion and the right use of learning, between the love of God and the love of letters, appeared in the writings, for instance, of Saint Jerome, Saint Augustine, and Tertullian.[10] These commonplaces affected literary composition in the Middle Ages; they filtered into the scholarship and literary endeavors of the Renaissance and gained new energy with the massive recovery in print of freshly edited patristic texts. Even in the seventeenth century, when scholarly possession of Greek patrology in its original language had revised certain conceptions of christian *paideia,* the story was still told that Saint Gregory Nazienzen converted Saint Basil from the vanity of secular studies.[11] Saint Paulinus of Nola, similarly, immortalized an *ars poetica christiana* when he wrote to his teacher, Ausonius, in the best latin rhetorical poetic form, that he had rejected Apollo for a new God, Christ: the English poet, Henry Vaughan, appropriated the hagiography of Paulinus to praise the sacred character of George Herbert and his writing.[12]

Patristic humanism may be defined, therefore, as that love of God and of human beings which pursues the recovery of the divine image in men and women by means of learning and the written word. Its theology takes a literary approach to truth, especially the truth of revelation, and seeks a moral end in the reading audience. Its psychology focuses on rhetorical technique and on the interpretation of analogy and of irony as a didactic method. It sees the mind as well as the heart as arenas of spiritual combat, classrooms for spiritual nurturance, where reason *and* faith reach toward a surpassing understanding. It addresses, in renaissance England, needed reform.

Part One of *Phyllyp Sparowe,* composed around 1505—at about the same time other christian humanists were addressing the problems of the spiritual formation of the laity in a dawning age of reform—brings such a definition of patristic humanism right down to earth, where it may take effect. The poem is a mock elegy of 844 lines lamenting the death of a pet bird who is styled as a schoolgirl's lover.[13] Jane Scroop, the historical woman whom Skelton refashioned as the fictional narrator of this portion of the poem, took offense at the sensual portrayal of herself; so did another reader, Alexander Barclay, author of the *Shyp of Folys,* who judged Skelton to be void of wisdom and the poem to be full of 'wantonnes'.[14] Skelton wrote Part Two of the poem within the year in his own poetic voice to mollify Jane; these epideictic commendations of her beauty and virtue, as well as a third section of the poem written years later, do not properly share in the poetic merit of the unified achievement of Part One.[15] What their very composition may suggest, however, along with the negative responses of some early readers, is the true success of Skelton's poetic medium. As modes of thought, irony deliberately evokes the confusion of appearance and reality in order finally to distinguish them, and satire exaggerates human foibles to provoke outrage and stimulate change in the audience.

The historical circumstances of Jane Scroop's life argue that pastoral concern informed by patristic readings motivated Skelton: he lampoons her with kindness in order to teach the truth.

The historical Jane Scroop lived with her widowed mother, six sisters, and one brother at Carrow Abbey, Norwich, where benedictine nuns undertook some of the responsibility for her education. Nineteen or twenty years of age at the time of the composition of the poem, Jane was not formally enrolled in the school but probably sat in on classes to pass the time.[16] Skelton, rector of the parish of Diss in the region of Norfolk where Carrow was located, enjoyed familiarity with both the Scroops and the nuns. His reductive treatment of literary conventions on the topics of love and death seems to represent a good paternalism exercised on a fatherless young woman. The instrument of the satire, the fictional Jane, is much younger than the historical Jane who read the poem, and Skelton uses the fictional girl caught up in literary confusion to teach the real Jane the security of revealed truth and tradition. Grief-stricken, the schoolgirl *persona* seeks suitable words to eulogize her pet sparrow, Philip; more profoundly, she seeks to know what to make of death. Skelton's major metaphor of the sparrow directs his lesson in interpretation for the real Jane: the sparrow may be read either as a type for lechery, as it was in classical literature, or as a figure of the soul saved from death, as it was in Scripture, or even as a figure of the Redeemer, as it was in the patristic tradition.[17] On the analogical foundation of Christ's exhortation to have confidence in the divine Providence that takes note of a mere sparrow's fall (Mt 10:28-31), Skelton moved his *persona* toward discovery of the theological message of his poem: faith in the doctrine of resurrection. To teach this lesson to the historical Jane Scroop, however, Skelton stylistically designed the poem as an artfully ironic treatment of monastic *opus Dei,* of scholastic questioning, and of humanist *lectio.* If divine watchfulness observes a sparrow's fall, then how much more does the

divine mind labor with love to bring the order of truth within
human reach in liturgy and in sound teaching.

Several aspects of the history of Carrow Abbey, like the
realities of the historical Jane Scroop's situation, shed light
on Skelton's social satire. Walter Rye, a nineteenth-century
historian of Carrow, which was founded in the twelfth century, considers it an obscure nunnery with some interesting
features. Carrow was under royal patronage and drew appli-
cants from the aristocracy; the guesthouse was popular, for
the nuns often entertained members of the higher classes who
judged the quiet of a quasi-monastic life to be preferable to
the bustle of an inn. Rye also notes a curious mixture of piety
and pettiness in the comments made by the nuns at various
visitations of the Ordinary in the years 1492, 1514, 1526, and
1532: the beer was too thin, the prioress had a favorite, some
sisters wore silk girdles, a murderer was given sanctuary.[18]
R.M. Phipson, citing an earlier, unidentified source, alludes to
the noteworthy role of Carrow in the education of young
women. The monastery school belonged, Phipson's source
says, 'to the good Shee Schools wherein the Girls and Maids of
the Neighbourhoods were taught to read and to work; and
sometimes a little Latine was taught them therein. Yea, give
me leave to say, if such Feminine Formation had still continued, provided no Vow were obtruded upon them, haply
the weaker Sex might be heightened to a higher Perfection
than hitherto hath been attained.'[19] Whether these opinions
possess full historical accuracy or suffer from a slanted view
of monasticism might be difficult to judge properly if we did
not have Skelton's poem. The very features of Carrow which
Rye and Phipson praise—its educational service to the neighbor-
hood—Skelton criticizes in his picture of nuns too fashionably
literate: their secular education of Jane leads her to make poor
use of reading and writing. As the historians question the petty
examination of faults and the genteel practice of hospitality in
the guesthouse, similarly, Skelton lauds the particular virtues
of monasticism: he blesses the vowed life of the religious in the

school of divine service, the moral usefulness of the examination of conscience and self-accusation, and the spiritual
hospitality which performance of the *opus Dei* gives Jane.

Phyllyp Sparowe begins when the fictional Jane refers to
the chanting of the Office of the Dead and to her literary
studies with equal emphasis. In the *horarium* of her education, the sacred work of God and secular *lectio* are inter-
twined. The first word of the poem echoes the Office whose
psalms mark off the hours of the day—*Placebo;* but the poem
quickly moves to interpret Scripture in question and answer
formulations not unlike those of the scholastic method. In
these questions, Skelton makes liturgical texts underscore
his ironic counterpointing of secular poetic convention to the
truth of the Word.[20] 'Who is there, who? / *Dilexi*' (ll.2-3),
that is, one who is a romantic lover, for 'I have loved, Dame
Margery' is how Jane, twisting scriptural words to her purpose,
responds to the interrogating nun. Then the girl punctuates her
conversion of the psalm to romance by humming the grave,
second melody line of the funeral sequence, *Dies irae,* 'Fa, re,
my, my'. With the next question and answer, however, in a
most scholastic manner, Skelton announces the significance
of the poem. The question addresses causality in the act of
mourning: 'Wheefore and why, why' (l.6)? The answer explains
the prayer for the dead, the souls in purgatory, on the basis of
faith in the immortality of the soul for whose sake, one hears
implied, 'swete Jesu' died. Intercessory prayer is one of the
ordinary functions of monastic life:

> For the sowle of Philip Sparowe,
> That was late slayn at Carowe
> Among the Nones Blake.
> For that swete souls sake,
> And for all sparowes soules
> Set in our bede rolles (ll.7-12).

Skelton's poem, like the Gospel, asks his audience to consider
the worth and the fall of a sparrow, for in the fall of a sparrow
is an allegory of the soul's development, for better or for
worse, in the truth, especially in the truth of language that may
either inspire or truncate spiritual growth. Then Skelton begins
to show his reader ironically that Jane does not know how to
love, to pray, to think properly about events in her life; her
difficulties, as he unfolds them, have much to do with her
abuse of the art of reading literature.

In the process of recording her grief, inventing a eulogy,
and searching for a fit religious response to death, Jane exposes the limitations of her *ratio studiorum.* As she rises to her
true *confessio,* however, her discovery of some essential
christian doctrines allows her to make an apt *conversatio
morum* with regard both to the interpretation of love and
death and to the reading and writing of literature. This process
establishes Skelton's design for providing the historical Jane,
his first audience, with a down-to-earth lesson in self-knowledge
and in the christian use of secular letters. By inventing the
persona of an awkward adolescent whose naivete in life and
in literature nevertheless possesses a certain humorous charm,
Skelton properly used the literary medium as a corrective
'mirror' and fulfilled his conviction that literature must contribute to the self-knowledge without which there can be no
spiritual growth. If the *persona* shows Skelton's projection of
his own awareness of sensuality on the character of Jane—in
whose 'mask' he acknowledges the struggle for chastity, too—
the voice of 'Jane' simultaneously resonates with Skelton's
use of patristic thought to qualify the image of love, literature,
and the life of the mind expressed by classical authors such as
Catullus, Ovid, and Cicero.

Constructing his literary mirror, Skelton amplifies two
short poems by Catullus in which the Roman poet rebukes his
amoral mistress, Clodia, for showing more affection to her pet
bird than to her lover.[21] In one of his poems Catullus aims to
persuade Clodia to love him; in the other he exaggerates

Clodia's grief at the death of her pet. Skelton's manipulation of these sources creates a narrative framework for Jane's voice, through which he practises both a renaissance art of 'imitation' that completely transforms the classical model and a medieval *Catullus moralisé*. Thus the character type of Clodia is completely hidden within the different appearance of Jane: Skelton's heroine is no aristocratic Roman woman of libidinous reputation, but an upperclass English schoolgirl of untarnished moral report. Jane is a comedienne and, unlike Clodia, no villainess; yet the english character stands in ironic tension with the roman, and the satirist must observe that Jane, in her familiarity with Philip, is dangerously blind to the powers of sexuality and language. Although merely a *potential* fall from grace is figured for Jane's soul in the fall of Philip to the devilish monastery cat, Gyb, Skelton's moralization of the classical love poems clearly surfaces in his irony. A christian poetry may not laud, by blind imitation, the morally unexamined pursuit of sexual desire, nor may poetry—whether it is Jane's or Skelton's own—simply collect ovidian myths and ciceronian modes of rhetorical amplification into new, contemporary images without revising their values. Poetry must cultivate humanely the image of the truth and the knowledge of divine love.

Not surprisingly, therefore, we find that Skelton's poem counters attitudes and techniques of Saint Jerome's letter to Eustochium on virginity to Catullus' poems to Clodia on desire. Jerome's nightmare in which he was judged to be a Ciceronian rather than a Christian appears to denigrate rhetoric in itself, but Jerome's language in telling his dream employs a strongly dramatic persuasion to the value of virginal chastity on his reading audience. That is, Jerome *uses* and does not *abuse* rhetoric. As a moral argument, the letter praises virginity by inspiring fear of the loss of it, for virginity, once lost, cannot be regained. If the apostle Paul struggled with the wretchedness of his body and prayed to be released from temptation, if ascetic men (Jerome among them—and Skelton)

are constantly tested in virtue, 'how must it fare with a girl
whose surroundings are those of luxury and ease?'[22] By making a comparison to his own keen struggle, Jerome mourns
the many virgins who are daily lost to the Church because of
loose social mores and reliance on their own poorly formed
consciences (22.5, 24; 22.13, 27). Skelton, the priest who
knew how difficult celibacy could be, playfully compared the
loss of virginity to Philip's death by murder: both loss and
death are irrevocable in the natural order. Philip, the sparrow
who finally figures Jane's own soul, may also figure any
clerical fellow of her acquaintance. Jerome appealed to
Eustochium to sustain the highest degree of chastity in her
chosen monastic state; her role as 'the first virgin of noble
birth in Rome' (22.15, 27) conferred a public identity that
brought with it great social responsibility. Skelton, similarly,
adapted the virtue of chastity required in the religious and
clerical states of life to Jane's situation by rhetorically exag-
gerating a sensual fantasy in its potentially deadly, and therefore truly nightmarish, moral effects. The way Jane loves and
loses Philip affects another 'soul' besides her own; the way she
fulfills or fails to fulfill a virtuous standard, similarly, exposes
the degree to which Carrow helps her develop in the super-
natural order either toward spiritual faithfulness or toward
sinfulness. Like Jerome, Skelton holds that the education of a
Christian should contribute to the resolution of moral ambi-
valences in literature and in life, not to the dissolution of
character.

Jerome directly satirized the wealthy widows who changed
their garb but not their self-seeking; they retained their sensual
habits but called themselves nuns (22.16, 28). So, too, Skelton's ironic treatment of Jane points to his satire on the Benedictines of Carrow; their black robes indicate that they have
purportedly changed their minds about worldly matters when,
in fact, the nuns nevertheless slavishly imitate contemporary
revivals of ancient secular literature without correcting the
classical vision by a christian standard of truth. Thus Skelton's

scholarly nun, 'Dame Sulpicia at Rome', professes more
humanism than religious doctrine. Her character functions
poetically as Skelton's criticism of the abuse of literature, for
she seeks literary fame more than the love of God and
neighbor.[23] Her name

> regystered was
> Forever in tables of bras,
> Because that she dyd pas
> In poesy to endyte
> And eloquently to wryte (ll. 148-153).

Skelton's satire appears partially in Dame Sulpicia's name, for
the *Carmen de temporibus Domitiani* of the classical poetess,
Sulpitia, was printed in Venice in 1498, and Dame Sulpicia
models herself on the poetess. So, too, Jane awkwardly emu-
lates the literary nun, striving to surpass her in rhetoric.

Jerome's self-revelation explained the experience of being
hauled up before the divine Judge and accused of being a
Ciceronian rather than a Christian; his admission testifies to
his sense of his own past sexual weaknesses and to his verbal
passion, as if the love of rhetoric partook of the same sensuality that might tempt him to an adulterous betrayal of his
call. By the time he finished his letter to Eustochium, he had
exhorted her to practise fasting, vigils, and austerity of speech
and fashion, encouraging her always to keep in mind the
model purity of the Blessed Virgin who was fittingly the
Mother of God (22.34-36; 22.38, 39). By the time Skelton
finishes his poem, similarly, he has led Jane through an examination of conscience and a *confessio* which reveal that she
has violated—in her clothing, speech, prayer, reading, and
physical familiarity with Philip—almost every rule of behavior
that Jerome had advocated to Eustochium. To see false nuns,
Jerome said, 'in their capacious litters, with red cloaks and
plump bodies, a row of eunuchs walking in front of them,
you would fancy them not to have lost husbands but to be

seeking them. Their houses are filled with flatterers and with
guests. The very clergy . . . kiss these ladies on the forehead,
and . . . take wages for their visits' (22.16, 28). With Rye's
comments on the guesthouse of Carrow ringing in our ears,
we may be reminded of Skelton's portrayal of Jane's behavior
with the clerical bird, Philip, whose intimacies she 'confesses'.
Often he

> wold syt upon my lap,
> And seke after small wormes,
> And sometyme white bred crommes (ll. 121-23).

Creeping into the openings of her gown and hood, or prettily
landing on her extended hand, Philip often exchanged 'Many
a prety kusse' with Jane (l. 361). In short, Skelton the literary
priest effectively opposed Jerome's Eustochium to Catullus'
Clodia as models of character for Jane; but that satiric opposition of antique characters revealed the more subtle, ironic
characterization of a classical poetess in the robe of an English
nun. The primary problem in the *ratio studiorum* of Carrow,
as exemplified in the character of Dame Sulpicia, is that it
might lead Jane, in turn, to think she is learning the ways of
Eustochium while she is inadvertently slipping down the
path of Clodia. As a eulogy, *Phyllyp Sparowe* is an encomium
on the dead bird. Skelton's point, ironically expressed by Jane
herself, is that Dame Sulpicia's rhetoric inadequately praises
Philip's virtues because the nun simply does not know them
all (ll. 154-158). Only Jane tells these 'virtues'—the powers
of the bird which she had known intimately—and only slowly
will Skelton guide her to admit their sensual nature to herself
in the public medium of the poem as *confessio*.

As obvious a structural parallel to Skelton's moral values as
Saint Jerome's letter to Eustochium provides, therefore, the
method of Skelton's instruction of Jane seems to depend on
augustinian thought. First of all, in the *Confessions* Saint
Augustine also placed the importance of classical rhetoric

in relationship to revealed truth. He credited Cicero's *Horten-sius,* an exhortation to seek true wisdom, with helping to lay the foundation of his intellectual conversion.[24] Saint Augustine's own definition of *confessio* as both the accusation of oneself and the praise of God has sometimes clouded the earlier patristic definition in which 'confession' meant primarily a testimony of faith motivated by the experience of conversion, by the suffering of martyrdom, or by the entrance into religious life; yet Augustine's autobiography included elements of conversion, martyrdom, and change of state. His 'confession' of sexual sins has received a disproportionate emphasis in western intellectual history and literature largely because of the description of Manichaeism and the related polarization of body and soul which he himself provided in the text of the *Confessions.*[25] Other augustinian texts, such as the *De doctrina christiana,* the *De ordine,* and the *De Trinitate,* seem to have played as important a role as the *Confessions* in influencing Skelton's views of sacred and secular literature, of the sequence of studies, and of the necessity of self-knowledge in the spiritual quest of the human person, the image and likeness of God, for the reality of God.[26] In the *De Trinitate,* for example, Saint Augustine had stated a correspondence between the image of the Holy Trinity in the soul and the proper use of its three faculties, memory, understanding, and will. By remembering, understanding, and loving, a person can accomplish many tasks of human *knowledge;* by remembering, understanding, and loving God, however, a person can perform the only work of *wisdom* possible to human nature, that is worship. This endeavor, the truest task of human life, begins with self-knowledge and leads to the justification of one's personal history.[27]

Jane's poetic exercise in self-knowledge methodologically serves the art of reading life as well as books in these three augustinian ways: attention to the role of memory; familiarity with the rules of understanding in the act of verbal expression and rhetorical amplification; and recognition of the

authoritative source of truth and love in Scripture by means
of reason and faith expressed by hearing and doing the Word
of God.

First, Skelton shows Jane experiencing the natural operations of memory. 'When I remembre agayn / How my Philyp
was slayn' (ll. 17-18), Jane says, recalling the event she needs
to understand, and setting forth the emotional motivation of
the poem. But her memory is muddled with odd literary com-
parisons of herself and Philip to an archetypal pair of lovers
whose separation came in a violent death:

> Never halfe the payne
> Was bewene you twayne,
> Pyramus and Thesbe,
> As then befell to me (ll. 19-22).

In the episode from Ovid, as Skelton well knew, the lion
merely scares Thisbe, whose mantle is picked up and bloodied
by the lion's mouth; Pyramus misinterprets the tainted mantle
as evidence of Thisbe's death, and consequently slays himself.
Seeing him dead, Thisbe commits suicide. The horrible pity of
the tale lies in the mistaken interpretation of the evidence, the
misreading of things.[28] Jane Scroop, in calling up this tale to
parallel the assassination of Philip by the monastery cat, Gyb,
sees no mistake in the lovers' judgment and adds to her mis-
interpretation of Ovid's moral by wrongly applying the case of
Pyramus and Thisbe to her own emotional state. Despite Jane's
uncritical reading of things, however, her relatively straightforward narrative recollection of emotion enables her to make
some sensible connections between the experience of the death
of her love, Philip, and its psychological and religious significance. Thus memory serves the purpose in the poem, as
Saint Augustine observed it does in life, of helping someone
'come to' her senses and know herself. Memory also leads
Jane, however crudely, to a perception of the creature's con-
tingency upon the Creator. The recollection of Philip deeply

moves Jane's affection, and this, in turn, evokes from Jane a prayer of helplessness, a prayer whose words are supplied her by the language of the liturgy. 'Unneth I kest myne eyes / Toward the cloudy skyes' (ll. 37-38), she says, paraphrasing Psalm 120, which is sung almost daily in the Office of Terce.[29] While still attending to the role of memory, Skelton slowly weaves his comparison of the sparrow and the soul—Jane's soul—by means of word-play and syntax. Jane in her sorrow falls like a sparrow: 'Halfe slumbrynge, in a sounde / I fell down to the grounde' (ll. 35-36). She confesses,

> I syghed and I sobbed,
> For that I was robbed
> Of my sparowes lyfe (ll. 50-62).

Finally she prays, 'Good Lorde, have mercy / Upon my sparowes soul' (l. 241). 'My *sparowe's* soul' may also be read as '*My* sparowe's *soul*'.

Jane's lesson in self-knowledge turns from memory to understanding in the rhetorical amplification which follows, lines 67 through 587 intermittently. Memory has instructed Jane in the kind of truth which nature learns by experience or knows by means of some moral tale—that is, the fact of death, the mystery of the fall, the effects of sin on the soul. The liturgy has instructed Jane to try to see her experience through the eyes of faith. Thus Skelton has Jane recite what she has learned in school, inventing rhetorical amplifications on the theme of death, in order to compare it with what she learns in the liturgy.[30] Jane surveys classical myths on hell, praying that Philip's soul be kept from the underworld 'Of Proserpinas bowre' and the 'dennes dark' of Cerberus (ll. 67-94); alludes to classical philosophers such as 'Socrates the wyse' who taught ways to understand death (ll. 98-107); mentions one of the more pitiful scenes in classical epic, Andromache's sorrow at the suffering of her 'Noble Hector of Troye', in the same breath has her own 'dedly wo' at the loss of Philip (ll. 108-114);

elaborates several fables on the themes of magical power as if
she could use it to quicken the bird (ll. 186-209); confuses
theories of history, both conventionally typing Noah and
Deucalion together and unconventionally referring to King
Philip of Macedonia (ll. 244-272); degenerates to a series of
curses against the murderer, Gyb (ll. 282-330); and finally,
fantastically invents a funeral Mass for Philip to be celebrated
by clerical birds of various sorts (ll. 387-582). Through Jane's
rhetorical amplifications, Skelton ironically comments on the
dangers of an education in rhetoric when it is not subjected to
a prior, logical demonstration of true doctrine. As Aristotle
well understood in his *Art of Rhetoric,* the ethical hazard of
persuasion was that its power could be used by charlatans to
present inappropriate opinions as truths worthy of action.[31]
The charlatanry at risk in Jane's rhetoric centers on the abuse
of literary interpretation. Both Jane's pictorial representation
of Philip on her sampler and her conflation of Scripture and
myth, for instance, abuse the christian purpose of literary
imagination. The 'icon' successfully inspires her prayer, but
only because her accidental pricking of her finger with the
needle while she embroiders Philip's image punctures the
solace and 'sport' of her fantasy (l. 218). The picture seems
to speak, and Philip warns Jane that she is 'in wyll' killing him
again; but in Skelton's satire, the same imaginative experience
causes Jane to throw her sampler down and pray for Philip's
soul (ll. 220-238). The allegorical mixture of Noah and Deucalion explicitly inspires in Jane a desire for revenge (ll. 273-281).
As in Jane's misapplication of Ovid's tale of Pyramus and
Thisbe, her attitude toward political history uncritically
accepts the moral validity of revenge, as if she were a follower
of Seneca rather than of Christ.

  Punctuating Jane's amplification of classical texts, however, are Skelton's many references to the psalms and readings
of the Divine Office. Each of these liturgical echoes recalls
Jane's mind to the reality at hand: the life and death of the
soul. Even her curses undergo a kind of moral transformation

on the strength of the truth of Scripture heard in the liturgy:
'Farewell, Phyllyp, adew; / Our Lorde thy soule reskew'
(ll. 331-332). After uttering maledictions on the savage cat,
Jane prays sincerely, for she now imagines Philip as a soul
being harrowed from hell. By revealing in Jane's interpretations, however humorous, the damning combination of a
rich familiarity with classical letters and a nearly complete
confusion as to how to read properly the texts of life, love,
death, and poetry, Skelton judges Jane's teachers, the nuns of
Carrow, by the effects of their teaching on her. Jane can cite
her *auctores,* but she does not yet consciously know how to
use secular letters to her soul's advantage by measuring her
experience and her learning against the revealed standard of
christian truth. In their excitement over literature, the nuns
of Carrow have apparently let their imparting of authoritative
religious doctrine slip. Only the faithful regularity of the *opus
Dei* and the Mass in benedictine life allows the Word of God
to cut through the muddle of Jane's mind, slowly, experien-
tially bringing her to a rational faith in the resurrection. This
'leading out' of her soul correctly educates her,

Skelton's satire of Jane's thought processes reaches its
greatest height when he presents Jane's foolish imitation of
her religious mentors in the celebration of the liturgy. Jane's
illogical deductions on liturgical practice are of the same order
as her misinterpretations of Ovid and Seneca, but to worse
effect. Because of the power of the Word of God and the
sacramental graces which flow from liturgical prayer, however,
Jane's greatest folly actually advances her on the way to the
knowledge of the truth. *Phyllyp Sparowe* had begun with a
reference to one of the nuns, presumably a superior, as she
conducted the Office of the Dead—in Jane's imagination for
the soul of Philip on whom Gyb has 'worrowyd' herself
(ll. 7-8; 29-30). Jane's poetic invention of a funeral Mass for
Philip documents her illogical imitation of Dame Margery's
behavior; if the nun can officiate liturgically, as is customary
in the singing of the Office in monastic houses, then Jane may

freely devise a poetic requiem quite apart from the usual
liturgical and clerical channels. As Jane strove to outdo
Dame Sulpicia in the vivid rhetorical description of Philip's
virtues, so the bird-Mass, the lengthiest rhetorical amplification in the poem, shows her striving to outdo both Dame
Margery and most of the clerical hierarchy in suitably bury-
ing her pet bird.

The significance of Skelton's presentation of Jane's invented Mass in his satire devolves, in part, from the augustinian notion that the only work of wisdom possible to
human nature is worship. As a sample of Jane's wisdom, the
bird-Mass compares to the 'parliament of fowles' in the best
chaucerian tradition; Robyn Redbrest is chief celebrant, a
popingay the deacon who reads the Gospel, and Chaunticleer
the cock the timekeeper. Jane's imaginative appropriation of
the canonical right to perform a Mass shows her reduction of
sacred ritual to the level of any other literary imitation; as a
reduction, the moral allegory of the bird-Mass functions in
the manner of the beast fable: animals who act like human
beings suggest a criticism of human beings who act like animals. The wisdom of Jane's 'worship' appears in Skelton's
satire, however, and surpasses the usual beast fable—another
classical genre—in Skelton's acute historical commentary on a
clergy in need of better theological education and less com-
pulsion to follow ceremony for its own sake, on monks and
nuns in need of a clear sense of their vocation, and on a
Church in need of general reform. The fact that East Anglian
psalters and liturgical books of the late Middle Ages had their
borders and capitals decorated with colorful portrayals of the
variety of birds reinforces the historicity of Skelton's poetic
image-making in his social satire.[32] In Jane's bird-Mass, moreover, Philip comes to represent both a foolish cleric and also
Jane's own seeking soul. The levels of the interpretation of the
analogy shift, heightening the satire, until Jane envisions the
immortality of her soul in the Image of God.[33] Like an orthodox celebration of the Divine Office and the Mass, the right

exercise of memory, understanding, and will in a good poetic
invention ought to lead the mind and heart to God and not
merely down the paths of eloquent fantasy for its own sake.
Consequently, even though Jane's poetic logic comically
misconstrues the dignity of the Mass, Skelton's logical satire
of contemporary religious abuses nevertheless establishes the
power with which the liturgy can apply a corrective to Jane's
mind. The medieval axiom *Auctoritas auget* stated that
'authority makes [things] grow'. On the strength of the
authority of patristic thought, scholastic method, and monastic worship, therefore, Skelton's development of Jane's Mass
of the birds becomes her stimulus to seek a true *conversatio
morum,* a willed changing of her ways.

In order to grasp Skelton's poetic design for Jane's religious and literary conversion, readers must appreciate the
scholasticism of her *confessio.* Initially Jane justifies her intimacies with the 'sparowe royall' who had the liberty of her
person (l. 158):

> And on me it wold lepe
> Whan I was aslepe,
> And his fethers shake,
> Wherewith he wolde make
> Me often for to wake
> And for to take him in
> Upon my naked skyn.
> God wot, we thought no syn—
> What though he crept so lowe? (ll. 161-169)

Flirtations with Philip seem foolishly innocuous, but Skelton
has dealt frankly with the potential lust in them in the classical and contemporary literary parallels that Jane cites. The
real matter of Jane's confession, consequently, has less to do
with her sensual behavior and more to do with her use of her
mind when she reads and writes. In this emphasis Skelton
presents the judgment of scholastic moral theology, which

was harder on sins of pride than on sins of the flesh.[34] His direction of Jane also fulfills scholastic concepts, for Skelton dramatizes Jane's foibles in order to form better her conscience and to bring her, persuasively and satirically, to *synderesis,* that is, to the application of general moral principles to her specific case.[35] Both Saint Jerome and Saint Augustine had developed the idea of the spark of reason—*scintilla rationis*—left in the nearly extinguished light of the fallen human mind into a notion of conscience. Scholastic theologians had, in turn, used these patristic sources to articulate an understanding of the way conscience operates.[36] Fundamental to all versions of the doctrine was the idea that conscience is the intellectual ability to tell the moral difference between good and evil; at dispute among scholastic theologians was whether conscience was also the power to choose the good and to avoid the evil.[37] The doctrine took shape on the premise that, after the Fall, men and women might only know truth fully insofar as they were guided by the divine gift of revelation. Without this gift of faith, even the best intellect would founder or, as Augustine observed in his own life, take a long time to come to the most elementary spiritual knowledge.[38] Jane's rectification of her conscience through *confessio* engages her in the self-knowledge of her mortal and immortal condition. Grounding her confession in truth, liturgical prayer produces in Jane an unexpected receptivity for solid and authoritative religious teaching. The liturgy, in short, even in Jane's reductive version of it in her bird-Mass, turns her thoughts to the keystone of christian theology, the doctrine of the resurrection. Thus Jane's confession not only functions as an admission of guilt but also as an expression of faith and a channel of grace.

Jane's faith, significantly, does not arise from renunciation of her love for Philip but from purification of her love for his sake. Still making analogies with classical literature, Jane in the Mass combines natural history with christian theological virtues that seem to appear, suddenly, in her mind. Philip, she surmises, may undergo in death the experience of the phoenix, the bird of Araby that rises, according to Pliny, from its own ashes as from a spark of fire. Jane's imaginary phoenix dons a black cope to bless the corpse:

> Of whose incyneracyon
> There ryseth a new creacyon
> Of the same facyon
> Without alteracyon,
> Savyng that olde age
> Is turned into corage
> Of fresshe youth agayne;
> This matter trew and playne,
> Playne matter indede,
> Whose list to rede (ll. 540-549).

The doctrine of resurrection is 'plain matter', plain truth. The phoenix celebrated by Pliny was christianized by Lactantius, one of the earliest christian poets and one much admired by Saint Jerome for his style.[39] By 'reading' the phoenix as the shadow or type of the resurrection, Jane begins the process of rectifying her conscience on the truths of sexuality and mortality; she engages, moreover, in the application of general moral principles to specific cases in the reading and writing of literature, for now, she says, she can rightly 'rede and spell' (l. 612).

Thus Jane's *confessio* leads through liturgical prayer to her *conversatio morum* just as the *ratio studiorum* of the reading list of classical texts at Carrow has led Skelton's reader, through the satire of Jane, to criticism of the nuns of Carrow and even to self-examination. Conscientiously now, Jane expresses an accurate evaluation of her literary abilities and limitations as she seeks to compose merely a little epitaph for Philip (ll. 605-606):

> But for I am a mayde,
> Tymerous, halfe afrayde,
> That never yet asayde
> Of Elyconys well,
> Where the muses dwell (ll. 607-611).

If Jane can now properly—that is, according to the teaching of grammar—read and spell correctly, the intellectual change corresponds morally to a conversion of her reading matter. Jane now reads not classical literature but medieval English literature which has, presumably, already been informed by christian doctrine and moral values. Thus she reads the *Canterbury Tales,* especially those which deal with love and marriage, and the romances of Tristan and Lancelot, the sorrows of Troilus and Criseyde, and all the many tales of good women and unfaithful men or bad women and long-suffering men (ll. 784-812). As she becomes adept in interpreting the truth of such literature, she also becomes an astute critic of the language and literary output of her own day. Instead of seeing herself among the latin authors, she numbers herself among writers for whom composition is an intellectual and moral struggle:

> I am but a yong mayd,
> And can not in effect
> My style as yet direct
> With English wordes elect:
> Our naturall tong is rude,
> And hard to be enneude
> With pullyshed termes lusty;
> Our language is so rusty . . .
> That if I wolde apply
> To wryte ornatly,
> I wot not where to fynd
> Termes to serve my mynde (ll. 770-783).

Jane knows that she needs to mature, to grow morally, intel-
lectually, and spiritually.[40] The english language needs to
mature, too—and, by implication, the english nation emerging
under the Tudors—if there is to be english christian citizenry
and literature that is spiritually reformed and not merely con-
formed to this world. In Skelton's view, such growth will express a lay and social manifestation of conversion of life.

The movement of *Phyllyp Sparowe* toward Jane's conversion of life outlines the depth of Skelton's application of
patristic tradition. When readers of the poem step back from
analyzing its sources in Saint Jerome, Saint Augustine, and
the scholastic theologians, the unity of the poem as an expression of Skelton's mind gathers once again in christian humanist
light. The particular patristic text that casts that unifying light,
communicating the major principles of patristic humanism to
renaissance thinkers, is Saint Basil's letter to young men on the
intellectual usefulness and moral limitations of secular literature.[41] Since this epistle, translated from Greek into Latin,
was widely published from the end of the fifteenth century
through the sixteenth century, Skelton may very well have
read it or, at least, become familiar with its major ideas, although he does not quote Saint Basil directly.[42] The letter
established as a christian humanist principle, for example, the
idea that education is for the sake of the soul. Only when one
capably understands the shadowy language and literature of
secular learning is one able to pursue appropriately the brilliant light of holy and revealed doctrine in sacred literature.[43]
Essentially, Saint Basil argued for the right use of secular
letters by making distinctions between the body and the soul,
their different values, and the different kinds of education each
requires. Basil explained that everything one does in this life is
but preparation for life after death, and that one ought not even
consider strength, beauty, or other human attributes worth
praying for. 'To the degree that the soul is more precious than
the body in all respects, so great is the difference between the

two lives.'[44] The earthly and heavenly lives have two ways of
knowing and two ways of being nurtured, Saint Basil tells his
nephews:

> Now to that other life the Holy Scriptures lead the
> way, teaching us through mysteries. Yet so long as, by
> reason of your age, it is impossible for you to under-
> stand the depth of the meaning of these, in the mean-
> time, by means of other analogies which are not
> entirely different, we give, as it were, in shadows and
> reflection, a preliminary training to the eye of the
> soul.[45]

Saint Basil maintained a clear sense of the primacy of revealed
truth while he tentatively affirmed the value of secular literature. Only on the basis of a discovered affinity between the
images of secular and sacred letters may pagan learning *not* be
without usefulness for the soul, he said. The christian reader
must, nevertheless, carefully select from secular literature
what encourages and resembles the truth; he or she must pass
over the remainder, especially anything that might damage
the life of the soul. Saint Basil's recognition of the primacy
of revealed truth and his insistence that learning serve the
development of virtue appealed to renaissance humanists. At
the same time, Basil's awareness that human knowledge is
propaedeutic to divine truth and that humanly devised analogies and divinely expressed doctrines have an affinity would
make sense to a scholastic cleric.

The patristic humanism of Skelton's *Phyllyp Sparowe* feeds
on Basil's definition of the order of truth and of the priority
of revelation. Skelton seems almost to have revelled in making
an analogy that would fulfill Basil's prescription. Thus, where
Basil addressed young men, Skelton addresses a young woman
and the nuns who teach her. Where Basil explained that secular literature might be read in preliminary training for the
reading of the Word of God, Skelton demonstrates a christian

ars legendi by manipulating the interpretation of several
classical pagan texts so that they conform in his poem to the
teachings of Scripture and the Fathers. Where Basil expressed
a principle of analogical interpretation between inferior secular letters and superior scriptural mysteries, Skelton *creates* a
literary analogy to a passage in Scripture. *Phyllyp Sparowe*
elaborates Christ's lesson of providential care in the fall of a
sparrow as a witty tudor instruction to a schoolgirl on the life
and death of the soul and on human and divine love. The
divine voice resonates from the depths of the poem as an
imaginative whole:

> And fear ye not them that kill the body and are
> not able to kill the soul; but rather fear him that
> can destroy both soul and body in hell. Are not
> two sparrows sold for a farthing? And not one of
> them shall fall on the ground without your Father.
> But the very hairs of your head are all numbered.
> Fear not, therefore; better are you than many
> sparrows. Every one therefore that shall confess
> me before men, I will also confess him before my
> Father who is in heaven (Mt 10:28-32, Douay–Rheims).

That Jane finally hears the Gospel in the exercise of imagination that corrects her *ratio studiorum,* informs her *confessio,* and motivates her *conversatio morum* is denoted by
Skelton's observation of the changing nature of her identifica-
tion with the sparrow, a type of the soul. When the poem
begins, Philip represents merely Jane's sensual little playmate,
a pet murdered by Gyb; loving the clerical Philip, though,
Jane identifies with him. Her longing pushes her, through
his death, to another sort of understanding of Philip and herself. Echoing Psalm 83, for example, Jane longs for her own
nest in the courts of the Lord relatively early in the poem.
She reflects here on Noah's ark, the type of the Church, and
says, 'I wolde have yet a nest / As pretty and as prest / As my

sparowe was' (ll. 263-265). Later in the poem her prayer is
less allegorical and more doctrinal. She has enough faith to
pray to God that 'Phillip to heven may fly . . . / To heven he
shall, from heven he cam' (ll. 580-582). Having begun by
praying for 'my sparowes soul / Wryten in my bede roule'
(ll. 242-243), Jane ends by acknowledging in her epitaph for
Philip that the bird who flies up to heaven and his true home
lodges as well in her own breast. The sparrow is, we recall, not
only a secular metaphor for sexual desire, but also a divine
metaphor for the christian soul loved by God (ll. 826-833).

The ancient christian poet and monk, Saint Paulinus of
Nola, developed the metaphor of the sparrow yet further in
one of his highly rhetorical epistles. Paulinus said that the sparrow was an image and likeness of the God–Man who used the
metaphor in the Gospel. The letter in which Paulinus suggests
that the metaphor figures the prototype of the new human
being, the only Son of God, is peppered with many of the
same scriptural allusions with which Skelton wove the invention of his poem:

> With body and soul in harmony with God's will I
> shall justly say: *I am alone until I pass.* What spar-
> row is this which represents perfected man, if it is
> not the sparrow which *hath found herself a house,
> and with the turtle hath made Thy altars, O Lord of
> hosts, her nest?* Perhaps this is one of the two spar-
> rows *not one of which falls on the ground without
> the will of the Father.* For the highest Sparrow fell
> in the flesh, yet He also rose again.[46]

At the close of Part One of *Phyllyp Sparowe,* therefore, the
historical Jane Scroop had the opportunity to see in the
mirror of her fictional counterpart the moral design of Skelton's tutelage in a christian *ars legendi.* To read the event of
Philip's fall according to the standard of Scripture and the
'shadowing' developed in Paulinus' metaphor invited Jane's

spiritual growth. Such an art of interpretation in the reading
of secular literature, if not completely congruent with the
monastic practice of *lectio divina*, nevertheless sympathizes
with its affective and contemplative aims by preparing for
them.

Skelton's poem has survived to invite later generations of
readers to use well and not abuse this art of reading. As Saint
Basil suggested, the christian reader ought to be like a bee who
gathers sweetness and light from poetry on the basis of its
analogy to Scripture, letting go of anything that might impede
the life of the soul.[47] Those who do not gather poetic significance properly will find only earthy humor in the secular
analogy of Skelton's clerical bird; those who do gather the
message of Skelton's irony will find, shining through witty
exaggerations, a divinely human sparrow. The first sort of
audience needs emphatically to hear the warning voice of the
satirist: mere indulgence in venereal love, while seeming play-
ful, leads to doom; and, if one sparrow was slain at Carrow by
the cat that devilishly prowls about like a roaring lion seeking
to devour souls, how many more schoolgirl souls may also be
lost to heaven through a literary education that lacks a christian
ars legendi? The second sort of audience may smile happily at
its own human folly because its newly gained self-knowledge
in reading the poem is the experiential parallel to the confident
discovery of the immutable truth of divine mercy. *Lectio* is a
form of spiritual combat; but *lectio* grounded in truth of doctrine is also a form of spiritual nurture and delight. So, too, is
Skelton's poetic composition. His view of the right way to read
and write makes a christian *arts legendi*.

With a similar understanding, Saint Jerome had warned
Eustochium not to seek to be over-eloquent and not to trifle
with verse; but he encouraged her to read: 'Read often, learn
all that you can. Let sleep overcome you, the roll still in your
hands; when your head falls, let it be on the sacred page.'[48]
The passion for sacred reading was ancient medicine for other
passions. It should come as no surprise, therefore, that a

scholastic cleric who loved both literature and revelation
should echo the exhortation. An old monastic saying observes
that 'repetition is the mother of learning', and so it often is in
the grammar school; but Skelton the university man and secular priest knew that *what* students were repeating mattered in
the life of the soul. Skelton's hope was that a young laywoman
educated in the precincts of a monastic house would carry
something of both monastic and scholastic approaches to truth
into her life. In this way she would become worthy of the
same commendations given to Our Lady, the virgin, mother,
and wife in whom apparent contradictions of state were mira-
culously harmonized: *Hac claritate gemina / O gloriosa
femina!*[49] His hope for a young woman, who did later marry,
was founded not so much on the wish to direct her into the
cloister as on the conviction that the spiritual values of cloister
and school had to be absorbed in lay life if each person were
to recover the image and likeness of God in the soul. When
Skelton 'asked the Fathers' how such a translation of values
might be effected, he found in them both an appreciation for
liberal arts education and theological training and also a strong
sense of the limitations and foibles of the human mind. Since,
however, the declaration of the truth of human nature is grace-
fully available in revelation, a Christian's satirical laughter at
human folly may pass *through* a literary mirror, almost mira-
culously moving from the cruel judgment of the cruelties of
moral wrong to the pleasures of divine mercy.

Like the well-known Spanish humanist, Juan Luis Vives,
who served the next generation of Tudors, Skelton the sup-
posedly medieval grammarian and scholastic cleric shows in
his art of reading and writing how much of the early renaissance humanist and rhetorician he also was. Vives' *Instruction
of a Christian Woman,* sent to Queen Katherine from Bruges
in 1523 on the subject of the education of the Princess Mary,
recommended the education of women and described a reading list that avoids Ovid but includes the 'chaste pastimes' of
the classical poetess, Sulpitia, on marriage. Those who read

and praise romances, Vives says, may well do so once they have read Saint Jerome or Holy Scripture and mended their lives: 'For often tymes the onely cause why they preyse them, is bycause they se in them their owne conditions, as in a glasse.'[50] So, too, like the Jerome who described a *ratio studiorum* for little Paula in a letter to her mother, Laeta, Skelton freely offered himself, former tutor to a prince, as a 'tutor and foster father' to Jane. He laughed with her and not against her. 'Let her treasures be . . . manuscripts of the holy scriptures . . . . But if she reads the works of others let it be rather to judge them than to follow them.'[51] *Phyllyp Sparowe* affirms that a monastery is neither a university nor a literary *salon;* learning never disturbs a monastery school, however, but the way truth is used or abused.

Vanderbilt University

232

NOTES

1.   For biographical information on Skelton throughout this essay, I am relying on H.L.R. Edwards, *Skelton: The Life and Times of an Early Tudor Poet* (London: Jonathan Cape, 1949).

2.   Erasmus's remark is quoted in Preserved Smith, *Erasmus* (New York, 1923) 62.

3.   Edward's biography is threaded with a discussion of Skelton's mix of scholasticism and humanism. For a summary discussion of Skelton's participation in the contemporary dispute over old and humanist grammar, see Alexander Dyce, ed., *The Poetical Works of John Skelton*, 2 vols. (London: Thomas Rodd, 1843; rpt. New York: AMS Press, 1965) 1: xxxiv-xxxix.

4.   John M. Berdan, *Early Tudor Poetry* (New York: MacMillan Co., 1920; rpt. Shoe String Press, 1961) 158, suppresses the question of theological interpretation by categorizing Skelton in 'the former age' not favorable to the men of 'new learning'. Eileen Power in *Medieval English Nunneries c. 1275 to 1535* (Cambridge, 1922) 590-95, treats the poem as little more than an amusement, a story about cats. In Stanley Eugene Fish, *John Skelton's Poetry* (New Haven: Yale, 1965), the satire but not the theological foundation of it, receives explication.

5.   Two contemporary and better known literary pieces which use the ironic mode in a similar way are humanist works, Erasmus's *Praise of Folly* and Saint Thomas More's *Utopia*. See Stephen Greenblatt's discussion, for example, of More's self-conscious 'playing' and search for a real self through the gradual cancellation of a series of shadowy selves in *Renaissance Self-Fashioning from More to Shakespeare* (Chicago: University of Chicago Press, 1980) 29-33.

6.   The continued use of Lombard's *Sentences* kept the sayings of the Fathers usefully current in the exercise of scholastic method in university curricula and theological training even as humanist production of new editions, translations, compendia, and *opera extant omnia* of the 'holy doctors' gained momentum through the sixteenth century. The *Liber de Scriptoribus Ecclesiasticis* of Abbot John Trithemius (Basle, 1494) listed writers of the Church from Clement the Roman to himself, providing both biographical information and a list of their works. The bibliography is prefaced by an alphabetical table of the writers by name with folio reference to their entries, and it includes a handy list of the commentators on the *Sentences*. Trithemius's bibliography quickly became the handbook of renaissance patristic studies while the work of

one of those 'commentators' on the *Sentences,* Dionysius the Carthusian, became a famous compilation of patristic opinion in a useful doctrinal order. His *De his quae secundum sacras scripturas et orthodoxorum patrum sententias,* 2 vols. (Cologne: Peter Quentel, 1535) helped establish the rallying cry of christian humanists who advocated a return to the sources of christian antiquity, 'ad fontes ipsos, Augustinum, Hieronymum, Ambrosium, Gregorium, Hilarium, Chrysostomum, Bedam' (II, verso of title page). See S.L. Greenslade, *The English Reformers and the Fathers of the Church* (Oxford, 1960), for an overview of the entry of patristic theology into sixteenth-century theology; Paul Morgan, *Oxford LIbraries outside the Bodleian,* 2nd ed. (Oxford: Bodleian Library, 1980) on manuscript and printed text copies of patristic writings available in the various college libraries; and William P. Hauugaard, 'Renaissance Patristic Scholarship and Theology in Sixteenth-Century England', *Sixteenth-Century Journal* 10,3 (1979) 37-60.

7.   A convenient survey of this patristic idea is George Maloney's book, *Man, the Divine Icon* (Pecos, New Mexico: Dove Publications, 1973).

8.   A bibliography of discussions of Christianity and classicism is a subject in itself, but a few places to start are: Edwin Hatch, *The Influence of Greek Ideas on Christianity* (New York: Harper and Row, 1957; rpt. 1970); Werner Jaeger, *Early Christianity and Greek Paideia* (Cambridge: Harvard Univ. Press, 1961); and Henry Chadwick, *Early Christian Thought and the Classical Tradition* (New York: Oxford Univ. Press, 1966). A recent, splendid study which reintegrates theological understanding of patristic doctrine with patristic spirituality in the context of classical thought is Andrew Louth's book, *The Origins of the Christian Mystical Tradition from Plato to Denys* (Oxford: Clarendon Press, 1981).

9.   The idea of the 'rule of faith' was especially elaborated by Saint Irenaeus in the *Adversus Haereses;* but see Louth, pp. 75-158, on the emphasis in practical spirituality on the incarnation of Christ and on the revelation of the Word of God in Scripture.

10.   See Harald Hagendahl, *Latin Fathers and the Classics: A Study of the Apologists, Jerome, and Other Christian Writers, Studia Graeca et Latina Gothoburgensia,* VI (Göteburg, 1958). See also Maurice Testard, *Chrétiens latins des premiers siècles: La littérature et la vie* (Paris: Société d'Édition 'Les Belles Lettres', 1981).

11.   In Henry Vaughan's *Flores Solitudinis,* 'Primitive Holiness', *The Works of Henry Vaughan,* ed. L.C. Martin, 2nd ed. (Oxford: Clarendon Press, 1957) 323-324. Although the version of the story with which I am familiar is this seventeenth-century one, it reflects Vaughan's own interest and use of patristic sources.

12.   See Herbert J. Musurillo, S.J., *Symbolism and the Christian Imagination* (Baltimore, Md.: Helicon Press, 1962) on the search in the early christian centuries for a characteristically christian mode of literary communication and on Paulinus's contribution, pp. 105-109. The first edition of Paulinus's works in the sixteenth century, *Epistolae & Poematae* (Paris: Badius Ascensius, 1516) actually published the pertinent poems by Ausonius with Paulinus's own epistolary answers to his teacher to immortalize the debate. See also my essay, 'Flores Solitudinis: The "Two Ways" and Vaughan's Patristic Hagiography', *George Herbert Journal* 7 (Fall 1983 / Spring 1984) 25-50.

13.   For the text of the poem I am using the most recent edition by John Scattergood, *The Complete English Poems* (New Haven: Yale, 1983) 71-106, and will indicate quotations by line number in my essay, which examines only Part One of the poem.

14.   As cited in Dyce, ed. *Poetical Works of John Skelton*, 1:xxxiv-xxxix. Cf. the statement of Thomas Fuller in *Anglorum Speculum, or The Worthies of England in Church and State* (London: John Wright, 1684) over a century later: Skelton was a 'satyrical wit' who touched 'three Noli me tangere's' and suffered for it: the grammarian, William Lilly, the local friars who then persuaded Bishop Nix to remove Skelton from his benefice on the charge that he practiced concubinage, and Cardinal Wolsey. The last mentioned, 'his too potent enemy, being charged with him with too much truth, so persecuted him, that he was forced to take sanctuary at Westminster' (p. 525).

15.   See Scattergood's notes on the dating of these parts of the poem, pp. 405-406.

16.   See Edwards, *Skelton: Life and Times,* pp. 102-114, for a summary of many of the biographical details of Jane Scroop's life.

17.   The patristic source of this commonplace is Paulinus, who transforms explicitly in his works numerous classical metaphors and literary structures, as explained by his modern editor and translator, P.G. Walsh, *The Poems of Saint Paulinus of Nola, Ancient Christian Writers,* 40 (New York: Newman Press, 1975) 3-20.

18.   *Carrow Abbey; Otherwise Carrow Priory; near Norwich, in the County of Norfolk: Its Foundation, Buildings, Offices & Inmates* (Norwich: Agar H. Goose, Rampant Horse Street, 1889) i-iii.

19.   As quoted in Rye, p. xli of the Appendix, *Carrow Abbey.* Phipson may have been citing Fuller's *Worthies,* edited and published in Norfolk in 1662, but I find no such passage in the London edition of 1684 which I have examined.

20.   On the liturgical framework of Skelton's poem, see Ian Gordon, 'Skelton's *Philip Sparrow* and the Roman Service-Book', *MLR* 29 (1934)

389-396, and F.W. Brownlow, 'The book of Phyllyp Sparowe and the Liturgy', *ELR* 9 (1979) 5-20.

21.   The two poems are 'Passer, deliciae meae puellae' and 'Lugete O Veneres Cupidinesque'. Catullus was available in early printed editions as well as in manuscript, the *Carmina* having been published in Venice in 1496.

22.   Jerome, Ep. 22.5-8, 24-25, *Principal Works of Saint Jerome*, ed. W.H. Fremantle, *A Select Library of Nicene and Post-Nicene Fathers of the Christian Church*, 2nd series (undated; rpt. Grand Rapids, Michigan: Wm. B. Eerdmans, 1979), 6,22-41. In the following comparison of Jerome's ideas with Skelton's, I shall refer to section and page number of Fremantle's edition in the body of my text.

23.   Cf. the monastic axiom on the tools for good works, as stated in *The Rule of Saint Benedict* 4;1-78.

24.   *Confessions* 3.4.7.

25.   See Peter Brown's discussion, *Augustine of Hippo* (Berkeley: Univ. of California Press, 1967) 158-181.

26.   See, for example, the *De doctrina christiana* 1.22-40 and 3.10-12 in conjunction with M.-D. Chenu's essay, 'The Symbolist Mentality', in *Nature, Man, and Society in the Twelfth Century*, ed. and trans. Jerome Taylor and Lester K. Little (Chicago: Univ. of Chicago Press, 1968) 99-145. *De Trinitate* 7.3, similarly, explains the centrality of love in the human being's recovery of the divine image.

27.   *De Trinitate* 14.15, trans. John Burnaby, *Augustine: Later Works* (Philadelphia: Westminster Press, 1955) p. 113. See *De Trinitate* 10 on self-knowledge, 11-13 *passim* on the trinities of sense, imagination, and faith, and 7 on faith seeking understanding. The discussion of Augustine's view of the mind's temporal journey to God in Louth, *Origins of the Christian Mystical Tradition,* pp. 148-158, clearly explains the workings of memory, understanding, and love.

28.   Which source of Ovid Skelton may be using is moot, there are so many, and he may be using a version of *Ovide moralisé* rather than the latin author. See Scattergood's note, number 21, p. 407, on *Metamorphoses* 4.55-166.

29.   Neither Gordon nor Scattergood notes this parallel.

30.   Erasmus's book on rhetorical amplification, *De Duplici Utraque Verborum ac Rerum Copia,* was first published in 1512, too late as a text to be behind Skelton's ironic treatment of the process of amplification, but not too late to give us some idea of the commonplace grammar-school practice of imitation of classical models which Skelton here satirically represents (Trans. D.B. King and H.D. Rix [Milwaukee: Marquette University Press, 1963]). Saint Augustine in the *De Trinitate*

15.20, pp. 146-47 in Burnaby's translation, offers an explanation of the search for the inward word of truth through memory and understanding. When the content of the word of human utterance is the same as the content of knowledge, then it is a true word having likeness to the Word of God.

31.   *Rhetoric* 1.5-6, 1360-1363.

32.   For this information I am indebted to Richard I. Schneider of York University, Ontario. See Scattergood's note, number 575, p. 409.

33.   See Louth's discussion of the making of analogies to God and to the spiritual life in the thought of Denys the Areopagite, who asserted   a preference for *unlike* symbols. Unlike analogies not only cause no illusion that one conceptually apprehends the divine Being but also force one constantly to move beyond the level of interpretation one exercises (p. 172). On the spiritual use of analogies in the Mass and in the Divine Office, cf. Thomas Merton's confidence in the liturgy and its truth: 'This is the secret of the psalms. Our identity is hidden in them. In them we ourselves, and God' (*The Sign of Jonas*, 1953; rpt. New York: Harcourt Brace Jovanovich, 1979, pp. 254-55).

34.   See, for example, Saint Thomas's 'De veritate', *Quaestiones Disputatae* 24.10-11, ed. R.M. Spazzi, 2 vols. (Rome–Turin: Marietti, 1954).

35.   See *Quaestiones Disputatae* 16-17, *Summa Theologia* Ia,79,12–13, and *Quodlibetum* 3.27.

36.   The term 'synderesis' shows up in Saint Jerome's *Commentary on Ezechiel* (PL 25:20–24) as he discusses the platonic three-fold division of the soul and allegorizes the four creatures who represent the evangelists to signify also four powers of the soul, the fourth, *synderesis scintilla* or *scintilla conscientiae* being represented by the   eagle   and   constantly   'sparking'   the   type   of the   sinner,   Cain,   to   reprent.   Saint   Augustine's term,   *scintilla   rationis,*   parallels this idea: 'Non in   eo   tamen   penitus   exstincta   est   quaedam   velut scintilla   rationis,   in   qua   factus   est   imaginem   Dei' (*De civitate Dei* 22.24.2; PL 41:789). Another passage in a doubtfully attributed text, *De spiritu et anima,* 10 (PL 40:785), amplifies the idea; the list of potential authors suggested by the Benedictine editors underscores how commonplace the idea was in patristic and scholastic thought. See also *De Trinitate* 12 and the *Retractions* 1.9.6. Saint Jerome's idea of *synderesis scintilla* and Saint Augustine's idea of

scintilla rationis were combined in scholastic theology, showing up in the work of Thomas, Bonaventure, and Duns Scotus, for example, as well as lesser figures, especially in fourteenth and fifteenth-century debates on illuminationism.

37.   See Timothy C. Pott's book, *Conscience in Medieval Philosophy* (Cambridge, 1980), for a convenient collection of translations of patristic and medieval texts on conscience.

38.   See especially Saint Bonaventure, *Itinerarium,* or *Journey of the Mind to God* 1.6, on powers of the mind distorted by sin and reformed by grace; see 1.7 on grace as the foundation of right will and the source of light for the penetrating reason. For Augustine, see Brown's biography, pp. 46-60.

39.   *Phoenix* or *Carmen de Dominica Resurrectione* was printed in the second volume of Aldus Manutius's anthology of christian poetry in 1502, but was available in a long manuscript tradition before that. Erasmus reports at the opening of his *Enchiridion* (1501 and subsequently) that Lactantius wanted to be a christian writer as good rhetorically as the pagan, Cicero, and that Saint Jerome loved Lactantius's style.

40.   The primary patristic source congenial to the idea of human maturation is Saint Irenaeus, *Adversus Haereses* 3.24-25, 4.20, and 4.38. Many of Irenaeus's ideas would have been communicated to the latin West through Augustine and Tertullian, but the sixteenth century saw the recovery of portions of the Greek and the publication of several new latin translations.

41.   'Address to Young Men on Reading Greek Literature', trans. Roy J. Deferrari, *The Letters of Saint Basil,* 4 volumes (London: William Heinemann, Ltd., 1934) 4:378-445.

42.   A latin translation of the letter under the title, *De legendis libros* was printed in Ulma as early as 1478. A 1499 edition in Paris and numerous other printings, including those in Brescia and Bologna before the turn of the century, imply the spreading influence of this patristic text. These early printings often used the translation of the well-known humanist, Leonardo Aretino, who also wrote with it an accompanying preface addressed to another humanist, Collucio Salutati. By 1531 the new translation of Raphael Volterranus appeared in Cologne, and in 1537 the letter was printed with a collection of humanist educational treatises by Pico della Mirandola, Agricola, Erasmus, and Melanchthon. See Luzi Schucan, 'Das Nachleben von Basilicus Magnus' "Ad adolescentes",' *Travaux d'humanisme et renaissance,* 133 (1973) with accompanying bibliography, pp. 15-22 and 233-247. The letter was universally well received from the beginning of the sixteenth century, its principles

absorbed, and its message harnessed to the cause of the advancement of literature; 'Ad adolescentes' is *the* patristic text for Skelton to have responded to.

43.   'Address to Young Men', trans. Deferrari, pp. 383-385.

44.   *Ibid.,* p. 387.

45.   *Ibid.,* pp. 385-387. The striving for virtue through the life of the mind, Saint Basil argues in this same passage, must be considered a form of spiritual combat, even the greatest form of such contests.

46.   Letter 40 in *Letters of Saint Paulinus of Nola,* trans. and anno-tated by P. G. Walsh, 2 volumes (Westminster, Maryland: Newman Press, 1966-67) 2:211-12. Cf. *Jerome,* Letter 22.17-18 and 29, for parallels.

47.   'Address to Young Men', 389-91.

48.   *Jerome,* Letter 22.17, ed., Fremantle, p. 28. In 22.18 Jerome urges Eustochium to keep watch at night 'like the sparrow upon the house-top' (p. 28).

49.   Scattergood cites Brownlow, 'The boke of Phyllyp Sparowe and the Liturgy' and refers to Caxton's primer, *O Gloriosa Femina* (1490, STC 15872), as explanations of this phrase which begins Skelton's commendations of Jane in Part Two of the poem (pp. 405-406). Al-though the phrase was conventionally used in anti-feminist satires and appeared generally in the roman rite, Skelton's use of it is primarily an allusion to the lauds hymn to Our Lady regularly sung in monastic houses.

50.   In Richard Hyrde's translation, *A very fruteful and pleasant boke callyd the Instruction of a Christian woman, made fyrste in latyne, by the right famous clerk mayster Lewes Vives* (London: Thomas Bertholet, 1541), sig. 5-12ᵛ. Vives cites Martiall on the 'holy precepts of matrimony' left behind by the classical poetess, Sulpitia (sig. 6ᵛ).

51.   Letter 102.13, pp. 195-96 in Fremantle.

Postscript: I am indebted to Arthur Kinney for the suggestion that Skelton's priestly and pastoral motives may help resolve apparent discrepancies between medieval and renaissance attitudes in his poems.

SILENTIVM

ENTHYMEME AND DIALECTIC:
CLOISTER AND CLASSROOM
Luke Anderson, O Cist.

A CAREFUL COMPARISON of the approaches to truth in the cloister and classroom in the early and later middle ages leads one to conclude that, besides the celebrated differences, there are some rather notable likenesses in the modes in which monks and schoolmen sought to penetrate the truths of faith.

The similarities are best explained by the simple fact that prior to any consideration of the special mental temper of either group, one must consider what is common to both, that is, their faculties and functions as men; for powers and operations rooted in a shared human nature will necessarily evince some commonality. Education and the special goals in any human life will profoundly modify a man's cast of mind, but abilities and their exercise will reveal a common origin.

This paper discusses some of the modifications which have affected the minds of monks and schoolmen in their respective environments, the cloister and the classroom; but it also more than hints at the similarities manifested in the search for and articulation of the truth.

As an introduction to the main thesis of this paper, we must review in this opening section several relevant points connected with our conclusions. We must look first at christian culture in general. St Augustine is credited with creating that culture, which grew out of the study of the liberal arts as applied to the sacred text. That tradition was vital and operative in the intellectual climate of the middle ages. The *trivium,* the literary-logical portion of the liberal arts, was especially pertinent to this medieval culture. And both rhetoric and dialectics thus became the special instruments for theological exposition. As we shall see, John of Salisbury is the brilliant witness to this twelfth century pedagogy. In the last part of our introduction we must study the roles of the abbot-educator and the *magister* or schoolman, with their proper functions exercised in their proper milieu.

The main section of this paper begins with an analysis of the enthymeme or rhetorical syllogism and this study will prepare us to appreciate the 'rhetorical' theology of the cloister. But we will also look at the dialectic method which offers us our best chance of appreciating nascent scholasticism and its full flowering into what we have chosen to call 'dialectical' theology. What is proper to each method and common to both, when well understood, should help us to understand the two approaches to truth. Finally, a more detailed investigation of the enthymeme in its properly medieval dress will reveal its authentic noetic force and its similarity to dialectical argumentation.

CHRISTIAN CULTURE AND THE LIBERAL ARTS:
A study of the basic pre-theological and classical education of medieval men gives us some insight into the diverse theological methods operative at this period. And an understanding of the liberal arts which formed and fostered verbal and

logical skills is especially pertinent to our inquiry.[1]

The *trivium,* i.e., grammar, rhetoric, and dialectic, constituted the more important segment of liberal studies at this
time; the three disciplines enabled the student to think correctly and to speak well. The second portion of liberal studies,
the *quadrivium,* i.e., arithmetic, geometry, music, and astronomy, formed other habits of mind, but received less attention.
The middle ages had received this bias from Aristotle himself,
who highly favored that disposition of studies which stressed
literary and logical talents as more nearly approximating the
ideals of liberal education. Christian appreciation of the liberal
arts was early articulated by both Clement of Alexandria and
Origen. Then during the late fourth and early fifth centuries
Augustine and Jerome championed classical learning for the
formation of christian culture. For this reason, we find even
the strictly catechetical schools offering a wide classical curri-
culum in their training.

When the barbarian invasions heralded the collapse of roman
culture and learning, two Romans, Boethius, *a logician,* and
Cassiodorus, *an educator,* assumed the task of preserving the
ancient learning for the use of the young christian culture.
Two sources, the *De artibus ac disciplinis liberalium litterarum* of Cassiodorus,[2] and the so called *logica nova* transmitted
to the West by Boethius, are especially helpful in understanding the cloister and the classroom of the middle ages.[3]

In their strenuous efforts to revive learning, Charlemagne
and Alcuin, and Alfred the Great in the eight and ninth centuries took their inspiration from these two Romans. But even
before the carolingian reforms, the liberal arts were well, if
variously, appreciated at York in England: (1) they were seen
as having a practical, functional value as they met purely
ecclesiastical and liturgical purposes; (2) they were also seen
as having an intrinsic value and being sufficient in themselves
as proper objects of study; and (3) they were given a dignity
and importance as the necessary introduction to the higher
studies of theology. And it is this last value that was to prevail.[4]

Alcuin, following Cassiodorus' scheme, instituted the *trivium*
and the *quadrivium* at Charlemagne's Palatine School; he manifested a certain predilection for logic, as is clear from a
knowledge of his *De dialectica.*[5] His famous disciple at Tours,
Rabanus Maurus, was destined to be the apostle of liberal arts
in Germany. The liberal studies which from England had
inspired France were passed on to a new generation of ger-
manic students.[6]

In England we see the *trivium* given a special impetus by
Anselm of Canterburgy in his *De grammatico.* The tract
treated of Aristotle's Categories and served as an introduction
to dialectic and as an instrument for theological investiga-
tions.[7] Beyond this, in Anselm's *De veritate* we find, together
with his threefold meaning of truth—logical, moral, and onto-
logical—new uses of dialectics not much to the liking of his
quondam teacher, Lanfranc.[8]

We know too that a little earlier, at Rheims, Gerbert of
Aurillac, later Pope Sylvester II, had used Boethius' commentary on Aristotle's *Topics* and Boethius's translation of
Porphyry's *Isagoge* in his teaching programs. But Gerbert's
original contribution to logic is to be found in his opuscule
De rationali et ratione uti; we have in this tract a witness to
the dialectical procedure at work in understanding the use of
'the proposition'.[9]

Still other uses of the liberal arts are seen in the school at
Chartres founded in the eleventh century; its concerns were
more properly classical and humanistic. From John of Salisbury, who has left us a lucid treatment of the verbal and
logical arts, we receive precious information on Chartres'
teachers. So, for example, Bernard of Chartres, as presented
by John, displays a singular love for classical learning, and
John documents Bernard's methods of teaching grammar.[10]
Bernard's statement that the men of the twelfth century see
better than their predecessors *not* because they have keener
vision or greater height, but because they are perched on the
shoulders of the ancient and giant sages, modestly expresses

Chartres' talents and accomplishments in the field of liberal
arts.[11]

Yet another teacher at Chartres, Thierry, in his book
Heptateuchon, lists the classical authors read at this school:
for grammar, Donatus and Priscian; for rhetoric, Cicero and
Marcianus Capella; for dialectics, Boethius and parts of
Aristotle's *Organon;* and for the *quadrivium,* Isadore of Seville,
Gerbert, Hyginus, and Ptolemeus.[12]

In Hugh of St Victor's *Didascalion* we find the study of the
liberal arts commended, and the incentive for this study in
the promise that solid grounding in these arts is the surer path
to all knowledge, and all truth.[13]

Thus the abiding influence of sixth century Romans, Boe-
thius and Cassiodorus, continued into the high middle ages.
And education theory and practice remained faithful to
Cassiodorus' admonition:

> It should be noted that both in Sacred Scripture
> and in learned expositions much can be learned
> from schemata, definitions, the art of grammar,
> rhetoric, dialectic, arithmetic and astronomy.[14]

We have a thirteenth-century witness to the high regard that
—when their usage in theological exposition had become
axiomatic—had for both *trivium* and *quadrivium.*

> Logic is good for it teaches us to distinguish
> truth from falsehood; grammar is good for it
> teaches us how to speak and write correctly;
> rhetoric is good for it teaches us how to speak
> elegantly and to persuade. Good too are geometry
> which teaches us how to measure the earth, arith-
> metic or the art of computing which enables us to
> estimate the brevity of our days, music which reminds
> us of the sweet chant of the blessed, astrology which leads
> us to consider the heavenly bodies shining resplendently

before God. But far better is theology which
alone can be called a liberal art, since it alone
delivers the human soul from its woes.[15]

Christian Culture in Rhetoric and Dialectics

The *trivium* in various and indeed uneven ways formed the
minds of medieval men. Nevertheless, after their mastery of
grammar, students could easily for one reason or another
emphasize either rhetoric or dialectic, though both disciplines
were mandated. It is the thesis of this paper that the cloister
favored a 'rhetorical' theology and the schools, enamored by
the *logica nova,* clearly favored a more 'dialectical' theology.

Proper understanding of the nature of rhetoric and dialectic might have avoided the preemptive claims made by both
monks and schoolmen for the land of theology when, in the
twelfth century, men began to experience a certain dichotomy in their traditional milieu. They saw differences as inevitably contradictory. The theology of the cloister seemed at
variance with the theology of the schools.

In Cassiodorus's quotation from Varro we find a beautiful
expression of the change in intellectual outlook:

> Dialectic and rhetoric are like man's closed fist
> and open palm.[16]

The use of *closed fist* to characterize dialectics and *open palm*
to indicate rhetoric was well stated. Moreover, Cassiodorus
had, so to speak, anticipated the twelfth-century dilemma, so
frequently seen as dichotomy; and he antecedently formulated
the elements of difficulty.

> ... one [dialectic] compresses its arguments
> into a narrow compass, the other [rhetoric]
> running about the fields of eloquence with
> copious speech; one [dialectic] contracting its
> language, the other [rhetoric] expanding it ...

> One [dialectic] comes to the school; the other
> [rhetoric] constantly proceeds to the forum. One
> [dialectic] seeks a few studious men; the other
> [rhetoric] seeks the great masses.[17]

Dialectic is seen here as fostering tight thinking: it is 'the close fist' aiming at the effective defense of truth. Dialectic compresses its arguments, chastens its language; it is exercised is a scholarly environment and is the instrument of studious men bent on exactness in thought and expression.

Rhetoric, by contrast, is more loose, more free; it is the 'open palm'. It expands and multiplies arguments, running about; and its language is rich and effusive and delights in eloquence. It delights when it informs and uses more than one mode of persuasion. It addresses the multitude, counts on an audience's talents and it is at home in the wide places of the forum—religious, political, and juridical gatherings. Exactness .in a scientific sense is not its only preoccupation.

Rhetoric was a very widely used instrument of theological systems in early christian thought. It is Augustine who best expresses agreement with the classical notion of moving men to the truth through the use of rhetoric. In his fourth book of *De doctrina christiana,* he champions the use of rhetoric, first recognizing its important role in greco-roman culture and then expressing his confidence in its usefulness in forming christian culture. Indeed, he asks, if the evil make use of rhetoric, why should not the good.

> . . . why should it [i.e., the faculty of eloquence]
> not be obtained for the uses of good in the service
> of truth, if the evil usurp it for the winning of per-
> verse and vain causes in defense of iniquity and
> error![18]

Inspired by Cicero, Augustine goes on to say that the orator's office is *to teach, to delight,* and *to move.* The teaching is a *necessity,* the pleasing, *a sweetness* and the persuading of the will to move, *a victory.*[19] Teaching has to do with *what* we have to say, and is primary; but delighting and moving some-one to some action grow out of the *way* in which one speaks.[20] Contrary to popular opinion, the *what* is far more important than the *way.* Rhetorical usage touches upon both theoretical and practical truths so that persuasion (moving) can be ex-clusively mental on one occasion, or both mental and voli-tional on other occasions. Augustine says that the christian teacher using rhetoric must at times instruct and at other times both instruct and move. In speculative or theoretic matters, that is, when 'truths taught are such that to believe or to know them is enough', then it follows that 'to give one's assent implies nothing more than to confess that they [i.e., taught truths] are true'. A practical truth demands movement. For in this case the teacher ' . . . must not only teach so as to give instruction, and please so as to keep attention, but he must also sway the mind' and he must do it 'so as to subdue the will'.[21] Following this well-established augustinian tradition, the rhe-torical theologians of the twelfth century dealt with dogmatic and moral issues of their day.

Let us look now at the dialectic theologians of the same era. Although Berengarius may have been responsible for the anti-dialectic movements of the late eleventh and twelfth centuries, the *trivium's* dialectic discipline remained a vital part of medieval education. We have already seen that Alcuin, then Gerbert and Anselm were genuine dialecticians and true 'fathers' of the movement. And John of Salisbury's marvel of medieval pedagogy, the *Metalogicon,* in explaining the con-temporary uses of the *trivium,* defines dialectic in this way:

> . . . it is that which accepts only what is or seems true . . . dialectic does not go to the extent of estimating utility or goodness. It remains for poli-tical (private, social, and civic ethics) to measure the latter . . . [22]

Dialectic does not concern itself with the kind of instruction that works to subdue the will; it instructs by way of *probable* truth. In order to stress the noetic quality of the *trivium* John of Salisbury tells us that logic is a *genus* and it has two *species:* the logic of dialectics and the logic of rhetoric. Then, taking his inspiration from Boethius, John goes on to say:

> . . . but those who would further broaden its [i.e., logic's] efficacy attribute even more to it. Indeed logic includes demonstration, probable proof, and sophistry.[23]

Demonstration, according to John, 'rejoices in necessity' and the listener cannot but assent, for the thing *must be,* as it is seen and as it is spoken.[24] In the area of less certitude, one deals with *probable proof,* the proof proper to both dialectic and rhetoric; the propositions in these argumentations are valid for all men, for some special class of men, or for the wise. Then, to clarify the meaning of dialectic, John says that it does not aim at *apodictic* teaching as does demonstration; nor does it *persuade* after the manner of rhetoric which also frequently seeks some action; nor does it *seduce* like sophistry with fallacies.[25] He concludes that dialectic only uses 'the ready instrument of moderate probability'.[26]

Moderate probabilities are expressed in language or speech, the vehicle for both dialectic and rhetoric; and rhetoric uses 'prolonged oration'; and dialectic speaks 'succinctly'.[27] John indicates the reason for this brevity:

> . . . the subject matter of dialectic consists in questions, and has reasoning or speech as its instrument.[28]

Abelard, the twelfth-century dialectician *par excellence,* exemplifies John's definition perfectly. In his famous *Sic et Non,* Abelard takes two statements, one positive or affirmative, the other negative, and then he attempts to compose the

differences. The statements, or more exactly the propositions,
are taken from one, or several, of the Fathers of the Church.
Abelard critically examines the *sic et non,* dialectically tests
the two propositions, and then works toward their *probable
accord* in a language that is succinct.[29] This process at face
value appeared as an onslaught of and affront to patristic
authority, a subjection of faith to reason. But this was not a
totally fair evaluation of Abelard's method.

Although Abelard had in Paris studied rhetoric under
William of Champeaux, his love for dialectics revealed itself
in his deep knowledge of Boethius' unfinished commentary
on the *Topics* of Cicero. In his *De dialectica,* he manifests
some clearly aristotelian influences, and repeats for the most
part Boethius' theory clothed in his own systematizing genius;
in the third part of this work he treats formally of the *Topics.*[30]
Abelard was not concerned with mental gymnastics. His purpose was to cultivate the ability to argue reasonably, and thus
to advance the truth.[31] He saw dialectics as a process of
criticism by which, sifting various opinions—opinions held by
all, by many or by a few more wise—one could come to the
principles of any body of knowledge.[32]

His process was rather traditional. He began his *enquiries*
with what Aristotle had called a 'dialectical thesis' or a paradoxical statement. For Abelard that meant a paradoxical
statement of one of the patristic Fathers which conflicted
with other statements of the same Father or statements of the
other Fathers. The *resolution* of the paradox ends in a dialectical
premise of proposition. This premise under one aspect appears
as a question (*non*), since it does not express full certitude. On
the other hand, the premise under yet another aspect appears
as a *bona fide* answer (*sic*), since its truth will commend itself
to all, to many, or to the wiser.[33] This method needed careful
handling and fear of its abuse was to lead to strong anti-
dialectical passions. Yet John of Salisbury could accept
Aristotle's method and saw no threat in it to his christian
faith:

> ... to find a line of inquiry by which we shall
> be able to reason from opinions that are gen-
> erally accepted about every problem proposed
> to us ... and avoid saying that which will
> obstruct us [i.e., lead to self-contradiction].[34]

Dialectic had a decidedly *preparatory* function as it worked
over the divinely-revealed data: it looked toward the formulation of first principles, toward definition and toward the
discovery of a 'middle term' in scientific demonstration.
Abelard had not attained to this perfection, but he shrewdly
guessed its possibility.[35]

The thirteenth century made another use of dialectic, not
as *preparatory*, but as *complementary*. This usage began
where proper demonstration had left off; it led one to make
tentative determination when probable conclusion was seen
as superior to no conclusion at all.[36] But again, Abelard had
not come to that state of perfection.

The preparatory dialectic was also known as *disjunctive*, in
as much as in a given discussion it did not see true demonstration as possible; it dealt with probable premises, arguments
from *convenience*, received opinions, and purely logical sup-
positions. In each of these cases probability was the limit for
proof.[37] The *conjunctive*, complementary dialectic method
was reserved for a later date. Meanwhile, probable arguments
and their probable conclusions were at the heart of the new
movement of dialectic theology.[38]

Conclusion

Cassiodorus calls the *Topics* the commonplaces that supply
men with fonts of argumentation. They are commonplaces
because these fonts are used by dialecticians and all the species
of rhetoricians, i.e., orators, poets, lawyers, and politicians.
But according to Cassiodorus rhetoricians argue in particulars,
dialecticians in generalities:

> . . . but when they [i.e., the arguments] demon-
> strate (not in the strict sense) a particular point
> they have to do with orators, poets and lawyers,
> and when they treat of general questions they
> clearly concern dialecticians.[39]

John of Salisbury repeats the teaching that *proof* is essential
to both rhetoric and dialectic.

> The art [of argumentation] is also most cogent
> in syllogisms, whether it is complete in its
> entirety . . . or hastens on to the conclusion
> by the suppressing of the middle proposition
> in fashioning an enthymeme. Therefore, this
> art [argumentation] is most effective in dispu-
> tation.[40]

Rhetoric and dialectics are species of logic because they both
search for proof. And medieval theologians made use of the
proofs proper to each discipline.

The goal of the rhetorician is to instruct and to persuade.
He ignores the possibilities of any conclusion other than the
conclusion he has freely chosen to defend, because his persuasion must frequently subdue the will and move to action.

The goal of the dialectician is to instruct. He freely considers
the possibilities and indeed sometimes the cogency of conclusions other than the one he is defending. He settles somewhat
uneasily for his probable conclusion and makes no effort to
persuade or move to action.

Applying this difference to men of the middle ages we can
say: the *claustrales* were patient, if not content, with the partial
nature of their understanding, and frequently through moralization ordered their arguments to action; the *scholares*, restless
and impatient with 'the probable', sought to widen and deepen
their understanding, and were concerned solely with forming
convictions. The rhetorical theologians addressed the crowd

and by multitudinous routes. The dialectical theologian spoke
to a select audience and followed a rigorous system. Both
offered proof for their conclusions.[41]

Christian culture: the cloister and classroom
   In the early middle ages a revival of the office of *teacher,*
i.e., *didaskaloi,* inferior to, but in consort with, the strictly
ecclesial teaching office, was seen in the persons of the abbot-
educator and the schools' *magister.* The abbot's claim to a
teaching office was based proximately on the Rule of St Benedict, and abbatial teaching methodology was largely rhetorical,
following the augustinian tradition. The magister's claim was
based on talent; his method was dialectical, and his inspiration
from the *logica vetus et nova* in the works of Boethius and his
translations of Aristotle's *Categories* and the *Perihermeneias.*

Abbot–Educator

   We are endebted to the hermits in the deserts of lower
Egypt for the concept of 'spiritual father'; the abba's function was viewed as a continuation of the teaching office as it
had existed in the early Church and is described by St Paul.
Cassian knew the 'spiritual father' tradition, approved of it,
and transferred it to the Western *coenobia.* In the *Rule of the
Master,* the use of 1 Cor 2:28 and Eph 4:11 as a commission
from Christ to the abbot seems exaggerated. In keeping with
his discretion, St Benedict in his *Rule* (cc. 2 and 64), drew a
more integral and realistic portrait of the abbot-educator. The
abbot's personal moral integrity and its power for instructing
and persuading his monks (reminiscent of the rhetorician's
personal qualities as an influence in argument) was not lost on
St Benedict: *words* may suffice in some instances to effect
some change in the monks' lives, but *deeds,* the personal deeds
of the abbot, are not to be neglected:

> . . . [he] is obliged to govern his disciples by a
> twofold manner of preaching . . . that is, he should

> show forth all that is good and holy by his deeds
> rather than by his words, so that he may declare
> the commands of the Lord to his docile subjects
> by words; but to the hard of heart . . . and the
> less intelligent let him demonstrate the divine
> precepts by his deeds.[42]

Nevertheless, the Abbot is obliged to teach objective truth:

> Therefore, the abbot ought not—which God forbid—
> to teach or ordain or command anything contrary to
> the law of the Lord; but let his commands and his
> doctrine be infused into the minds of his disciples
> as the leaven of divine justice.[43]

But it is also true that the abbot must at times persuade his
disciples and subdue their wills and move them to action.

> . . . at the dreadful judgment of God an account
> will be given both of his teaching (*doctrinae suae*)
> and the obedience of his disciples (*obedientiae dis-
> cipulorum*).[44]

When St Benedict set the conditions governing the choice of
an abbot, we see again qualities necessary to the orator. The
abbot is to be a man with personal merit (*merito vitae*) and
personal learning (*sapientiae doctrina*). These are the elements
of instruction and persuasion that make an orator credible.[45]
These conditions are repeated in the same chapter: the abbot
must be well-versed in the divine law; he must have virtues
which recommend him for the position of leadership.[46]

The monastery, according to St Benedict, is a school of the
Lord's service.[47] It is a special school; for it promotes ascetical
and mystical performance. The thrust of the education is practical: it does teach some theoretic truths, but by the way of
persuasion; it especially persuades men to act. In this it differs

from dialectical and demonstrative procedures. The monks, in keeping with Aristotle's definition of rhetoric, 'deliberate' with the aid of their abbot 'on what course is best set and followed'. Moreover, because the monks have chosen a rich simplicity of life and thought, the abbot as teacher has no need for either prolonged or complicated arguments when speaking of 'alternative possibilities'. This too is a mark of rhetorical practice.

Thus it is that the content and purpose of the abbot's teaching profoundly influenced the *invention* and *employment* of argument. As a monastic educator, he had to make use of the art of rhetoric, and needed 'the power to see the possible ways of persuading'. For this purpose he used both *enthymeme* and at times *example* to form his arguments.

In the cloister, then there was a lively interplay between the abbot (orator) and his monks (audience), between the orator's eloquence and the audience's emotional and intellectual response. In the chapter house the abbot's finely sculptured rhetorical argument and the mental and affective acquiescence of his monks lent harmony to life. In so austere an environment, imaginative speech and creative listening combined paradoxically to create a beauty of life altogether unique and especially claustral.

Magister–Educator

The *magister* began as a dialectician; only with time did the art of demonstration come into existence and captivate the minds at the schools. The *magister* differed from the abbot-educator. His purpose was other than *moving to action* or *enlightening for motion.* His qualifications were also different: his personal moral virtue was not essential; intellectual acuteness was. His audience was different: he spoke to *scholares,* students, not to *claustrales.*[48] Yet probable premises and probable conclusions as central to the argumentation did unite the teaching efforts of both magister and abbot.[49]

A *magister* was celebrated for his knowledge, for his perception of problems, for the formulation of his argument, for keenness in debate, in a word, for his dialectical skills. In this atmosphere, the *scholares'* personal feelings and aspirations could only hinder the process of finding truth. They were docile of mind in the sense that they were open to being *rationally* convinced. Illustrations and concrete images were pedagogical instruments, but learning was above all the personal assessment and acceptance of a truth only in virtue of its probability or certitude. In a strictly dialectical conclusion, the mind has a commitment to one side of a contradiction, but entertains some genuine fear that the opposite side of the argument may prove true. The rhetorical conclusion simply aims at convincing the listener to accept one side of the contradiction, without giving any attention at all to the possible truth of the other and opposite side. This is frequently because some action must be taken and decision cannot easily be postponed. Poetry, like rhetoric, inclines toward one side of a contradiction by stressing its attractiveness.

Dialectics also more clearly manifests the basic elements in the learning process. The *magister* is nothing more than the *extrinsic instrumental* agent in the learning process. But the *scholares* are the *active agents,* and theirs is the principal causality.[50] St Thomas would assert in his time that neither magister and physician do more for student or patient than foster the conditions in which self-functioning and the vitality of the intrinsic operations of the natural powers are stimulated and restored.[51]

While the *magister* desires scientific knowledge, he must work at this dialectically. He must work with 'probabilities' and refine the concepts and words that will later serve as middle terms in his argumentation. Chenu has pointed out that congenital nature of finished scholastic conclusions and the *Sic et Non* method used so skillfully by Abelard.[52] As proof of this process of reduced contradictions and increased probabilities Chenu quotes from St Thomas' commentary of the *Metaphysics,* Liber 111, c. 1:

Now it is expedient for him who wants to come
into the knowledge of some truth, to know the
doubt-causing difficulties that are raised against
that truth, because the solving of problems that
one doubts about is a coming into truth . . . .
And, therefore, in order to know what the
truth is, there is great value in seeing into the
reasons of contrary opinions.

Sites of Learning

It is Cassian, founder of a monastic school at St Victor,
Marseilles (404), who first introduced the search for learning
into monasteries. Indeed until the early years of the eleventh
century the centers of education were largely monastic.
Notable exceptions were celebrated cathedral schools at
Toledo, Seville, and York.

The monastic schools trained monastic candidates in sufficient Latin and the basic skills of the liberal arts. Such education was essential if the monk hoped to execute his choral
obligation and *lectio divina* with intelligence, devotion, and
dignity. Cassiodorus witnesses to the need of this education.

. . . the monk will derive a certain advantage from
this book [i.e., Fortunatianus' book on Rhetoric
111, 13ff] since it seems not improper for him to
adapt to his own uses that which orators have profitably applied to disputation. Duly cautious, he will
pay heed to memorization, as applied to *divine reading (lectio divina)* . . . he will foster the art of delivery
in reading the divine law aloud [community reading];
and he will, moreover, preserve a careful manner of
speaking in chanting the psalms (*in choro*).[53]

When students not destined for claustral life were admitted
to monastic schools, a number of conflicts surfaced. For
this reason, Benedict of Aniane was instrumental in having

this practice condemned in 817, and to some extent abolished. This led to the formation of separate schools for externs; but these schools remained under monastic control. By the late eleventh century these extern schools were already well established and had frequently joined themselves to cathedral schools under episcopal control.

It was at these centers and at a few monastic schools that the fascination with the new logic and dialectics took root. It was there too that application of the new learning to theological reflection gave rise to new intellectual tensions. And although the cathedral schools catered to the formation of men destined for the clerical state and cathedral positions, other strong influences directed these schools on the way to becoming the great universities of the thirteenth century. Thus, the cloister and the classroom grew further and further apart:

> . . . the *magister in sacra pagina* has taken the place
> of the abbot, and his exegetical concern replaces
> monastic paternalism. It is no longer a *collatio*
> he offers, it is a *lectio*.[54]

Nevertheless, despite real differences, the modes of proof in argumentation for both cloister and classroom were very much alike. Both the spirit and the letter of the *trivium* relate rhetoric and dialectic to each other: they are species of logic.

INVENTION: DISCOVERING THE ARGUMENT
From Cicero's *De inventione*, medieval men accepted uncritically the five works proper to the rhetorician: *invention*, the discovery of arguments powerful enough to persuade; *arrangement*, the placement of arguments in due order; *proper expression*, the adaptation of words to the arguments; *memorization*, the lasting comprehension of words and arguments; and *delivery*, the harmonious adjusting of voice and gesture to words and arguments.[55]

When investigating the twelfth-century 'rhetorical' theologians, our chief interest is in *invention* because this concerns the art of devising arguments which are either true or resemble true argumentation. Both the dialectician and the orator see invention's purpose as rendering an argument 'probable' and to that degree 'credible'.[56] Through invention, then, rhetoric's conditions of 'wise reflection' and discourse 'nowhere uninstructed' are fulfilled.[57]

Although it is undeniable that monastic theologians reveal 'style that is dignified and graceful', it is our contention here that the noetic aspect of these writings determines the poetic, and that arrangement and proper expression are in the service of invention. In keeping with the aristotelian, ciceronian and augustinian traditions, medieval monastic authors favored argument over style; they favored exact verbal expressions, and propositions calculated to appeal to the mind. Cassiodorus, following this tradition, speaks of two modes of argumentation: induction, and imperfect syllogism, i.e., *enthymeme* and *epichirema*. Induction, he defines as: ' . . . a statement which by the use of clearly known particulars seeks to gain approval for the generalization with which the induction began'.[58] The imperfect syllogism is 'suitable for orators rather than dialecticians', he says; because 'to gain credence it employs an argument which disregards the laws of the syllogism'.[59] The abbreviated or imperfect syllogism is called an *enthymeme;* when it is either extended by emphasizing an argument, or extended by advancing an argument, it is called an *epichirema.*[60] In treating of the enthymeme, therefore, we also treat of its two forms of extensions.

The Enthymeme

Enthymeme is defined by Aristotle as the 'orator's demonstration'.[61] It is, therefore, a genuine, if rhetorical, argumentation, although it lacks the power to produce proper demonstration.[62] Under its aspect of certitude enthymeme is more like dialectics since it does produce *probably* true conclusions.[63]

> Neither rhetoric nor dialectic is the scientific
> study of any one separate subject: both are
> faculties for providing arguments.[64]

However, the enthymeme is 'a sort of syllogism'.[65] It sets about
to persuade by a kind of demonstration. Proof of some kind is
necessary 'since we are most fully persuaded when we consider
a thing to have been demonstrated'.[66] And although the enthymeme may at times appear in a loose syllogistic form, it
differs from perfect and scientific syllogisms in as much as it
infers either (1) from merely probable premises or (2) from
signs.[67] But unexpressed propositions are virtually present
because without them argument is simply not possible.

The cloister used imperfect syllogisms in deliberative,
demonstrative and, more rarely, quasi-forensic eloquence.[68]
And the three vehicles of persuasion listed by Aristotle, distinct but conjoined, applied to each species of rhetoric. The
first means of persuasion is the *character* of the speaker:
something of his personal virtue and nobility of nature lends
special credibility to his words. The orator reveals himself as
one who can safely be believed. The second, and related,
vehicle of persuasion is the *disposition of the hearer;* the
listener is favorable to being persuaded. He reveals a good will,
or its opposite, toward the subject matter and the orator.
Finally, the *intrinsic* power of the discourse, rooted in the
very nature of argumentation must facilitate persuasion.
Hence we conclude that the genuine rhetorician must 'be
able (1) to reason logically, (2) to understand human character and goodness in their various forms, and (3) to understand
the emotions—that is, to name them, to know their causes and
the way in which they are excited'.[69] But it is reasoning
logically that is the essence of true eloquence, according to
the constant tradition.

> It follows plainly, therefore, that he is best
> able to see how and from what elements a

syllogism is produced will also be best skilled in
the Enthymeme, when he has further learnt
what its subject-matter is and in what respects
it differs from the syllogism of strict logic. The
true and the approximately true are apprehended
by the same faculty.[70]

The medieval cloister frequently furnishes us with a fine combination of the vehicles of rhetorical persuasion. The character of a revered abbot, combined with the high ascetical and
mystical aspiration of his monks, lent additional credibility
to an already finely moulded argument. On the other hand,
scholares, despite the docility and curiosity proper to students
and the genius of a famous teacher, disengaged themselves
from all that did not rest on proof. The dynamism lay in the
argument, the *sic et non,* and not between the person of the
speaker and listener.

The Uses of Enthymeme

We shall now examine a few samples of the use of enthymeme taken from Sermon 28 of St Bernard's *Super Cantica
canticorum.*[71] Our study will attempt to show how powerful
is this essentially cognitive instrument of argumentation, the
enthymeme, and how forcefully it secures persuasion. As
Aristotle taught: the argumentative avenue of persuasion per-
tains to the essence of both the science and art of rhetoric.[72]

After an introductory word on how St Bernard used invention to settle upon the middle term of his argumentation, we
will investigate his use of the enthymeme in proving (1) that
Christ is *both* black and beautiful, and (2) that the *eyes* see
only *blackness,* but that the *ear* perceives the *beautiful.* The
transitional argument joining these statements attains to *the
persuasion achieved by proof* by drawing upon the two forms
of rhetorical argument: enthymeme and example.[73]

Our introductory text is: 'She is black, but beautiful'.[74]
The 'she' is the bride of the Canticle of Canticles and in our

text 'she' is the Church, the bride of Christ. St Bernard first
shows his faculty of discovering available means to persuade
us of the truth of this paradoxical proposition: black, but
beautiful.[75] The first element in building the enthymeme is
the invention of a binding force or middle term for the premises. St Bernard chooses the concept and word 'blackness' to
bind the argument. The bride's blackness is attributed to her
compassion and to her participation in the vulnerability
shared by all the members of the Church:

> —the bride has preserved the inner brilliance of her
> ornaments, *because* she is black (compassion) [76]

> —the bride relieves and heals the sicknesses of
> passion in others, *because* she is black and
> accepts the blemishes of the flesh (compassion) [77]

> —the bride has zeal for moral brightness and for
> the prize of beauty, *because* she is black and her
> complexion grows dark (compassion)[78]

Thus, says St Bernard, ' . . . the bride does not deny her
blackness but excuses it'.[79]

In the above propositions the term blackness unites the
subject, the bride or Church, to the predicate beautiful. And
this middle term is truly causal in the logical construct. But
the term lacks any *intrinsic* probative force; and in a dialectical or demonstrative thesis such usage would be in varying
degrees inadmissible. Again, in this sermon, the term will have
a variety of meanings: so, for example, the human nature
assumed by Christ in association with sinful mankind will be
one of the meanings given to blackness;[80] blackness is also
applied to actual sin;[81] and blackness is the life of the senses
as they impede the act of faith.[82] But this term has its general-
ity and extension conferred on it and its value is extrinsic.
St Bernard has invented and imposed its meaning and then

hinged his argument on this meaning.

Now St Bernard sets up a new thesis: Christ, the bride-groom, is black and beautiful. He is likened to Solomon of whom scripture says: he is black. Christ too 'presents this black exterior' but within is the brightness of divine life: *. . . foris niger, in cute niger, non intus . . . Intus divinitatis candor.*[83]

Then St Bernard moves on to a reference to the Jacob-Esau story. This allows him to use an extended *refutative* enthymeme to argue his point: Christ is both Esau and Jacob, black and beautiful, even as Jacob was Esau. Now the logical tool of conjoining these two incompatible propositions, the *refutative* enthymeme, will issue in *two* conclusions, opposed to one another, corroborating one another, and thus validating one another.[84]

The argument in form:

<table>
<tr><td align="center">*1.*</td><td align="center">*2.*</td></tr>
<tr><td>1. the *hands* of Esau—black</td><td>1. the voice of Jacob—beauty</td></tr>
<tr><td>2. what we as humans *see,* i.e., 'coverings' and these are *ours*—black</td><td>2. what we *hear* from him is *his*—beauty</td></tr>
<tr><td>3. the form (or coverings) we *see* is *mortal, subject to death*—black</td><td>3. the *words* Jacob *speaks* are *spirit and life*—beauty</td></tr>
<tr><td>4. we *see one thing*—black</td><td>4. we *believe some thing* else—beauty</td></tr>
<tr><td>5. our *senses* tell us he is *black*—black</td><td>5. our *faith* declares Him *fair and beautiful*—beauty</td></tr>
</table>

6. If he is *black,* it is in the eyes of the foolish—	6. to the *faithful* He is wholly *beautiful*—beauty
He is *black.*	He is beautiful.[85]

If we look at this schema vertically, we observe two distinct arguments. When we study the schema horizontally we discover six sets of propositions which nourish each of the arguments. The terms black and beautiful in the conclusions are linked analogously to related concepts. The terms Esau, coverings, mortality, seeing, sense life, and foolishness are concepts related to darkness and predicates applied to the subject, Christ, the bridegroom. The terms Jacob, voice, hearing, spirit and life, faith, and believer are, by contrast, related to beauty and also applied to Christ. The incompatibles are conjoined even as each of the six propositions refute each other.

The more complex materials out of which the enthymeme is constructed are the propositions. These propositions are argued from either probabilities or signs. When they express what *usually happens* in a given category *of things contingent* and *variable* they are called probabilities; in the case at issue, voice, hearing, and faith have contingent relations.[86] The sign, on the other hand, supports a statement either as moving from the particular to the universal or as universal to the particular.[87] In this case, St Bernard moves from particulars to a more universal truth: faith comes by hearing. But this sign-proof is refutable and fallible as soon as one poses the question: What has 'Esau and Jacob' to do with 'faith comes by hearing'?[88] The middle terms are only extrinsic and concomitant to the final subject and predicate in both probabilities and signs. Clearly the rhetorical syllogism is imperfect.[89]

In this sequence of arguments there are any number of *lacunae:* the root of the argument is not clearly stated from the beginning; the links in the whole chain of arguments are made, but not tightly secured, and the order of procedure is

somewhat haphazard.[90] Yet the text truly instructs the
hearer and its arguments can persuade him; for the listener
perceives that the arguments are drawn from common
knowledge and he is able to supply his own connections even
without an explicit statement from the orator. In brief, the
probable premises and the signs and their implication lead to
probably true conclusions. And though the conclusion could
on the face of the evidence be refuted, one can choose in favor
of its truth.[91] The refutative nature of this enthymeme, however, is of a different nature: in a brief space two opposing
arguments are each defended and each of the conclusions
clarifies the other: Christ *is* black and beautiful, but black *is
not* beautiful.[92]

The transition from the subjects of the bride and the bride-
groom to the subjects of hearing and seeing is formalized by
St Bernard in his deft use of *example,* the other usual device in
rhetorical argumentation.[93] Here the attitudes of Herod, the
centurion and the repentant thief *as example* are explained.

> He [Christ] is black, then, but beautiful: black
> in the opinion of Herod, beautiful in the testimony
> of the penitent thief, in the faith of the centurion.[94]

The faith of the centurion becomes the topic for another
refutative enthymeme. St Bernard remarks that the man who
declared: 'Truly this man was the Son of God!' had to have
perceived his beauty. Yet, he adds, it must be asked: 'What
did the eyes of the beholders see, but a man deformed and
black . . . '[95] He concludes that we have a dilemma: 'How did the
centurion see the beauty of the crucified . . . ?'[96] For St Bernard, St Mark the Evangelist, solves the problem.

> And when the centurion, who stood facing him,
> saw that he thus cried out and breathed his last,
> he said: 'Truly this man was the Son of God!'[97]

According to St Bernard, then, it was the *voice*
of Christ, *heard* by the centurion, that inspired
his belief; while Christ's black face revealed his
black humanity, his voice revealed his beautiful
divinity. Indeed, this man (black), and *seen* as
such, is the Song of God (beautiful) and recognized *by his voice.*

The conclusion reached concerning the centurion introduces
a third and final *refutative* enthymeme. The thesis examines
two of our human senses, presumed, at first, to be not only
different but incompatible: the sense of seeing and the sense
of hearing. To put the argument in form we would say: Hearing is compatible with faith; but seeing is not compatible with
faith; therefore, hearing is not compatible with seeing.

> . . . hearing succeeded where sight failed.[98]

> Appearances deceived the eyes, but truth
> poured itself into the ears.[99]

> The eyes saw him to be weak, detestable,
> wretched, a man . . . but to the ear the Son
> of God revealed himself, to the ear he made
> known his beauty.[100]

Then in an apparent digression, which in fact anticipates a
statement of hearing's spiritual function, St Bernard says
that not all ears are disposed to receive the faith that comes
by hearing. He goes on to distinguish two kinds of hearing.
To exemplify this, he says that he finds a certain propriety
in St Peter's severing the temple servant's ear. Because,
although Jewish, the servant's ear is uncircumcised. Peter's
act in the garden circumcised the servant's ear and now it is
open to truth and freedom. This illustration is substantiated
by the fact that the uncircumcised centurion on calvary had
manifest faith and hence circumcised ears.[101] And thus is

proven that faith comes by hearing.

After establishing the ambiguity present in the hearing faculty, St Bernard now turns to a *demonstrative* enthymeme to compose those differences so very deliberately fostered in setting up the *refutative* enthymeme. He cautiously begins to prepare a composition of contrasts.

- Sight is nobler than the power of hearing.
- But sight is reserved for the face to face vision of God.[102]
- When man *listened* to the suggestions of the devil, his punishment was the loss of sight.[103]
- The ear sinned, and the sight suffered the punishment.[104]
- Therefore, faith must return by the route through which it was lost, i.e., hearing.

To a degree this argument composes the actions of hearing and seeing; while they are different actions, they are not at all incompatible. Sin made them incompatible, and hearing renewed by faith will lift the punishment from sight, and sight will be the faculty for vision.

Then St Bernard continues to compose apparently contradictory propositions in order to complement, to extend, and to corroborate his advancing argument.

- Life must follow the same pathway as death, i.e., what was *lost* by hearing, i.e. *sight,* must be *regained* by hearing, i.e. *sight.*
- Let there be light in the wake of darkness and the antidote of truth after the poison the serpent spread.
- Hearing will heal the *troubled eye,* and then the *healed eye* can serenely contemplate him whom the *sickly eye* cannot see.[105]

This argument composes hearing and seeing at a still higher

degree. Proper hearing will restore proper seeing as has been explained in the centurion's experience: good hearing gave him the sight of the crucified as Son of God. Hearing thus nurtures sight.

St Bernard concludes this section with an ultimate resolution of what was originally presented as refutative.

> Therefore, hearing is connected with merit,
> sight with reward.[106]

Scripture is seen as the font of this doctrine, for the prophet says: 'You will give my hearing joy and gladness.' (Ps 50:10) Of sight we read: 'Blessed are the pure of heart, for they shall see God.' (Mt 5:8)

The last statement of this resolution is given succinctly:

> The eye that would see God must be cleansed by
> faith as it is written: 'He cleaned their hearts by faith.'[107]

Clearly the argumentations presented in these passages are sophisticated, studied, and well ordered. The necessary inferences can easily be made by the audience. The text may appear to merely run about 'the fields of eloquence' and 'indulge in copious speech' and 'expanding language'. But in fact, the 'open palm' method is genuinely scientific. And the skillful use of enthymeme assures us of the exactitude proper to the art of rhetoric.[108]

Dialectic Usage

Let us now, by contrast, look at one example of 'close-fisted' argumentation and the use of dialectic with its contracted language and compressed reasoning.[109]

In this schoolman's text, we will find a dialectic argument sober, curt, and infinitely tighter than our rhetorical syllogism.[110] The subject had to do with the faith that is necessarily prior to vision, a truth taught by St Bernard as he

composed his arguments on hearing and seeing. In form, our
present text reads:

> The perfection of the rational creature is the
> vision of God.
>
> But being taught by God is necessary to the
> vision of God.
>
> Therefore, the perfection of the creature is his
> being taught by God, in a relationship of disciple
> to master.[111]

Here there are three fundamental concepts: the perfection of
the rational creature; God, the teacher; and the vision of God.
The middle term *vision* applies first to the rational creature as
its recipient, and then to God the teacher who mediates this
vision through his teaching. In the conclusion, the rational
creature is a disciple, and *recipient* of God's shared knowledge
(faith) and God is *donor,* i.e., *per modum addiscentis a Deo
doctore.* Here neither the character of the author nor the
emotions and feelings of the reader have any essential role in
the argument. The appeal is only to a reasoning faith: the
vision is offered by God the teacher; it is received by the
rational creature as disciple.

In a final conclusion, St Thomas wonderfully puts his
concepts together:

> *Unde ad hoc quod homo perveniat ad perfectam
> visionem beatitudinis, praeexigitur quod credat
> Deo, tamquam discipulus magistro docenti.*[112]

But St Bernard's conclusion on a similar subject is not less
exact:

> *Et ut scias etiam Spiritum Sanctum hunc in animae*

*spirituali profectu ordinem observare, ut videlicet
prius formet auditum, quam laetificet visum: Audi,
inquit, Filia, et vide. (Ps 44:11) Quid intendis
oculum? Aurem para.*[113]

CONCLUSION

In the cloister, truth was sought after and elaborated upon
through the artful use of the enthymeme. Truth was also pursued and expounded in the schools through the appropriate
method of *sic et non.* Both the rhetorical syllogism and the
dialectical one searched for 'topics' or lines of argument that
were either general or special.

During the medieval students' *trivium* training the 'topics'
were of a general nature; as the students advanced some of
them applied either their rhetorical or their dialectical skills to
the special domain of theology. Aristotle had already alerted
his students to the importance of this distinction; for as the
content is more specified, the methodology is less self-
conscious.

> Missing this distinction, people fail to notice
> that the more correctly they handle their parti-
> cular subject [in our case, theology] the further
> they are getting away from pure rhetoric and
> dialectic.[114]

Thus, any criticism of either monastic or scholastic theology
must carefully consider this distinction whenever or wherever
faulty premises or inaccurate conclusions appear. The 'uses'
of reason on the data of faith must answer both the laws of
faith and the laws of reason. This altogether necessary tension
has frequently led to premature verdicts of 'rationalism' or
'fideism', when, in fact, an author was still wrestling with the
problem of faith seeking understanding and using dialectics or
rhetoric, and using them either well or poorly.

New Ringgold, Pennsylvania

NOTES

1. John of Salisbury (1125–1180) is an articulate witness to twelfth-century liberal educational practices and a staunch defender of the classical understanding of the *trivium.* His complete works are found in Migne, PL 199. The *Metalogicon,* translated by Daniel D. McGarry (Berkeley and Los Angeles: University of California Press, 1955) is the fundamental source for this paper. The english translations are from McGarry.

2. Cassiodorus (477–570?), *De artibus ac disciplinis liberalium,* PL 70:1149–1218. His teaching on dialectic with some borrowing from Varro is already more developed than his teaching on the other liberal arts. Cf. PL 70:1167–1179. For his rhetorical teaching, see columns 1157–1166.

3. Manlius Severinus Boethius (480–524?). His translation of Porphyry's *Isagoge,* with two commentaries (one from Victorinus' translation), translations of Aristotle's *Categories* and a commentary, translations of the *Perihermeneias* (Interpretations) and two commentaries, the unfinished commentary on Cicero's Topics, and his own studies of syllogisms, and divisions constitute the *logica vetus.* His translations of the *Anaytics–Prior* and *Posterior, Sophistic Arguments* and *Topics* were unknown until the mid-twelfth century and constitute the *logica nova.* For the complete works of Boethius see PL 63, 64. Of special pertinence for this paper, see 64:639–672; 609 ff; 1007 ff.

4. C. J. B. Gaskoin, *Alcuin: His Life and Work,* (New York: Russell and Russell, 1966) Chapter IV, pp. 33–40.

5. Alcuin, PL 101:949–976.

6. Rabanus Maurus, *De clericorum institutione;* PL 111. In this work he transmitted the educational ideas of Augustine's *De doctrina christiana.* See also PL 111:613–678.

7. Anselm of Canterbury's complete works are in PL 158 and 159. *De grammatico,* PL 158:561–582.

8. Anselm of Canterbury, *De veritate,* PL 158:461–482.

9. Gerbert of Aurillac, (Pope Sylvester II), PL 139:157–168.

10. John of Salisbury, *Metalogicon,* Bk. 1, c. 23; McGarry pp. 67–71 ff.

11. *Ibid.,* Bk. 111, c. 4; p. 167.

12. Thierry of Chartres, *Heptateuchon,* Cf. John of Salisbury, *Metalogicon,* Bk. III, c. 5; p. 172.

13. Hugh of St. Victor, *Didiscalion,* Bk. III, cc. 3, 4, and 5, PL 176: 811–838.

14. Cassiodorus, *An Introduction to Divine and Human Readings*. Translated with Introduction and Notes, Leslie Webber Jones, (New York: Columbia Press, 1969). In the following pages the english translations will be taken from this work. The *De artibus ac disciplinis liberalium litterarum* is sometimes spoken of as 'Secular Letters'. Bk. 1, c. 27, #1, of the 'Divine Letters' is the source of this text, which occurs on page 127.

15. Jacob of Vitry, in G. Compayre's *Abelard and the Early History of Universities* (New York: 1893) 200.

16. Marcus Terentius Varro (116-27 B.C.), a roman rhetorician, wrote nine books of *Disciplines* now lost; to the usual seven liberal arts he added medicine and architecture. The same teaching is found in Isidore, *Etymologiae* II.XXIII. 1-2, and is traced back to Quintilian's *Institutio Oratoris* II.XX, 7 ff. Cf. Cassiodorus, *Secular Letters,* Bk. 11, c. 111, #2; p. 159.

17. *Ibid.*

18. Augustine, *De doctrina christiana,* IV. 2. 3. English translation taken from The Nicene and Post-Nicene Fathers, edited by P. Shaff, (New York: Charles Scribner's Sons, 1887) Vol. 2:575.

19. *Ibid.,* IV.12.27; p. 583.

20. *Ibid.*

21. *Ibid.,* IV.13.29; 583-4.

22. John of Salisbury, *Metalogicon,* I.15; p. 46.

23. *Ibid.,* II.3; p. 79. Cf. also Boethius, *De diff. top.,* IV; PL 64: 1205ff.

24. John of Salisbury, *Metalogicon* II.3; p. 79: 'Demonstrative logic flourishes in the [basic] principles of the [various] sciences, and progresses further to deducting conclusions from these. It rejoices in necessity. It does not pay much attention to what various people may think about a given proposition. Its sole concern is that a thing must be so. It thus befits the philosophical majesty of those who teach the truth, a majesty which is a result of its own conviction [that it is teaching the truth], and independent of the assent of its listeners.' N. B. This last phrase *independent of the assent of its listeners* is the decisive element in demonstrative truth, as opposed to both dialectical and rhetorical truth, and it can be said that *if* such a demonstrative position is possible it is the preferred truth. But the problem is that this type of truth, for a variety of reasons, is not always attainable.

25. *Ibid.* (Cf. also Aristotle, *Topics,* Bk. I, c. 10, 104a-8-9.)

26. *Ibid.*

27. John of Salisbury, *Metalogicon* II.12; 102: 'Rhetoric, which aims to sway the judgment of persons other than the contestants, usually

employs prolonged oration and induction, owing to the fact that it is addressed to a larger number of people and generally solicits the assent of the crowd. Dialectic, on the contrary, expresses itself succinctly, and generally in the form of syllogisms, for it has one judge alone: an opponent, to convince whom is its sole goal and purpose.'

28. *Ibid.*

29. See Abelard, PL 178:1465–1466.

30. According to John of Salisbury (*Metalogicon,* III.6.), Abelard, the Peripatethic of Pallet, developing new doctrines as well as elucidating old ones, had some acquaintance with Aristotle's *Topics.* But this seems to have come to him indirectly through Boethius' commentary of Cicero's *Topics* and through Thierry of Chartres in the *Heptateuchon,* and Boethius' own *De diff. topiciis.* John, on his part appears to have had direct contact with Aristotle; but John was some thirty-five years younger than Abelard.

31. Concerning the purposes of inquiry, Aristotle wrote: ' . . . we must say for how many and for what purposes the treatise [*Topics*] is useful. They are three—intellectual training, casual encounters and the philosophical sciences . . . For the study of the philosophical sciences it is useful because the ability to raise searching difficulties on both sides of a subject will make us detect more easily truth and error.' *Topics,* Bk. I, c. 2, 25–28, and 34–36.

32. Aristotle, *Topics,* Bk. I, c. 10, 104a, 8–10 and 11: 'Now a dialectical proposition consists in asking something that is held by all men or by most men or by philosophers . . . provided it is not contrary to the general opinion.' See also Cassiodorus, *Divine Learning: Dialectics,* III.15; pp. 172–175.

33. Aristotle, *Topics,* Bk. I, c. 10, 104a, 3–35.

34. *Ibid.,* Bk. I, c. 1, 100a, 8–23.

35. The three major functions of dialectics are carefully distinguished by St Thomas in the thirteenth century. In the early middle ages, dialectics had a distinctly 'disjunctive' function: it merely set up the questions and was satisfied with probable answers. Later, dialectics were seen as a *preparation* for demonstration and as *complementary* to demonstrative processes. St Thomas treats of the disjunctive or more strictly dialectical function as opposed to demonstrative function: 'Nam inventio non semper est cum certitudine. Unde de his, quae inventa sunt, iudicium requiritur, ad hoc quod certitudo habeatur . . . quandoque quidem, etsi non fiat scientia, fit tamen fides vel opinio propter probabilitatem propostionum ex quibus proceditur . . . et ad hoc ordinator *Topica* sive *Dialectica.*' St Thomas, *In libros posteriorum analyticorum,* Prooemium, #6.

36. John of Salisbury, *Metalogicon,* IV.8; pp. 214-215. See also St Thomas, In *I De anima,* lect. 1, #55: 'Si quis ergo assignet definitionem, per quam non deveniatur in cognitionem accidentium rei definitae, illa definitio non est realis, sed remota et dialectica. Sed illa definitio per quam devenitur in cognitionem accidentium, est realis, et ex propriis, et essentialibus rei.'

37. St Thomas, *In Metaphysica* IV, lect. 4, #576: 'Dialectica enim potest considerari secumdum quod est docens et secundum est utens. Secundum quidem quod est docens, habet considerationem de istis intentionibus, instituens modum, quod per eas procedi possit ad conclusiones in singulis scientis probabiliter ostendendas; et hoc demonstrativa facit, et sedundum hoc est scientiam.'

38. John of Salisbury, *Metalogicon,* II.13 and 14; pp. 103-107.

39. Cassiodorus, Secular letters, II.III.17; p. 176.

40. John of Salisbury, *Metalogicon,* III. 10; p. 192. Note the special use of enthymeme.

41. Aristotle, *Rhetoric,* Bk. I, c. 1, 1354a—1-6.

42. St Benedict, *The Holy Rule* (St Meinrad: Grail Publication, 1956) [Abbreviation: RB] 2: 'Ergo cum aliquis suscipit nomen Abbatis, duplici debet duplici debet doctrina suis praeesse discipulis, id est bona et sancta factis amplius quam verbis ostendere . . . duris vero corde et simplicioribus, factis suis divina praecepta demonstret.'

43. RB 2: 'Ideoque Abbas nihil extra praeceptum Domini, quod absit, debet aut docere, aut constituere, vel jubere: sed jussio ejus, vel, doctrina fermentum divinae justitiae in discipulorum mentibus conspergatur.'

44. RB 2: 'Memor sit semper Abbas, quia doctrinae suae, vel discipulorum obedientiae utrarumque rerum in tremendo judicio Dei facienta erit discussio.'

45. RB 64: 'Vitae autem merito, et sapientiae doctrina eligatur, qui ordinandus est . . . '

46. RB 64: Knowledge: 'Oportet ergo eum *doctum* lege divina . . . ' Leadership: 'Castum, sobrium, miseridordem et semper superexaltantem misericordiam judicio: ut idem ipse consequator.'

47. RB, *Prologue.*

48. M. -D. Chenu, *Toward Understanding St. Thomas,* trans. by Landry and Hughes, (Chicago: Henry Regnery, 1964) p. 17.

49. John of Salisbury, *Metalogicon,* III.6; p. 177.

50. St Thomas, *Summa Theologiae,* 1, q. 117, a. 1, [ST].

51. ST 1, q. 117; a. 1, obj. 1: ' . . . just as the inward nature is the principle cause of all healing, so the interior light of the intellect is the principle cause of learning.'

52. Chenu, 181: 'The questions that are inspired by the formal *sic et non* are not always brought to demonstrations. Due to the most diversified of reasons the first of which is that the objects undergoing study do not require a demonstration, more often than not arguments and their conclusions remain within the limits of the probable (in the Aristotelian sense of the word). The latter is a vast variegated domain in which, seemingly, the mind should feel ill at ease, but in which, in reality, the mind proves her true keenness and her finest balance.'

53. Cassiodorus, Secular Letters, II.11.16; pp. 157–158.

54. Chenu, p. 237.

55. Cassiodorus, Secular Letters, II.11.2; p. 149. The source of this doctrine is Cicero's *De inventione,* 1. 9.

56. John of Salisbury, *Metalogicon,* IV.8; p. 215.

57. Cassiodorus, Secular Letters, II.11.11; p. 155.

58. *Ibid.,* 12; 156.

59. *Ibid.,* 12 (p. 156) and 14 (p. 157): 'An enthymeme, therefore is rendered into Latin as a mental concept and is usually called an imperfect syllogism by rhetorical writers. For this form of proof consists of two parts, since to gain credence it employs an argument which disregards the law of syllogism.'

60. *Ibid.,* 15; p. 157. 'An epichirema, as we have said above, is a rather extended treatment of the rhetorical syllogism proceeding from deduction and differing from dialectic syllogism in amplitude and length of language, on account of which it is assigned to rhetoricians.'

61. Aristotle, *Rhetoric,* Bk. 1, c. 1, 1355a—7: 'The orator's demonstration is an Enthymeme, and this is, in general, the most effective of the modes of persuasion.'

62. John of Salisbury, *Metalogicon,* IV.5; p. 211. In this chapter, outlining the contents of Aristotle's *Prior Analytics,* Bk. II, cc. 23–25, John furnishes us with the discussion on the sources and uses of enthymemes.

63. Aristotle, *Rhetoric,* Bk. 1, c. 1, 1354a—1.

64. *Ibid.,* c. 1, 1356a—31-34.

65. *Ibid.,* c. 1, 1355a—8.

66. *Ibid.,* c. 1, 1355a—6-7.

67. Aristotle, *Prior Analytics,* Bk. 11, c. 27, 70a—9-11.

68. Aristotle, *Rhetoric,* Bk. 1, c. 3, 1358b—1-8.

69. *Ibid.,* c. 2, 1356a—23-25.

70. *Ibid.,* c. 1, 1355a—10-15.

71. *S. Bernardi Opera,* Vol. 1, *Sermones super Cantica canticorum,* 1-35, (Roma: Editiones Cistercienses, 1957) [Abbreviated SC]. The text of special interest here is Sermon 28 (pp. 192-196). The english translation used here is Bernard of Clairvaux: *On the Song of Songs,*

(Kalamazoo: Cistercian Publications, 1976) 3:88-93.
72. Aristotle, *Rhetoric*, Bk. 1, c. 1, 1355b—26, 31-36.
73. *Ibid.*, Bk. 1, c. 2, 1356b—4-5.
74. *Song of Songs*, 1:4.
75. Aristotle, *Rhetoric*, Bk., 1, c. 1, 1355a—35.
76. SC, 28. 1. 20-21; pp. 192 and 193.
77. *Ibid.*, 1.3-4; 193.
78. *Ibid.*, 1.4-5; 193.
79. *Ibid.*, 1.1-3; 193.
80. *Ibid.*, 2.7; 193.
81. *Ibid.*, 10.29-30; 198.
82. *Ibid.*, 11.15-16; 200.
83. *Ibid.*, 2.17-18; 193.
84. Aristotle, *Rhetoric*, Bk. II, c. 22, 1396b—20-27.
85. SC, 28.3.17-22; p. 194.
86. Aristotle, *Rhetoric*, Bk. 1, c. 2, 1357a—35-40.
87. *Ibid.*, Bk. 1, c. 2, 1357b—1-20.
88. Aristotle, *Prior Analytics*, Bk. II, c. 27, 70a—2-35.
89. *Ibid.*, Bk. 11, c. 27, 70a—20-25.
90. Aristotle, *Rhetoric*, Bk. II, 2. 22, 1395b—24-28.
91. *Ibid.*, 1395b—30-33.
92. *Ibid.*, Bk. II, c. 23, 1400b—25-29.
93. *Ibid.*, Bk. I, c. 2, 1357b—25-30.
94. SC 28. 3. 22-23; p. 194.
95. *Ibid.*, 4, 27; 194.
96. *Ibid.*, 4.1-3; 195.
97. *Ibid.*, 4.4-6; 195.
98. *Ibid.*, 5.9; 195.
99. *Ibid.*, 5.9-10; 195.
100. *Ibid.*, 5.10-11; 195.
101. *Ibid.*, 5.12-16; 195.
102. *Ibid.*, 5.18-20; 195.
103. *Ibid.*, 5.22; 195.
104. *Ibid.*, 5.25; 195.
105. *Ibid.*, 5.20-25; 195.
106. *Ibid.*, 5.25; 195.
107. *Ibid.*, 5.28; 195 and 5.1-2; p. 196.
108. Cassiodorus, *Secular Letters* (from Varro), Bk. II, III, 2; p. 159.
109. *Ibid.*
110. St Thomas, *Summa Theologica*, 11-11, q. 2, art. 3.
111. *Ibid., corpus.*
112. *Ibid.*
113. SC 28. 7. 20-22; p. 196.
114. Aristotle, *Rhetoric*, Bk. I. c. 2, 1358a-8-9.

ABBREVIATIONS

Acta SS	*Acta Sanctorum.*
CC	Corpus Christianorum.
CCSL	Corpus Christianorum Series Latina.
CSEL	Corpus scriptorum ecclesiasticorum latinorum.
DSp	*Dictionnaire de Spiritualité.* Paris, 1932–.
Ep(p)	*Epistola(e)*
ET	English translation
MGH	*Monumenta Germaniae Historica.*
PG	J.-P. Migne, *Patrologiae cursus completus, series graeca.*
PL	J.-P. Migne, *Patrologiae cursus completus, series latina.*
SC	Bernard of Clairvaux, *Sermones in Cantica canticorum*
ST	Thomas of Aquinas, *Summa theologiae.*

CISTERCIAN PUBLICATIONS INC.
Kalamazoo, Michigan

TITLES LISTING

THE CISTERCIAN FATHERS SERIES

THE WORKS OF BERNARD OF CLAIRVAUX

THE WORKS OF WILLIAM OF SAINT THIERRY

THE WORKS OF AELRED OF RIEVAULX

THE WORKS OF GILBERT OF HOYLAND

THE WORKS OF JOHN OF FORD

Texts and Studies in the Monastic Tradition

* *Temporarily out of print*   † *Forthcoming*

Temporarily out of print   † *Fortbcoming*